STANDING WATCH

MARITIME CURRENTS: HISTORY AND ARCHAEOLOGY

STANDING WATCH

American Submarine Veterans Remember the Cold War Era

Jonathan Li-Chung Leung

The University of Alabama Press
Tuscaloosa

The University of Alabama Press
Tuscaloosa, Alabama 35487-0380
uapress.ua.edu

Typefaces: Scala Pro, Scala Sans Pro, and Avenir Black

Cover image: Illuminated by rays of sunshine peering through broken cloud cover, a sailor on the missile deck of an unidentified ballistic missile submarine observes as the USS *Sam Houston* (SSBN-609) enters Holy Loch, Scotland, 1963. In August 1979, a Soviet trawler snatched a practice torpedo shot by the *Sam Houston*, touching off a tense diplomatic standoff between the two countries; courtesy of the National Archives (USN 711325)
Cover design: David Nees

Library of Congress Cataloging-in-Publication Data

Names: Leung, Jonathan Li-Chung, 1987– author.
Title: Standing watch : American submarine veterans remember the Cold War era / Jonathan Li-Chung Leung.
Other titles: American submarine veterans remember the Cold War era
Description: Tuscaloosa, AL : The University of Alabama Press, [2019] | Series: Maritime currents: history and archaeology | Includes bibliographical references and index.
Identifiers: LCCN 2018038929| ISBN 9780817320126 (cloth) | ISBN 9780817359577 (paper) | ISBN 9780817392505 (e book)
Subjects: LCSH: United States. Navy—Submarine forces—History—20th century—Anecdotes. | Submariners—United States—Interviews. | Submariners—United States—Biography. | United States. Navy—Sea life—Anecdotes. | Submarines (Ships)—United States—Anecdotes. | Veterans—United States—Interviews. | Cold War—Anecdotes.
Classification: LCC V858 .L48 2019 | DDC 359.9/3092273—dc23
LC record available at https://lccn.loc.gov/2018038929

To Marvin,
and all others whose lives are measured by the number of stories they left untold.

In memory of
Fred Carneau 1922–2014
Chuck Nelson 1941–2016
and
Dave Koch 1940–2017

Contents

Preface

The din of whirring fans drowns out the electrical buzz coming from the overhead fluorescent lights as a dank and musty odor wafts through the wardroom on this stifling summer day. This smell indiscriminately permeates everything, from my hair and skin, to the shirts worn by the fine gentlemen seated around me. It's an eclectic mix of diesel fuel and hydraulic fluid, remnants from two decades ago, actually. But I tell the men, "You're not close enough until you can smell your neighbor!" They laugh. They laugh because they know it is true. So they slide across the bench seating and squeeze in tighter, until they are shoulder-to-shoulder, thigh-to-thigh, and sixteen of us are fitted around an average-sized dining table. But this of course is not your standard dining table. It also doubles as an operating table, when one of your shipmates goes under the knife.

I introduce myself. Half of the men I know already; the other half had spoken to me only once before, on the phone, before eagerly accepting my invitation to cram into a hot, muggy compartment with more than a dozen of their brethren. We go around the table. They say their names. Fire control technician (third class) Robert Walters introduces himself. "Bob," he says. "With one 'O.'" Just in case we needed clarification. After all, they are very thoughtful gentlemen.

Fred Carneau begins a story. He is the elder statesman of the group. Although he did not enter the submarine service until 1947, he had enlisted in the Navy soon after the outbreak of World War II. He talks about being at Normandy on a tank landing ship during the Allied invasion of France, talks about seeing men blown out of the water, and talks about receiving fire from the Germans still nestled on shore. No big deal . . . because the gunfire, he remarks, was only from "small arms." Garth Lascink, seated next to me, gently gives us a reminder. "Fred," he quips, "You're just as dead with a small arm as you are with a big arm!" The room erupts in laughter. They laugh because they know it is true.

After all, Garth is young enough to still be Fred's son. No one ever shot at him. Collie Collins, a hospital corpsman seated at the corner of the table, is the only other person in the room who saw combat. He received a Purple Heart in Korea. Everyone else had it easy. Relatively.

The older veterans always claim that the youngsters had it especially easy. Seated across from Fred is Chuck Macaluso. Chuck is a youngster. He retired from the Navy in 2001, when Fred and Collie had already been drawing Social Security for years. These youngsters, the old salts exclaim, had everything handed to them and didn't know how to do anything for themselves! Everyone laughs. It is the clichéd refrain older generations haze their younger counterparts with. But they laugh because they know it's *not* true.

In reality, I am the only youngster. When these gentlemen introduce themselves to my school-age friends, some of them tell my friends that they are my "grandfathers." I do not dispute this. Because, in actuality, they consider me a member of their family.

These gentlemen are submariners. They are submariners from the Cold War, a war they fought with the utmost dedication and patriotism. But they never made it to the front page of the paper nor to the nightly six o'clock news. No, they never fired a shot. And no, no one ever shot at them . . . for the most part. But just like their more famous predecessors from the World War, they have a history to keep alive. "So then, what was it really like?" I ask. This is their reply. This is their story.

Acknowledgments

There was a point when each time I opened up a new book to read, I would skip this section. "What was the purpose," I asked myself, "In reading all the names of all these people I didn't know and would never meet?" Eventually, I would have to go through the whole process of writing my own book in order to appreciate how much meaning this section holds for any author.

I am a firm believer that all my successes in life are as much, if not more, a product of all those who have helped me along the way, than they are of my own ability. And undertaking a project of this magnitude has really reinforced this sentiment. To be sure, there would have been no book without the wonderful veterans answering my barrage of questions, but this final product would also not exist without the multitude of people who took it upon themselves to coax it out of me.

First and foremost though, special thanks go to the seventeen submariners featured in this book: Bill Bryan, Fred Carneau, Collie Collins, Herb Herman, Bob Jackson, Garth Lascink, Chuck Macaluso, Mark Manzer, Chuck Nelson, Alan Nolan, Chris Stafford, Mike Stephens, Bob Sumner, Dave Vrooman, R. G. Walker, Bob Walters, and Gary Webb. Every Monday for two months in the summer of 2008, these men enthusiastically trooped down to the USS *Blueback* to share their stories and experiences with me. They shared their camaraderie with me and made me part of their family. R. G. Walker deserves additional mention here. If I had to single out one person on whose shoulders the success of this project rested, it is R. G., who, as manager of the *Blueback*, helped me organize the veterans for the interviews, undertake the massive logistical operation of feeding the crew, plan for the interviews with insightful advice, and make the sacrifice of giving up his volunteers to me, delaying or postponing projects he had, so that I could spend more time with these amazing people.

Additional thanks go to Alta Fleming, Tamee Flanagan, and executive chef

Charles Simmons, all of Bon Appétit Management Company. They made sure that our entire crew was more than well-fed with cuisine of the highest order.

Several friends who were key to the initial project-planning phase include Nick Kourtides, who helped me acquire the necessary recording equipment for my interviews, Sonia Lee, who provided invaluable advice on how to conduct an oral history project, and Brian Bernard, a Naval ROTC instructor and qualified submariner who aided me with technical and conceptual advice.

Throughout the entire project, I had the privilege of being assisted by my good friend Corey Walden, who was responsible for the copious amounts of documentation, note-taking, and logistical demand necessitated by the magnitude of my ambition. Corey also proved his worth as a marvelous question-generator during our pre-interview planning sessions, and his sage advice throughout the next ten years was critical in shaping this book. Another childhood friend, Ryan Fish, cheered me on from this book's infancy to its maturation, and also designed the sublime timeline that accompanies the text in the introduction.

At the Naval Historical Center (now the Naval History and Heritage Command) at the Washington Navy Yard, Gina Akers shared with me her tremendous enthusiasm for my project and helped me archive it in the Operational Archives. At the Ships History Branch, Bob Cressman and Greg Ellis shuttled back and forth from the "vault" to make sure I had everything I needed and continued to keep me entertained as I navigated through the mountain of documents growing on my desk. Six time zones west at the USS *Bowfin* Submarine Museum and Park at Pearl Harbor, Nancy Richards and Charles Hinman played the role of gracious hosts and helped me dig deeper into their extensive archives of Pacific Fleet submarines.

In helping me ease the financial burden of such a massive project, a debt of gratitude goes out to my alma mater, Swarthmore College, which funded my interview project during the summer of 2008, as well as to Alaska Airlines/Horizon Air, which shuttled me all over the country for fourteen years.

Heartfelt appreciation is extended to a few friends who helped mentor and guide me when I started volunteering as a docent on the *Blueback*: Tylor Doherty, the late Pat Patterson, and three of my interviewees: Garth Lascink, Alan Nolan, and R. G. Walker. Special mention also goes to Nancy Stueber, Russ Repp, John Farmer, Carol Cruzan, the late Dave Koch, Scott Thingelstad, Steve Myers, and all of the employees and volunteers at the Oregon Museum of Science and Industry, who eagerly allowed me to bounce my project ideas off of them.

In addition, I am deeply grateful toward Gannon McHale and Chris Drew, two amazing authors who shared with me their philosophies on writing, as well as their experiences and journeys through the web of challenges and gratifications they encountered, and offered me their encouragement, advice, and support.

The long journey toward publication gained traction during a chance discussion with fellow *Blueback* volunteer Dave Thompson, who connected me with his former captain, Fred McLaren. Fred introduced me to the publisher of his first book, the University of Alabama Press, and I reached out to Dan Waterman, who became thoroughly invested in my work and was instrumental in helping me create a final product that we could all be proud of. During the editing process, Joanna Jacobs and Annalisa Zox-Weaver expertly shepherded this book through the obstacle course, shearing off all the unruly wool, and the rest of the championship team at the University of Alabama Press guided the book to completion. Roll Tide.

And in turning back the clock, it would be a travesty if I did not acknowledge all the wonderful friends and teachers who have unconditionally supported me over the years, from Swarthmore College, from the University of Pennsylvania, and especially from the Beaverton School District, where I grew up with the confidence that I could accomplish anything I put my mind to.

Finally and most importantly, I would like to thank my entire extended family. From my mother and father, to my aunts and uncles and grandmothers and grandfathers, they all saw a precocious little boy and raised him into a young man who never lost his childhood interests and passions. Bravo Zulu.

STANDING WATCH

Introduction

The Sailors

I am proud to serve with these men. Not in the same way they dutifully served their country in their vibrant youth, but with the same passion and enthusiasm they serve today. The seventeen men featured in this book are all in one way or another, connected with the USS *Blueback* (SS-581), the US Navy's last diesel-electric powered attack submarine, now a floating educational resource and tribute to submariners at the Oregon Museum of Science and Industry in Portland. These seventeen, all qualified submariners themselves, come from diverse backgrounds in both time and geography, but they share a common bond today in their work to preserve a piece of American history. They volunteer their time, most of them either on the maintenance crew, or as docents. All of them volunteered for their country.

This is a unique group. Often known only for an aura or mystique of clandestine secrecy, the submarine service has been subject to popular misconception. My ultimate goal is to tell the story of the submarine force during the Cold War, from the perspective of, and as experienced by, the submariners themselves. This isn't the biography of Admiral Rickover, or the story of the Special Projects Office that was responsible for tapping cables and spying on the Soviets. This is the story of everyday men, who lived their job around the clock, oscillating between monotonous routine and unparalleled excitement. This is not a story about politics or naval bureaucracy. It is a story about pride and service. This is the human face of the story.

Although some key biographical information about my interviewees is provided in appendix A, a brief introduction here is necessary so that the stories that follow can be placed in an appropriate context. Appendix C lists different rates and ranks, and the timeline presented in this introduction will serve as a useful reference. Of the seventeen Navy veterans who are featured in this

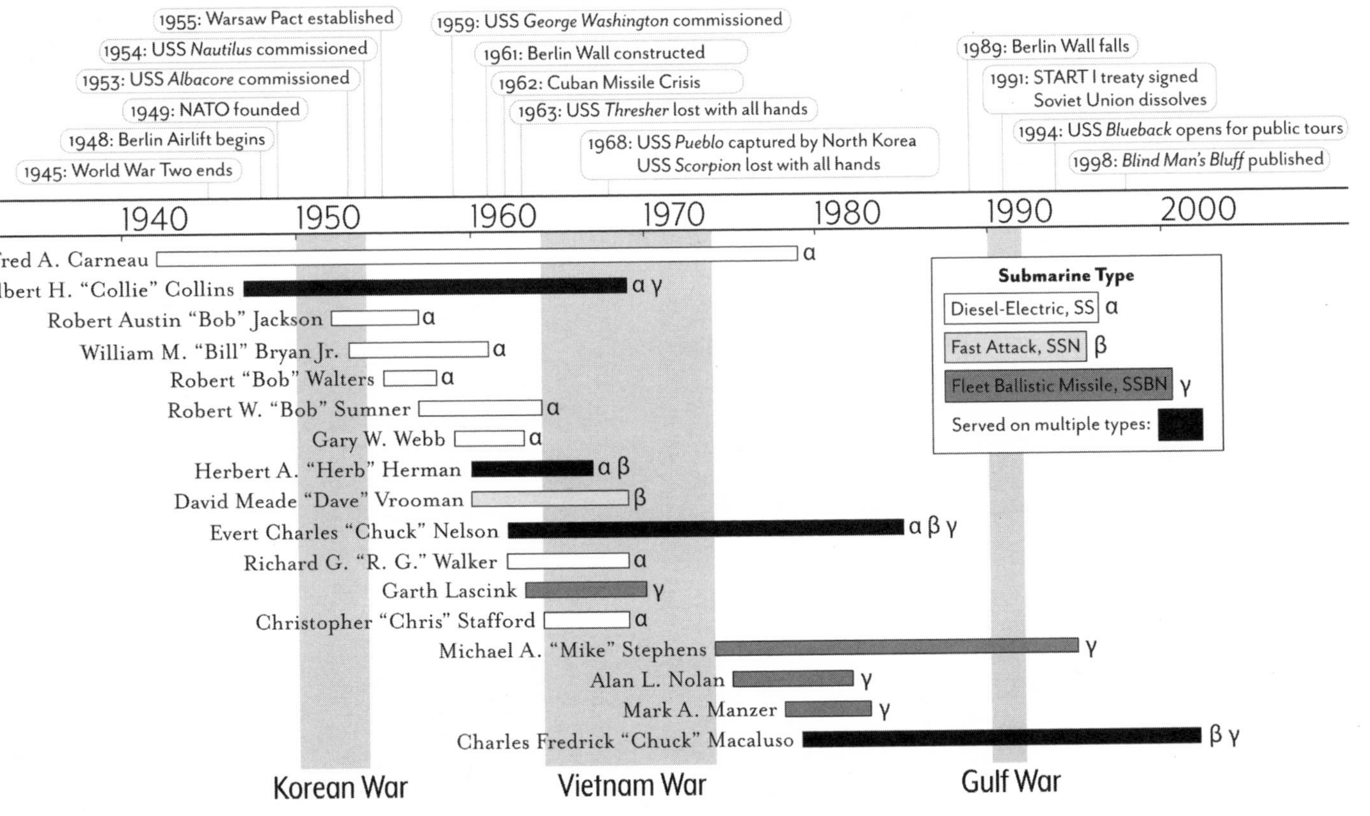

Career snapshots of *Standing Watch* interviewees. Design by Ryan Fish.

book, all of them are submarine qualified. All but one of them left the service in an enlisted rate, ranging from third class (E-4) to senior chief (E-8). Chuck Macaluso retired as a chief warrant officer (W-2).

Of the sixteen enlisted men, four of them (Bill Bryan, Fred Carneau, Bob Jackson, and Bob Sumner) worked as enginemen. Three of them (Mark Manzer, Alan Nolan, and Gary Webb) received their specialty training in sonar. In addition, there are two missile technicians (Garth Lascink and Mike Stephens) and two electronics technicians (Herb Herman and Chuck Nelson) in the group. Macaluso was also an electronics technician before his promotion to the warrant officer ranks. The remaining five include a hospital corpsman (Collie Collins), a machinist's mate (Chris Stafford), an electrician's mate (Dave Vrooman), a commissaryman (R. G. Walker), and a fire control technician (Bob Walters).[1]

The only men in the group who exceeded a decade of service individually were the four chiefs (Carneau, Collins, Nelson, and Stephens) and Macaluso, the warrant officer. The first of our volunteers to enlist was Carneau, who joined the Navy in September 1942 as the Second World War heated up, and was dispatched across the Atlantic on a tank landing ship (LST) to Oran, Algeria. His first taste of battle soon followed, as the invasion fleet roared ashore on the Italian beaches of Sicily and Salerno in late 1943. At Omaha Beach in Normandy, France, his war duty reached its epic climax during a cameo appearance following the D-Day landings in June of 1944. Carneau left active duty at the conclusion of the war and transitioned into the Naval Reserves. In 1947, he joined the submarine service with a tour of duty on the USS *Entemedor* (SS-340), and eventually qualified on the USS *Stickleback* (SS-415) in 1952. He retired from the US Navy as a senior chief in February 1978. Just over a year later, Macaluso, then a wide-eyed teenager, reported to boot camp with no inkling that he was about to embark upon the beginning of a twenty-two-year career on five different submarines. By the time he retired in 2001, the Cold War had officially been over for a decade. Between Carneau's enlistment and Macaluso's retirement, our fifteen other volunteers served their tours of duty, covering every single year of the Cold War and witnessing the whole spectrum of geopolitical possibilities, from détente to the brink of nuclear Armageddon.

But besides ranks, ratings, and the eras of service, one of the most significant factors dictating the experiences submariners went through was the type of submarine they served on. From the end of the Second World War in 1945 to the fall of the Soviet Union in 1991, the US Navy utilized three primary types of submarines.

Immediately following the surrender of the Axis powers, the United States worked feverishly on improving its submarine designs. The old diesel-electric fleet boats, admirable mainstays of the submarine service throughout the entire conflict, faced several pronounced limitations. First, the hull design forced these boats to operate like submersible warships instead of as true submarines. Complete with an unwieldy conning tower and deck guns, the fleet boats were significantly faster steaming on the surface than cruising underwater. Also, because their diesel engines required fresh oxygen for combustion, the old fleet boats always had to surface once their battery life was exhausted. Running the diesels to charge batteries came at an extraordinary cost though. Not only was the submarine's key tactical advantage—stealth—compromised but this operating vulnerability also often forced a submarine to relocate to safer waters for recharging, effectively removing it from action for an average of six hours every time.

With the fall of Germany in May 1945, Allied troops moved in to quickly seize and inspect the new-generation *Kriegsmarine* Type XXI U-boats, advanced cousins of submarines that had for years terrorized the North Atlantic. Due to the rapidly dwindling resources available to the German war machine, Type XXI U-boats were never produced at a rate fast enough to be deployable in full force.[2] It was without a doubt a lucky break for the Allies because these submarines were far superior in design to anything the Americans had. By taking a page from German engineering, and with the aid of two captured Type XXI U-boats, the US Navy's Bureau of Ships went to work to reshape their flotilla of diesel boats; what resulted was the GUPPY program.[3] The deck guns were removed, the conning tower was reshaped into the more hydrodynamic shape of a sail, the hull was streamlined, and the battery capacity was increased to improve the underwater efficiency of the fleet boats. Furthermore, the big drawback of diesel propulsion was ameliorated with the addition of the snorkel, which now allowed American submarines to recharge their batteries while submerged.

Eleven of our seventeen submariners served on at least one diesel boat. Of these eleven, eight of them served only on diesels. The other three (Collins, Herman, and Nelson) also made the transition to nuclear-powered submarines; these three men are included in our total of nine that served onboard nuclear-powered boats.

Nuclear propulsion was introduced to the world on January 17, 1955, when the USS *Nautilus* (SSN-571) broadcast her historic message: "Underway on nuclear power."[4] The groundbreaking achievement allowed submarines to extend their mission length. They would no longer have to constantly refuel or even get dangerously close to the surface to snorkel. Gone were the noisy diesel engines. And now with an essentially unlimited energy source, electrical power could be utilized to provide other essentials: fresh water from distillers and pure oxygen from the electrolysis of water. There was one small disadvantage, though. On battery power alone, the older diesel fleet boats were still quieter than nuclear submarines, which were unable to entirely mask the sounds emanating from their reactor and propulsion machinery. Irrespective of this downside, the page had turned. The atom had replaced the fossil fuel, underwater anyway.

Combined with a revolutionary development in hull design that was christened with the USS *Albacore* (AGSS-569) just a year before the arrival of the *Nautilus*, nuclear propulsion could now be melded with the hydrodynamically superior teardrop-shaped cylindrical hull to produce a completely new era of undersea warfare: the fast attack submarine. Also known as hunter-killers, or simply attack submarines (hull prefix: SSN), the fast attacks revolutionized heretofore uncharted waters in submerged speed and performance. Not only were they ideal for operations against any enemy surface vessel or submarine but fast attacks were also perfect for covert operations. And, at the same time, a completely novel mission was being developed for the submarine force. Already the gold standard for its hunter-killer and intelligence-gathering operations, the Navy now added strategic deterrence to the repertoire of the Silent Service.

These nuclear-powered fleet ballistic missile submarines, colloquially known as boomers or FBMs (hull prefix: SSBN), were specifically designed to serve as one leg of the US strategic deterrent tripod (along with Air Force strategic bombers and silo-based intercontinental ballistic missiles). In the back-and-forth arms race of the Cold War, the Soviets had managed to put the first ballistic missile submarine out to sea. But the US Navy, already experienced in deterrent patrols from the days of the Regulus program, quickly countered with its first boomer, the USS *George Washington* (SSBN-598), commissioned in December of 1959. *George Washington* carried sixteen Polaris submarine-launched ballistic missiles (SLBMs) and ushered in a new era of strategic deterrence.[5] While Regulus guided missiles required submarines to surface prior to firing, Polaris SLBMs could be launched underwater. Now, as the theory went, the idea of a preemptive strike by the Soviet Union to disable the American nuclear weapons arsenal was rendered obsolete because it would be impossible to guarantee that all the boomers could be located and taken out. The United States had finally produced a legitimate second-strike option. Stealth raised the stakes again.

Of our nine veterans that served on nuclear-powered submarines, five served only on boomers. Two served only on fast attacks, and the other two (Macaluso and Nelson) served on both varieties of nuclear-powered boats. But regardless of which types of submarines each individual served on, each man had taken his own unique path to earn membership in one of the most exclusive clubs in the US Navy.

The Interviews

The idea for this project was hatched in the early hours of Easter Sunday, April 16, 2006, and took on a sense of urgency when beloved submarine veteran and friend James "Pat" Patterson passed away that November. Patterson was our only docent who had actually served onboard the USS *Blueback*, and he took me under his wing when I started leading tours as a baby-faced fifteen-year-old with a still-sometimes squeaky voice. As I volunteered on the *Blueback*, weekend after weekend through four years of high school, and then summer after summer through four years of college, I had the privilege of becoming close friends with many of these veterans, which granted me the unique opportunity to share in their experiences. This book is the culmination of my realization that these memories will not last forever. Furthermore, despite their remarkable service to their country, these men have often gone unnoticed and unrecognized. As such, this work also serves as a tribute to them. With these inspirations in mind, I designed this project with authenticity as a primary goal. Before we started the interview sessions, I made sure the veterans understood that what is important to them is important to me. It is not about what they think I want to hear. It is about what they want to tell. People make history, and history is ultimately the grand compilation of all these individual stories and perspectives.

As a result, I decided to conduct the majority of these interviews in a group discussion format. This construction of the interviews allowed the veterans to interact with one another, providing opportunities for them to either reinforce each other's points, or to counter with contrasting examples. Hearing other submarine veterans talk about their experiences also undoubtedly helped bring back many memories for the men, and essentially provided cues from which they could comment and discuss each other's narratives. A group setting most accurately replicated the social fabric of life onboard a submarine and allowed the sailors to be more comfortable and candid. The weekly group interviews were organized thematically, with each of the eight total sessions focusing on certain specific aspects of submarine life. This thematic organization also serves as the primary basis for the different chapters in this book. Structuring these interviews by themes (as opposed to by time or chronology) helps us make broad generalizations that encompass the experiences a typical submariner went through during the Cold War. A sample size of seventeen is obviously far from scientific and not perfectly representative of all the varieties of experiences a submariner could have encountered. But it nonetheless provides a detailed snapshot of a secluded society and is definitely diverse enough for us to discern a common occurrence from an isolated happening.

Oral History and Methodology

Oral history presents very rich and nuanced first-hand perspectives that contribute to a more complete understanding of history. Qualities of the human experience, such as emotion and humor, are often lost in the documents of the recorded past. But these qualities are no less important to the way we process our memories and construct culture. For example, the words "pride" and "service" have very different meanings to a sailor who spent twenty of his prime years in the Navy and to a politician who loads a speech with these two words on Veterans Day. Without proper context, we may not hear the difference. The sailor has defined years of his life, and oftentimes his worldview, based on these concepts. The politician is digging for catchphrases that accentuate another purpose, which even if noble in intent, is often lived only through the experiences of others. Oral history allows us to peel back the layers and reveal the underlying emotions. This was my primary motivation for making these interviews the centerpiece of this book. Such a construction strikes at the hearts of more traditional academic historians, who find it difficult to determine how oral history should be incorporated into the field. But the preservation and accessibility of history is of at least equal importance to the study of history as is a groundbreaking thesis and its interpretive analysis. Ivory towers are meaningless if we do not build doors and stairs (or elevators) inside them.

The use of oral history as the basis for a narrative also comes with limitations, however. Many of the perspectives that were shared by these sailors probably changed and evolved over time. The memory of an experience after five years, after ten years, or after twenty years differs from the actual objective event. The canvas, paints, and outline of the landscape all remain the same, but it is impossible to create an exact duplicate. Beyond dates, names, and places, history becomes quite subjective, and any attempt to cover this gray area comprehensively will undoubtedly be incomplete. Additionally, memories can be biased, and any reader who served onboard submarines may very well find an anecdote to be contradictory to his (and now her) own experiences. Other memories may even seem exaggerated or embellished, sometimes with fanciful figures of speech. These occurrences are an inevitable result of human storytelling. But contrary to what academic history has ingrained in us, to emphasize the verification of every fact presented, or to take narratives at their most literal interpretation, would be missing the point here. In these cases, context and intent are very important. A reader should instead ask, "Why did the speaker choose these words (or numbers)? What point is he attempting to emphasize? What emotions are embedded in his statement?" In the narration I've woven around the oral histories, I've tried to strike a balance between presenting my own conclusions and allowing the reader to formulate his or her own.

Equally important to document in this introduction is what this book is missing. Beginning our study by delineating what we have and don't have allows us to take the following oral histories at face value. For example, this book omits the experiences of submariners from other racial and ethnic backgrounds. Their stories and perspectives are invariably very different and are definitely part of the complete picture. Initially limited in the role they were allowed to play in the service, many stewards onboard submarines were of African American or Filipino descent. This omission was not intentional, but rather a byproduct of the available sample during the interview phase of the project. This book also does not utilize any interviews from naval officers, with the exception of one sailor (Chuck Macaluso) who rose from the enlisted ranks to become a warrant officer. The original project included interviews with a junior officer; but regrettably, he opted to withdraw before the book reached publication. Although the junior officer's perspectives provided a helpful contrast with the other narratives, this book is definitively built on the foundation of the enlisted experience in the submarine service.

Writing Oral History

When it came time to transpose the often-chaotic dialogue from the interviews into readable prose, I went in search of the oral historian's elusive compromise. On one hand, the interviews can be reproduced with complete accuracy by leaving in every nonsensical word, in addition to "umms," "uhhs," and other similarly constructed awkward pauses. At the other end of the spectrum, the oral historian may decide to take many liberties and remove all superfluous verbiage, perhaps even rearranging words and sentences to this end. In order to capture emotional cues and to give my interviewees each a distinct voice, I decided not to alter common English speech patterns, even if they are grammatically incorrect in theory. For example, I deliberately avoided editing commonly perceived errors in subject/verb agreement or verb tenses, and instead chose to duplicate them faithfully. Additionally, I left in certain terminology that didn't necessarily provide the right connotation but was nonetheless clear in terms of what the speaker was trying to describe. Examples include "closed vs. shut," "maps vs. charts," and "doors vs. hatches." But I have also tried to improve the readability of the spoken word, making comprehension easier. To accomplish this goal, I decided to omit any extraneous words and sentences that detracted from what I believed to be the speakers' intents and purposes for making their statements.

And in order to more effectively convey these intents and purposes to the reader, I occasionally inserted my own words into the quotations. These modifications are enclosed by brackets. I also asked my interviewees to review my transcriptions for errors. If they requested cosmetic alterations, I made them without indication. If their suggested modifications changed the meaning of the text, I inserted those changes with brackets as well. In other instances, the reader may encounter unfamiliar acronyms, technical terminology, and submarine slang within the quotations. To preserve the natural flow of speech, I chose to have these words and phrases explained in the endnotes, unless they are crucial to a basic understanding of the text.

I have exerted every effort to ensure that each quoted word exists as a result of my conscious decision to have it included. But throughout the process of writing this book, I will inevitably have made some errors in judgment. I take full responsibility for these errors, irrespective of their origin.

Beyond *Standing Watch*

Readers with greater interest in the history of the American submarine service during the Cold War should refer to the bibliography for more resources. From the very beginning, I wrote with the intention of making this book a complementary piece to the other historical studies heretofore published. Addressed in this book's epilogue, *Blind Man's Bluff* by Sherry Sontag and Christopher Drew is generally accepted as the point of entry into this field. Memoirs by high-ranking officers and scientists (William Anderson, Alfred McLaren, Dan Summitt, etc.) are the most commonly encountered contributions. These career retrospectives additionally provide a different context for the literature on Admiral Rickover, which is also fairly comprehensive, but the topics addressed by these works are mostly not covered within the scope of this book. The short section in chapter 4 on Admiral Rickover (Kindly Old Gentleman) exists solely because of his outsized influence on people he never even met. Our contribution to the study of the admiral is to show a different perspective of what Rickover was like as a person through the lenses of sailors who saw him as a mythical creature. If a reader desires to further plumb the depths of the admiral's administrative prowess, myriad books cover this topic from different angles.

Works on the enlisted experience are much sparser; comprehensive memoirs like *Stealth Boat* by Gannon McHale are few and far between. Some books include compilations or brief excerpts of the enlisted experience. Paul Stillwell edited a volume of individual recollections from the diesel-boat era, and Glenn Knoblock explores the dynamics of race in his study of black US submariners through 1975. These works are all foundational brushstrokes of a painting still in its infancy. With this book, it is my hope that a semblance of something recognizable and colorful will begin to appear.

But every experience is still individual and unique. The reader will join our seventeen sailors in a time machine, and accompany them as each man relives his most difficult challenges and his biggest accomplishments. Whether surrounded by the putrid essence of their own puke, or the fresh and salty sea breeze on a rare foray to the surface, our veterans share perspectives and emotions that illuminate the darker corners of the Silent Service.

It is June 16, 2008. Glistening off the glass high-rises of downtown Portland, the sun is still flashing brightly on another beautiful Pacific Northwest summer evening. On the opposite bank of the Willamette River, the USS *Blueback* peacefully rests at moor. Her gentle rolling in the river's current belies an appetite for adventure during thirty-one years of Cold War service. Although seemingly still and serene from a vantage point on the water, there is much more activity within the hull of the old war machine. I turn on the recorder.

I
Adventure's Beginning

Joining the Navy

Although one-third of our volunteers joined the Navy from Portland, it is almost by sheer coincidence that everyone ended up in the same room, sitting around the same table. These men entered the US Navy from various backgrounds and for various reasons. Their enlistment periods stretched across seven different decades, the equivalent of a lifespan. Furthermore, some of them had never met one another before, even though they volunteer on the same submarine. So when it came time to ask the first question of a two-month-long interview project, I decided to keep it simple and slightly personal. I settled on a question that everyone would have a different answer for, yet would also provide a common basis from which they could get to know their peers better, and in a more comfortable setting. So I simply queried, "Why did you join the Navy?" Their responses here serve as a personal introduction to each individual, and help transition to their anecdotes in the rest of the book.

1942—**Fred A. Carneau:** I went to work at the shipyard up in Bremerton, and we were working on one of them little escort carriers. We waited three months for steel, and I got tired of welding guys' cleats to the deck and throwing welding wire at the ducks, so I went down and joined the Navy.

1947—**Elbert H. "Collie" Collins:** I joined the Navy to go into what they called V-12, to be a doctor. I didn't have enough money to keep competing against everybody, so I joined the Navy. And so next thing I know, I'm in! I said, "You're not going to screw me over; I'm going to take that V-12 exam first, to find out if I can pass it, and then I'll sign up." So I took the exam, and I passed for V-12. I said, "Hot damn, I'm going to school," so then I enlisted for six years. While I was in boot camp, the sons of guns cancelled

V-12 and I had signed up for six freaking years! Now that was a mistake. Next thing I know, I'm in for six years, and I thought, "You're not going to screw me over . . ." until the Marine Corps got me.[1]

1952—Robert Austin "Bob" Jackson: World War II broke out, I was about eight, and my brother volunteered a day or two after the war broke out. He was stationed at Long Beach, Washington, and my folks and I would go down there and visit him. At that time, looking up to him—the role model that he was, I knew that I wanted to get into the service, and someday that I would get in the Navy. Of course, World War II had a great influence on my life, and so I actually enlisted in the Navy before I graduated from high school. And I knew when I joined the service, that I was going to sub school. There was a submarine [at] Swan Island, and I'd gone aboard that boat, and I just volunteered for sub duty.

1953—William M. "Bill" Bryan Jr.: I just went down and joined the reserves, to . . . I guess make more money, I thought. Went to sub school right out of high school; I had quit school. I was out of school a year—and that's what started the reserve thing. My mother said, "I don't care how long you take to get out of school—you're going to have that diploma." I told my dad; I said, "Bullshit!" He says, "Mmm . . . you're going to get that diploma!" So anyway, I went back and finished up and that was it—went on active duty right out of sub school.

1955—Robert "Bob" Walters: I was going to the University of Washington. At that time, ROTC was required up there. And the ROTC was the Army ROTC, which was not my forte, so I joined the submarine reserves up in Seattle, took after that; didn't go to boot camp, went to six weeks of submarine school in San Francisco, Hunters Point, "A" school for two weeks, and "B" school for four weeks. Came back to Seattle, [and] said, "I want to go active," and went active. Main reason I went active was . . . the girl I was chasing around joined the convent.[2]

1957—Robert W. "Bob" Sumner: I was living in New Mexico, I was getting ready to graduate from high school, and I was running around with a bunch of guys that probably weren't the best in the world. Some of them got killed, [got into] car accidents and everything else, and I decided that I probably needed to change my life. So I went down to [the] Navy recruiter, and signed up. My mother was more than happy to sign the papers.

1959—Gary W. Webb: Well, I had a choice, I guess. At the time that I was going through high school, why it was common knowledge with the guys I run with that you had a choice: you either enlisted or you got drafted.

Enlisting in the Navy would get me what I wanted, where if I just hung around, why you'd get drafted into the Army probably. I didn't particularly care for that, so I went ahead and enlisted.

1960—Herbert A. "Herb" Herman: Actually, I wanted to become a nuclear physicist. That was the days of the Sputnik. I didn't have any money to become a nuclear physicist, so I wound up going in the Navy and going to nuke school.

1960—David Meade "Dave" Vrooman: Well, my dad was in the Navy, so there was never any question what I was going to do. So as soon as I got old enough, I joined the Navy.

1962—Evert Charles "Chuck" Nelson: When I was a senior in high school, that was in about '59, early in the year, like February, a bunch of recruiters got together and they all had one show for the whole senior class, and I thought, "You know, that didn't sound bad; they had some interesting things." So I thought, "Let's beat the draft; I'll join the Coast Guard Reserve." Off I go, after graduation, we went on down to the Bay Area, Alameda. They had their Coast Guard base there, the boot camp. I did my time in the Coast Guard Reserve; it's only six months. When I got out, I was going to college, [and] got into a car accident. Now you're not supposed to drive without insurance, I know that, but it cost me a little bit of money, and I said, "Well, let's see what they got back in the Navy." They started this nuclear power program, and I thought, "You know, that's probably a good education, and they're building civilian plants, so it's a good job future." So I signed up for it.

1962—Richard G. "R. G." Walker: I got out of high school and didn't know what I wanted to do. Didn't want to go to school, went to school anyway—decided I really didn't want to go to school. And then, [I] watched too many John Wayne movies, [and] that TV show *The Silent Service*, [so] my brother and I both signed up for submarines. We're getting ready to go and they gave our physical and they said, "Well, there's something wrong with your brother . . ."

"Well, what [does] that mean?"

"He's not going and you are!"

1963—Garth Lascink: Now I'm graduated from high school, and I'm getting ready to go to Long Beach State, to go to college, and end up buying a car. Then I got in a fight with my dad, because he says, "How in the hell you going to pay for college if you're buying a car?" And on and on; we got in a little bit of a fight. So I says,

"Well, I can always join the Navy like you did!"

"Go ahead! Be my guest!"

Anyway, to join, I says, "Well, I'll join; I'll go in for three years," cause they had what they called a "kiddie cruise." If you went in before you're eighteen, you could do three years, get out by the time you're twenty-one. So I says, "Hey, that sounds good," so I got my mom talked in to go down and sign the papers with me. And then I wanted to go into submarines. [The recruiter] says, "We got a deal for you, young man; we have what we call a Polaris Electronics field," something like that. He says, "You're in for three years. If you get along fine, if you finally get through, then you go for six, but other than that, you're on a three-year kiddie cruise." So anyway, I joined that program, and what happened was if you keep going on, next thing you know, you got to do six years, because you went to two years worth of school. So that's how I got in. After that, it was all downhill!

1964—Christopher "Chris" Stafford: When I was in high school, one of my friends got an invitation to go down to the Naval Reserve Center, just for an instructional type of thing—letting everybody know what's available. So he suckered me in along with some other guys, the neighborhood buddies, to go down to listen to the spiel. And at the time, Vietnam was starting to get hot and heavy. I don't know if it was an intelligent decision on my part, or whether it was just dumb luck. I [thought], hey, the submarine community is a really tight-knit community, and it interested me; you could kind of call your own shots. You weren't going to be walking around in the mud in Vietnam. So while we're there, we took an aptitude test, and they call you up, "Hey! You did pretty good on the aptitude test; why don't you come down and talk to us?" So I went down and talked to them and had a pretty good deal going, and I go, "Sure, what the heck? Why not?" So I joined the Naval Reserve when I was seventeen.

1974—Michael A. "Mike" Stephens: Graduated high school, [and] knew a whole bunch of things I didn't want to do. It was a little lumber town I grew up in, and I knew I didn't want to work in the woods, didn't want to work in the mill. Didn't think I was smart enough to go to college, so I talked to the Air Force recruiter, and he was a jerk. So I went next door and talked with the Navy guy, and next thing I know, I was headed to San Diego.

1975—Alan L. Nolan: Coming from Montana, a place where there's not a lot of jobs, I had to do something. Couldn't afford to go to college—my folks weren't going to be able to help me much with that. And I already kind of had an idea in my mind, already wanted to be on a submarine, probably cause of the movies I watched while I was growing up. I had a brother that was in the Navy. And he was on submarines. I think that's probably the reason that I joined the Navy—mostly because of, one, it was a job, it was a way to get some education, [and] maybe a little chance to see some of the world.

1978—**Mark A. Manzer:** For me about a year after high school, working a minimum wage job, and still not being ready for school, I thought the Navy would be a good choice at the time.

1979—**Charles Fredrick "Chuck" Macaluso:** I was just starting my senior year in high school, and went down to the recruiter in September. My recruiter was a submariner—he kind of impressed me. So I was kind of hooked; I signed up on the delayed-entry program, told my mom; she cried, and then eight months later, I graduated from high school on a Tuesday night, and Thursday morning, I was in boot camp. That's how it started. I was seventeen.

Entering the Submarine Service

Not all of our volunteers joined the Navy with one eye on the Silent Service. For each person who entered with a piqued interest in submarines, there was someone else who never planned on being awarded his dolphins. An undersea equivalent of the golden or silver wings worn by an aviator, dolphins are insignia pins awarded to submariners who have passed the arduous qualification process. It is important to keep in mind that the submarine service is, and has always been, a volunteer service, even in the darkest and most desperate days of the Second World War. Simply stated, this is not a job for just anyone. Not every man has the disposition and the faculties to spend extended periods of time confined to several small, cramped compartments, isolated from the outside world, rarely seeing daylight, while sharing this environment with sixty to over 100 of his closest compatriots.

As one of those who made a decision early on, Gary Webb was steered toward the submarine service due to financial considerations: "I came out [from boot camp], second in my company, and because of that honor, when they were interviewing us, why they said, 'Where would you like to go?' And I asked the key question that any eighteen-year-old would ask:

'Where can I make the most money?'

'Well, submarine service, you can make good money . . . '

'Okay, that's where I'll go.'

And being that I was high enough in my company at boot camp, I automatically got sub service."

Others such as R. G. Walker, Garth Lascink, and Alan Nolan were inspired to serve onboard submarines because certain aspects of the service made lasting impressions on them even before they joined the Navy. Whereas Walker and Nolan watched too many movies, Lascink recalled a real-life encounter:

> My dad was a chief, in the Navy twenty-six years. When I was a kid, growing up, I'd see him. He was a destroyer man basically, but he would tell me about the submarine service and how it was a pretty good service, a good place to be, even though he wasn't in it. And then I attribute . . . going into the submarine service because he took me as a kid one time, down on one of the old diesel boats, after the Korean War—we went onboard. It's like going on a pirate ship. I mean, these guys had these big old beards, and they're all grody and stuff, and you go, "Man, this is cool!" For a young kid, I mean . . . it's like watching *Pirates of the Caribbean*, right? I mean, these guys are nasty-looking down there, so that must have imprinted in my brain.

Mark Manzer was similarly inspired, but gravitated toward a different aspect of submarine life. "[I was] kind of a romantic when I joined the submarine service. When I was in junior high, I read a couple of books [that] talked about submarine exploits in World War II, and I thought that was pretty cool, and I thought, you know, that's a camaraderie I'd like to experience."

Dave Vrooman wanted to sign up for the submarine service from the start. Although initially denied entry because of medical considerations, he eventually found the right loophole that would get him where he wanted to be. As he recalled, "I got to boot camp, found out that I couldn't get into sub school because of my vision; but then I went to a destroyer and I found out that if I got into [the] nuclear power program, they didn't have those restrictions on vision. [So I] got into nuclear power, then submarines."

For some of the other veterans, it took much longer to find their way into the submarine service. As Collie Collins remembered,

> This was another one of my smart deals. I had just come back from five years of sea duty, and for a corpsman, that is exceptional; I mean, usually year-and-a-half, two years at the most. I had five years at sea, reported to Bremerton, wife just had a child, and things are going good. I've been on the beach about six months. [Then] I wanted to get a dental appointment; you couldn't get a dental appointment [at the time]. [But] they were needing guys for submarine service; they would take

> [those] people to the head of the dental line. I knew I wanted to go to submarines eventually, so I thought, "I'll volunteer for submarines; lets me get done with my sea duty, you know, but I got to get my teeth fixed." So me and six other guys all went in and got our teeth fixed. I sat in that chair for two-and-a-half hours. They took fillings out of my mouth I didn't even know I had! So we got all done with that; they sent us out to Keyport for the submarine pressure test, and we closed the door. One guy wanted out immediately, cause he was claustrophobic. Soon as they started [to] put the pressure on, another guy wanted out. Next thing you know, I was the only one out of seven to pass the damn thing. But you're not going to screw me over, because you know, you got independent-duty school to go to, and submarine school, and all this, and I thought, "Shit, honey, don't worry about it; I still have another year or two on the beach before I ever go back out to sea." Wrong! I had to go home that next day and explain to my wife why we were going to New London immediately. You can't trust the goddamn doctors! They wrote me up in such a way that I didn't even have to go to independent-duty school. I'm reading the thing . . . "Who the hell is this guy they're talking about?" Oh, that first two or three years we were married . . . it was kind of iffy there.[3]

Other sailors had the Silent Service find them. Bob Sumner was well on his way to a career in the surface fleet when his destroyer escort was assigned on a deployment to the Western Pacific area of operations (WESTPAC). Little did he anticipate the end of that deployment changing his destiny:

> When I got out of boot camp, I was initially sent up to Astoria, Oregon. There was a naval reserve fleet; it was called Tongue Point Naval Reserve Fleet. And it was all the old World War II troop transports that were sitting on the mud. So I came up here for about three months. And then I got sent down to San Diego onboard [the] USS *Bridget*, and we departed almost immediately for WESTPAC. About six months, we were over in WESTPAC. I was in the fire room; I was a fireman, and talk about hot . . . Not the most popular place in the world to be. When we got back, operating in San Diego, we were operating with some submarines, in antisubmarine warfare games. And the captain came on one day and asked [if] anybody would like to ride a submarine: "See if that's something you'd like to do." And I put my hand up immediately, so I went aboard the USS *Aspro*, and rode it for three or four days. I just knew right away that's what I wanted to do. And so I put in for submarine school right away.

Submarine School

Submarine school was considered to be the unique training phase that revealed whether prospective submariners were fit for duty beneath the waves. The program was designed to weed out those considered unfit, essentially through natural selection. If a sailor couldn't complete every step of the training, he was effectively prevented from serving on a submarine.

But if a sailor performed well in training and earned high marks in class, he was given preferential treatment when it came time for duty assignments. As Bob Sumner recalled, "Shortly after I had taken the third-class boiler tender test, I was transferred to New London for sub school; while I was in sub school, I got third-class boiler tender. Then when I graduated out of sub school, I was fairly high in the class, and so they assigned me to *Sea Poacher,* which at that time was rumored in the fleet [to be] one of the best submarines on the East Coast, which sounded pretty good. Key West sounded pretty good." Gary Webb was even offered a choice: "I did well in sub school, so when it came time for billets, I was second in my class, and they said, 'Where would you like to go?' And I says, 'What've you got on the West Coast?' And they had about three or four submarines in Hawaii and they had a couple in San Diego, and I said, 'I'll take that one in San Diego,' and I reported aboard the second of December, 1959."

All but one of our volunteers attended submarine school. The lone exception was Fred Carneau, our only World War II veteran. As he explained, "The war got over, so it was in [1947] . . . I went into submarines, and being as I went in as chief, I didn't [have to] go to sub school."

As most of our veterans attended submarine school in New London, Connecticut, they all went through essentially identical training, even over different decades. And for all of them, their defining experience as students was the escape tower training. As Webb recalled, "Bottom line, sub school, the biggest thing . . . was going through the escape [tower]. We made two eighteen-footers, and a fifty-footer, and that weekend, anybody who wanted to could go do a 100-footer, and I elected to do that—that was a lot of fun." But for most other prospective submariners, "fun" was not the best description of the experience, nor of the wait. "Daunting" seemed to be the more appropriate word. As it wasn't until the final weeks of sub school that one would finally be subjected to the challenges of the escape tower, Collie Collins added, "You would sit there for the several weeks while you were in class, and for three or four weeks, you'd sit there, and you'd look at that big sucker there, [thinking] 'Oh shit!'"

The stated idea behind this training facility was to ensure that all submariners knew how to conduct and survive an escape ascent in the event that a submarine was disabled in shallow-enough water. However, the probability of sailors actually applying this training to a real-life situation was extremely low, because the chances were quite slim that any emergency would occur in conditions favorable to this sort of escape method. Thus, there were other reasons all submarine school students were required to go through the tower. These included giving instructors the opportunity to evaluate the psychological behavior and physical reaction of each sailor in this sort of high-pressure environment, both figuratively and literally.

The water in this tower was about 80 degrees, and the inside chamber wall was painted with mermaids. Also inside the chamber were Navy divers, whose job it was to facilitate the training. As Webb recalled, "That was one thing I thought was real amazing, is when you're going through the escape chamber, the Navy divers would be operating off of the top of [the tower], and they would be coming down to fifty feet and staying there for five to six minutes with no breathing apparatus whatsoever."

The adjacent holding chamber was small, cramped, noisy, and hot . . . and then the water level started rising. The sailors were instructed to take three deep breaths before they entered the escape tower. As Garth Lascink recalled, "They're flooding and pressurizing at the same time. I can remember thinking, 'I hope the hell he shuts this off before this sucker gets up to my nose.' I felt sorry for the shorter guy." Collins happened to be one of the shorter guys: "When we went through the chamber, I'm the shortest guy; I actually had to get two guys to [support me]. And I'm up there saying, 'Who wants to go first!?' I had to go, or else I was going to drown!"

As one prepared for the ascent, he was under strict orders to follow clearly defined guidelines. Failure to comply could result in serious, potentially fatal, bodily harm: "We stood on a platform, outside the compression chamber. You duck down, you step out on the platform, you stood there until one of those divers tapped you on the shoulders. Once he tapped you on the shoulder, then you let go, and you went to surface, blowing all the way to the top."[4] If a sailor failed to continuously exhale on the way to the surface and instead regressed to the natural instinct of holding his breath, one of the divers would punch him in the abdomen, forcing the release of air. This was a crucial part of the ascent procedure, as the decreasing water pressure over the duration of the ascent would cause the air in one's lungs to expand. Failure to exhale would allow air pressure to build up inside the lungs and eventually cause them to rupture.

There was so much emphasis placed on breathing correctly that those who messed up en route had their ascent cut short and were forced to repeat the test. As Lascink remembered, "If you didn't breathe out, they'd hit you in the stomach. So when you're standing up around the ring up above, you could see bubbles that would come up just normally. But if a guy got tapped, all of a sudden, [you'd see a burst], and everybody [watching] would go 'Whoa!' And they'd pull these guys [out]. They have these bells on the side they throw you into, yank you in from there. So [you] had to go back down again." Collins recalled how "One other corpsman left his glasses on. Halfway up, he lost it and decided he was going to go after it. One of the [divers] grabbed him and kneed him right where he lived, doubled him up like a small ball, and just stuck him ever so gently into [the bell]. They did not screw around." But even those who successfully completed the ascent did not always make it out unscathed. One common injury that occurred would be seen in sailors bleeding from the ears if they failed to physically adjust to the quick pressure change. These men would immediately be ushered into decompression chambers so that they could readjust. If the ascent was too fast, another common danger these sailors faced was decompression sickness, when a gas embolism or bubble would form in the bloodstream from formerly dissolved gasses. Commonly known as "the bends," this was a particular concern because it could result in permanent neurological damage. Although it was rare for someone to experience "the bends" in the escape tower (due to the limited time one was subjected to high pressures), the Navy took no chances. As Collins continued,

> We had one corpsman—had been out drinking pretty good the night before, and he was whizzing up a storm. One of the signs of an embolism is you got to urinate. And he had to urinate when we're down below. I'm the first one up; [he] was the second one up. They ask [us]: "How do you feel?" He said, "I have to whiz!" [So] they jerked him up and threw him in the [decompression] chamber. I said [to the supervisor], "He had to whiz before we left!"
>
> "Oh really?" So he went over there: "How are you?"
>
> "Fine!"
>
> "Do you still have to go?"
>
> "No . . ."

One aspect of the ascent that frequently changed over time was the sort of assistance one could rely on while going up. When Bill Bryan went through the twenty-five-foot and fifty-foot ascents in 1955, sailors were allowed to guide themselves with a knotted rope, and instructed to go "Hand over hand, and don't you reach too soon!" Less than a year later, the rope was abandoned, and sailors were instead ordered to free ascent, or "Follow the bubble." By the time Lascink went through in 1964, he noted that Steinke Hoods, a protective mask and life preserver unit covering the head and neck, were standard issue for the escape tower.

But with or without assisting equipment, completing the ascent successfully was much easier said than done. It took R. G. Walker several attempts to finally make it:

> We marched down there . . . excuse me, we walked down there, since we couldn't march. Got down there, we're looking at the tower, and the guys kept saying, "Are you alright!? Are you alright!?"
>
> "Why?"
>
> "You're pure white!"
>
> [Then] we get inside the thing; they start dividing us up into groups. First group goes up, gets in the chamber, does their thing; next group [goes up]. Meanwhile, I'm getting whiter and whiter . . . So they get us in there, and they start flooding it up. Then they turn the pressure on—the screaming noise, and the air is hotter than hell; [we're] sucking this hot air in, and I must have put a glow out or something, cause the guy in there says, "Are you okay!? Are you okay!?" So they give you the instructions and you step out; come my turn, I get down there, look up—let all my air out! The guy grabs my neck and grabs my shorts, shoved me back underneath there . . . "What's wrong with you!? Try again!" And then [next time], the guy reaches over and grabs me from the side [bell], hits me in the guts: "You got to blow out! [Or I'll] put you back in!" It took me three times to get through that son-of-a-bitch.

But even Walker can be considered a success, because it was not uncommon to see several sailors in each group refuse to enter the chamber in the first place and flunk out.

In addition to the escape tower, the sailors were subjected to a pressure chamber test. As Lascink explained,

> They put us in this great big chamber full of guys, and you're in there . . . what we call "asshole to bellybutton." You got your legs spread; this guy's in front of you, [facing away]. So they take you down; they're going to check you out [to see if] you can equalize. Then you get down there—run some pure oxygen to make sure you don't come up with oxygen narcosis. And the guy says, "Keep ahead of the pressurization. You don't want to get behind, cause you won't be able to catch back up." So to pressurize, you hold your nose, blow against your nose, and your ears start popping. Some of these guys really get with the program, right? So we're going down, going down, and next thing you know, we're down probably about 100 feet or whatever. The guy in front of me—his finger slips off. And he had a cold, I think, because he put a green caterpillar out of his nose, onto this guy's shoulder blade! Now, I'm laughing,

> the guy behind me is laughing . . . and if you're down there, everybody sounds like Donald Duck. So now the chief in control is saying, "You guys shut up!" And he sounds like Donald Duck! And as soon as he says that, the whole thing's roaring now! He's lost total control; you got all these ducks in there just talking and laughing like hell—and this guy's got this big loogie on the back of his shoulder. And this guy was livid up there, the chief in charge: "I'm going to flunk all you guys! What the hell's going [on]?" And everybody's pointing back here . . . Oh my God, that was so funny!

Bob Walters went through submarine school at Hunters Point in San Francisco. Because this facility did not have an escape tower, Walters later completed that particular test at Pearl Harbor. But while at Hunters Point, his first test was in the pressurization chamber: "They put us in the diving chamber, brought up the pressure to 55 pounds, and [at] about 35 pounds, a friend of mine from Seattle—he started screaming his head off. His teeth . . . the fillings were not right. So they pulled him out; he was no longer there. I thought, 'Jesus . . . you know? Wow . . .'" If dental fillings were improperly inserted with a bubble of air trapped underneath, pressurization could cause the teeth to blow apart. Lascink pointed to this danger as one of the main reasons the Navy required everyone to go through a dental check before a submarine deployed.

Another distinguishing trial of submarine school happened near the beginning of the course, when every man would be subjected to psychological evaluations. As Webb recalled, "The other thing that was difficult was the first week, [when] we had sit-down interviews with the shrink. Each one of us spent about three hours talking with him, and I would say we lost about fifty percent of our guys."

As a hospital corpsman, Collins was able to see these evaluations from the other side, later on in his career: "You took those tests, every half a day for the first week, either morning or afternoon. We would sit up there and grade these, and they're looking for guys who are either out to the left or the right. And we wanted a shade of gray." With regard to these psychological tests, Lascink pointed to one difficult question that left a lasting impression: "It was like, from 1 to 7 or 1 to 10, you grade what you think about this . . . and the question was: 'What do you think of body odor?' But I'm going now, 'Wait a minute. I'm going into submarines. Those suckers smell like a pig sty, right?' So if I say I like it, they're going to go, 'Whoa, what's the matter [with him]?' But if I say I don't like it, you're not going, so you're sitting there going, 'But do I be 5 or do I be a 6, or 4,' or what do you be, you know?"

Another standard evaluation administered to every sailor was a color recognition test. After scoring one such test, Collins remembered,

> I got my ass chewed up like you would not believe. I flunked the young ensign right out of the Academy. I was doing the physicals up there, and this kid was colorblind. And I marked him down colorblind, and I dropped his ass, just that easy. A week later, I get a call. The administrator's office—they want to know if I dropped this ensign so and so. And I said, "Yeah, I did. My signature's there." He said, "Well, his dad's contesting it." I thought, "Well, who the hell's his dad?"
>
> Yes, the admiral came back and he wanted to see the test. He wanted it run right in front of him; he didn't believe it. So we have a test; it's twenty-six colored checkers. And they got numbers on one side, colors on the other. And you dump them out here on the table, and you give him a rack, and he's got to go from the shade of black here over to the reds and greens. And you had to line them up. Then when you turn them over, you [count] 1, 2, 3, 4, right on down. Well, I did that test, and his dad found out he was colorblind.

But passing this seemingly insignificant test is critical because the identification of many control panel indicators onboard a submarine is dependent on color. In addition, red/green indicator lights and numerous valves would be simply indistinguishable to a colorblind person.

Prospective submariners were also subjected to a hearing test. Although Herb Herman suffered from some high frequency loss, he knew exactly how to pass the test: "They give you a hearing test with the phones, on a bench. There was a whole row of people, and you sat down, you mark the tones. [So] I made sure I sat next to a sonarman!"

And as a result of the intense battery of evaluations, tests, medical checks, and physical stresses, the attrition rate was high; frequently, one would see less than half of the original class graduate. From standard class sizes of fifty students, Sumner remembered that twenty to twenty-five graduated; that number was only nineteen in Webb's class; and in Collins's class of corpsmen on the medical track, a mere twelve students made it through. But even with so many sailors flunking out, submarine school did not come close to simulating the actual training a sailor would have to go through before he was truly qualified to serve on a boat.

Specialty Training

Besides the obligatory submarine school, most sailors received other standard technical training through classes known as "A," "B," and "C" schools. To acquire basic proficiency in a specialty rating such as fire control technician or engineman, sailors completed "A" school. If they desired advanced proficiency, many sailors would be given an opportunity to continue their studies in "B" school. "C" schools were offered as focused training courses for specific pieces of shipboard equipment, a radar unit for example. Additionally, several of our volunteers pursued unique qualifications that required separate, intensive training programs. These included diving school and nuclear power school.

Collie Collins ended up in nuclear power school, but not by his own design:

> I was on the *Catfish*, and it was a training boat at the time. And they would send these young kids to the boat, and we'd get them qualified, and send them to nuclear power school. But they kept sending us corpsmen . . . Well, I knew one of us [would] go to nuclear power school. So I would get these guys qualified, get the dolphins in about eight months—didn't know shit when they left, but they got their dolphins. [They'd] qualify, and I'd ship them off to nuclear power school, [while] I stayed on that *Catfish*. I had it made. Then they sent me a Seventh-day Adventist . . . wouldn't go to school or the boat on Friday or Saturday. Of course, he'd come back on Sunday; there'd [be] nobody there. I'm looking at the seventh month, then the eighth month. [I] keep thinking, "I got to get you qualified," and the skipper would say, "Is he going to be ready to go?" And I'm saying, "I'm hoping so!" Needless to say, he didn't get qualified, so I ended up going to nuclear power school! That's how I ended up there, whether I wanted it or not. And I didn't.

Exceptions like Collins aside, the specialty rating of enlisted personnel determined whether one would attend nuclear power school. Most sailors who worked in the engineering spaces of nuclear submarines were required to go, as this training was relevant to the job description. For officers, however, there was a little more at stake.

After the Navy opted for an all-nuclear underwater fleet, all officers on track for a career in submarines were required to be nuclear-qualified, as the top three slots in the officer community onboard all nuclear-powered submarines were held by nuclear-trained officers: commanding officer (CO), executive officer (XO), and engineer. In the 1960s, as Garth Lascink noted from the USS *Mariano G. Vallejo* (SSBN-658), most of the junior officers were not nuclear-qualified. But as Mark Manzer and Mike Stephens both observed a decade later, non-nuclear-qualified officers became a rarity onboard, with the few exceptions being perhaps a supply officer or a weapons officer. Supply officers were usually the youngest on the submarine; they were assigned to handle all the administrative and logistical duties. And because officers weren't required to be nuclear-qualified as a weapons officer when they moved up the ladder, this particular position ended up being less desirable. As Stephens noted about officers in the pursuit of commanding their own submarine, "They didn't want to be weapons officers because they were all geared towards the big tea kettle."[5]

Later in his career, Chuck Macaluso went to diving school:

> I was at Coronado. It was just a five, six week school. However, there was a week there called "pool week," and the first day of pool week, they took everybody to the deep end of the pool, and you buddied-up. Everybody had to take their boot laces off, and your buddy tied your hands behind your back with one lace, and your ankles together. And they threw us in the 25-foot deep end and told us, "You need to float for fifteen minutes." And that scared the crap out of me. Cause if you didn't have a lot of body weight, it was kind of hard to get that balance, to the bottom and up. And later in the week, on the final day, was "shark day," when the instructors would be up at the top of the pool; you're down below in your scuba with your buddy, and you're not supposed to surface without your air. Your air is down below in a tank, not up there with them. And so I ran out of air, and I surfaced, and they start screaming at me. If you surface twice, you're out. So the next time, they hit me harder, cause they knew I came up the first time. And they had my hoses tied, my mask was ripped off . . . They had me upside down; they were punching me in the stomach. And then they pulled the regulator away . . . and I just blew bubbles, until . . . my vision started going . . . and I almost passed out underwater. He saw that, he took the regulator, he put it in my mouth, and boom, the vision came back. And I passed. It was like, *that* close. And there was puke floating around all over the pool. Everybody was vomiting or getting sick . . . That was an interesting week.

Lascink went through similar training in Hawaii some twenty years earlier, diving initially in a pool, and then later in the open sea, off Barbers Point, Oahu. Scuba training there required the divers to go through the escape chamber again: "One of the things you do, is you go through that tower, but this time you go out with just the air in your lungs, free ascent. So you pick out a bubble as you go up, and if it starts getting away from you, you hold in air; if you get close, you blow out more air. I was going up, and there's people coming up behind, and the next thing I hear is: 'SWIM!' It's like God, talking underwater . . . to somebody behind me that had less body fat. Most people [could] go up with their body fat, but there's a few people that'll have negative buoyancy and head down. So they're telling this guy to swim." Overall, the physical demands on divers were intense, and as Lascink added, "You're just trying to make it through there; it's kind of scary for awhile . . . That was one place I was glad to get out of, when I finally got through there, and got my qualification to be a diver."

Although scuba school was undoubtedly challenging, Lascink cited the wet trainer at Pearl Harbor as his most salient training experience. Designed to replicate various damage conditions, including battle damage, the wet trainer simulated flooding in different submarine compartments and created a realistic live-action environment where sailors could learn to prepare for and conduct repairs under extreme conditions: "They'd take the senior guys off the boat, put them in the tank down in the pit, turn the water on, start that stuff coming in, and invariably, the boat was lost. That was the best training I ever had in the submarine service. And once [you have the experience], you can stop [the flooding]. Of course, it gives you false confidence because these lines, the pressure . . . is not very much. But you could stop it before it got to your ankles, once you knew what you were doing in there. But it was interesting to see chiefs and first-class . . . losing the boat . . . That kind of opened your eyes. You really never had any practice doing that stuff, until they put that wet trainer in." The wet trainer had only been recently installed at the time Lascink went through, for just a couple years before, facilities for damage control training did not even exist. It is a difficult leap of imagination from the present day, where damage control simulations form an integral part of basic training.

On a recent tour of a training facility in St. Marys, Georgia, Bill Bryan expressed unexpected surprise at the changes that had taken place over several decades. When Bryan joined the Navy in the early 1950s, "We got training, and I thought we got good training. But if you compare that to what they get today, the crew that's off—trains, trains, trains. It's everyday, eight, ten, twelve, fourteen, sixteen hours a day. As compared to us, we trained when we [were] aboard, but when you left that boat, you went whichever way. You either went home or you went to the barracks or whatever. But if you take the difference between today and then, they get one whale of an amount of more training. I'm sure the boat is much more complicated today than it was when I was on it, but the mishaps that can happen [are still the same]."

Even out at sea, the crew is constantly drilling for a whole plethora of emergency situations. Macaluso recounted one such drill that took an ironic twist: "On my last patrol, before I got off the *Kentucky*, we were doing our afternoon drill set. I was the drill monitor in control [room]. We had a simulated fire onboard. Everybody in the control room has EAB [masks] on, except me and this other guy. And him and I are looking at each other, and we start smelling something burning. No one else can smell it—they're all on EABs. And this control panel behind us starts smoking and burning. Nobody [else] notices it! We actually had a fire start during the drill, right next to me, and I'm the drill monitor! I had to stop the drill and actually fight [the fire]."[6]

Collins, the hospital corpsman, was also baptized with on-the-job training. And just like Macaluso's trial by fire, Collins's drill turned into the real thing. During a practice emergency as part of an Operational Readiness Inspection (ORI), the evacuation of simulated casualties from the USS *Catfish* (SS-339) didn't go as planned: "Our first ORI, in the forward engine room, the [drill monitor] picked this guy and laid him right down on the [deck]. He said, 'Fire in the engine room!' [I] went running back there, [saw the casualty] laying there—I had to get him out, so I grabbed him, put him on my shoulder, [like] a fireman carrying . . . I went running for that hatch going into the mess hall . . . ['Bang!'] [We both] went down. That was my first surgery on the boat. Eight stitches! I was called 'Nurse' for the next couple of weeks!" News of this story spread fast, and as Collins noted, "In the medical [community], you screw up, and it's just like a telephone service. A bunch of old ladies . . . Everybody knows, 'Hey, he did something,' and boy, it just goes out."

Bob Walters originally wanted to go to school for specialty training as an electronics technician (ET), but was told that there was no room for additional ETs. Undeterred by this closed door, his inquisitive nature led him to a different opportunity:

> I figured I'd be chipping paint for the rest of my life. [But] I'm a junkie. I went over to the beach and bought a servomotor and a book on how servomotors work. I'm sitting there on my bunk, and this other chief walks through and says, "Where'd you get that!?"
>
> "Don't give me no shit, chief! Here's the receipt!"
>
> "No, no, no! How would you like to go to school?"
>
> So I went to fire control school [instead]. It was a twenty-six-week school, and the thirteenth week, right after we got our radios built, this guy comes around looking for Walters: "Get your ass packed and out of here; you're going back to the boat, cause you're going to WESTPAC."

To pass a rating exam, though, was sometimes less than straightforward. Herb Herman was a nuclear reactor operator, but like all reactor operators, he had no specialized rating, and was thus rated as an electronics technician. This of course meant that all reactor operators had to take the advancement exam given to ETs: "You took the test on sonar, and radios, and radar, and you never knew anything about them. So I studied my butt off for that first-class test, and I passed all the electronics parts, but I flunked the military requirements! Then I took it again and passed, but that was ridiculous!"

And then there was the case of Bryan, whose enrollment in yeoman school seemed to be nothing out of the ordinary, but instead ended up being critical in allowing him to strike, or earn his rating, as an engineman (submariners in training were known as strikers):

> I think I'm the only person in here, that was a yeoman [who] ended up being a third-class engineman. The only thing I forgot to do, was [to] not sign that piece of paper. I was supposed to go to engineman school, and when they said, "Off you go," and I finally looked at it really close, it said "yeoman school." He said,
>
> "Well, your clerical was the highest when you took all the tests . . ."
>
> "Bullshit, I want to be an engineman!"
>
> So I went to yeoman school. But I'll tell you what, it's the best deal that ever happened, because when I went for third [class], third engineman was frozen. If you absolutely hit everything right, you couldn't make it. They wouldn't give it to you. So the yeoman says, "Oh, there's an engineering yeoman's test. Take it and you've got it!" Aced it, made it, the old man in ninety days, changed me back to engineman, and I became an engineman. But if I had not gone to yeoman school, I would've never made third. So there's all kinds of stories in this business.[7]

The First Time

As it were, nothing could have possibly prepared these men for their initial experiences onboard a submarine, where the learning curve was often steep and unforgiving. Reactions like Bill Bryan's "Oh shit!" to Mike Stephens's "What the hell did I get myself into this time!?" were the norm. Dave Vrooman was immediately immersed into the submarine lifestyle when he first boarded the USS *Plunger* (SSN-595): "The first time I went onboard, I went down the engine room hatch, and there was an air leak. I don't know what was going on, but it took them guys over an hour to find out where that air leak was, and I just thought to myself, 'What am I doing [here]!?'" Garth Lascink revealed a little trick submariners played to baptize the newcomers: "For the new guys, we tie a string on the bulkheads, so when we dive down, we say, 'Watch the string.' And of course their eyeballs are getting bigger [as] the string starts [slackening]. Then you say, 'How many times you think that hull can compress like that before it won't come back?'"

Bob Walters received a rousing welcome from Mother Nature: "My first time—I was on a reserve cruise. I did pretty good in 'B' school, so they gave me three days on the *Queenfish*, out by the Farallon Islands. I was in the rack, for about two-and-a-half days, sicker than three dogs. The Farallon Islands are right off of San Francisco Bay, and I don't think the water is ever calm out there." Shortly after, Walters was assigned his first boat:

> They flew us down to Vallejo, and kept pretty short strings on us there, then put us in blues, and flew us to Hawaii. Got off the plane, and it was about 105 degrees—just hits you like an oven. Went to the barrack there, had liberty and everybody said, "Don't go to Hotel Street." So guess where we went . . . Then the guy in the jeep hauled me off to what he said was the *Caiman*. And here's this beautiful ship sitting alongside 1010 dock; put my orders in there, gave it to the [watch]: "This isn't the *Caiman*. *Caiman*'s over in drydock." So I went over to drydock, and here's this, what looked like a junkyard. They were trying to put it [back] together. They had living barges, and [took] me up to the top deck, where the wardroom was—met the captain and executive officer, and those guys walked me aboard, shook my hand, and as far as I'm concerned, those guys walked on water. [Then there was] this one guy, wearing a brown hat, and my first question to [him], I said,
>
> "How do you tell the difference between a chief and an officer?"
>
> "You dumbshit, the chiefs don't have gold on their hat."

For as much as the brotherhood and camaraderie of the submarine service is emphasized by submarine veterans today, this respect was rarely accorded to newcomers. As Chuck Macaluso recalled, "The first time I stepped on the boat, I was scared to death. And then I couldn't find the head, and I had to go to the bathroom. I was running around looking . . . and no one would help you. They'd just call you, 'Non-qual, go figure it out!' And then when I first stepped on [my] second boat, I just got down the hatch, wasn't on the boat five seconds . . . An a-ganger came over and [stuck] his tongue in my ear. I guess he was just kind of testing me out to see what I'd do, so I . . . grabbed his nutsack. And he never bothered me again. We got along just fine. You just had to deal with the situation. When you're a new guy, you're a new guy, and you'd better be ready for anything."[8]

Nor was Collie Collins exempt from the customary awkwardness of stepping into foreign territory:

> The first time I was ever onboard, I felt silly as shit. I went on a school boat in New London. A friend of mine, a kid I'd been in the service with, with the Marines also, was [in the] ship's crew. So he invited me onboard Monday morning for breakfast before I reported into class, up at Submarine Medicine. It was a December . . . snow, New Lon-

don snow all over the place. We went aboard his boat, he opened the hatch, we went down, we had breakfast. I had to get out to go, while he went forward into Hogan's Alley [to] change his clothes. And they kind of left me alone to go up the after [battery hatch]. I climbed up, and it was closed, and I turned the thing this way and it didn't open. I turned it [that] way, and it didn't open. I'm thinking, "Oh, shit . . ." I see guys walking by down below, and I don't want to be stupid and ask them how you get out of this goddamn thing. [So] I kept [turning] . . . and I was up there probably turning that damn knob at least five or ten minutes. And then somebody topside opened it up. And when [he] did, it sprung up, and I'm hanging on it! And I felt so goddamn stupid! And the deck watch says, "What's up, Doc?"[9]

Bob Sumner had a marginally more embarrassing experience:

I wore civvies down to Key West on the bus, and then I had to change . . . all I had was blues, my thirteen-button blues . . . in the bus station. When I bent over to tie my shoes, I ripped my blues, from your crotch all the way up to your ass. And this is all I got to wear to go report onboard the boat. So I get on the base, Marines guarding the gate—sneak by them with my ripped pants. I get on the pier, and the guard at the gangway—told him I was reporting onboard, so he sent me back to [the] after battery hatch. I went down. Of course it's like Saturday or Sunday afternoon, and they're all sitting there watching movies, [and] I'm going down the after battery hatch with my ass ripped out. So you know what kind of impression I made right there. Anyway, I get down to the bottom of the ladder, and there was somebody waiting to take me up to the captain; he was onboard, so by the time I got up to his stateroom, word had already got to him that my pants were ripped out. And so I handed him my orders, he opened them up, looked at me, and he says, "What the [hell] are we going to do with a third-class boiler tender on a submarine with your goddamn blues ripped?" I said, "I don't know! I'd like to be in the engine room!"

Qualifying

Generally taking anywhere from five months to over a year, the qualification process was designed as a rigorous on-the-job program that trained each submariner in all critical aspects of the boat's operation and of the technical systems onboard. Upon completion, qualified submariners were awarded their dolphins, which signified their achievements—silver breast insignia pins for enlisted men, and gold for officers. The dolphins elicited a tremendous amount of pride from submariners, because they were hard earned, not given: "The day you put those dolphins on your uniform, that defined you as somebody altogether different. It was a proud day to be able to wear them, and it identified you as being of a small cadre of people—only a few people get to do that kind of [job]."[10]

Due to the magnitude of accomplishment connoted by the awarding of dolphins, there was a widely understood taboo that those who weren't qualified had not earned the right to display the dolphins. Chuck Nelson remembered one instance when he saved a young sailor from making this mistake: "Just before I got out, I was going over to Hawaii. This guy comes in, and I was wearing civilian clothes, and he sits down alongside me. He's real happy, he's wearing his dolphins and everything. I said, 'Hey great, where are you going?' We're talking, just chatting back and forth. I says, 'Oh by the way, you just got out of sub school, right? I'll tell you what. I'll tell you a little secret. Don't be seen wearing those dolphins. You check aboard with your dolphins on . . . '

'Well, I just got through sub school!'

'That only starts it . . . '

He would've been dead meat coming aboard one of these boats!"[11]

In reality, submarine school was just a phase of basic training that taught prospective submariners a mere fraction of what they would eventually have to learn. When Collie Collins first reported onboard the USS *Catfish*, any illusions he had about how well his sub school training prepared him were quickly snuffed out by the chief of the boat (COB), the most senior, and leader, of the enlisted men aboard. As Collins explained,

> You come out of sub school, you [think] you know what's going on, but you really don't. You [have] a job, but things are going to change; you might go into mess cooking. I went [onboard] with a wide-open idea that I was going to be a corpsman. When I first got there, I pulled an old corpsman deal that didn't work worth a shit with the COB. I reported on a Friday afternoon so I could go on liberty. If you do that at a hospital, they're going to send you away for the weekend, give you your liberty card and you're gone! [Instead] I immediately went to work on the air compressors. I didn't [even] know what an air compressor looked [like]. Man, I learned right quick. The chief came in and said, "God, I'm glad you're here. I just need another body! Air system is going to be one of your major things, so here's a good chance to learn. They're stripping it down. That's right down your line; it's the best thing you can do." [Even so], I was so happy when I got my own boat, the *Catfish*. I thought, "Hot damn, that is mine!"

The amount of time it took to qualify varied widely, and was dependent on a multitude of factors, but would for the most part range between several months to a year, with exceptions on both ends of the spectrum. The middle of the pack included Bob Walters (six months), Bob Sumner (seven months), Dave Vrooman (eight months), Bill Bryan, Fred Carneau, and R. G. Walker (nine months), and Collins (ten months).

On the shorter end of the time frame was Gary Webb, who qualified in just five months. As he explained, "The main reason I qualified as quick as I did is because I wanted the privileges of being qualified, watching movies and stuff like that." Another quick qualifier, Chuck Macaluso, recounted, "When I got on my first boat, and I had to get my dolphins, I started [during our] refit in Guam, and my goal was to get one signature per off-watch. And so I never slept. I wasn't watching movies—I was out there studying and getting signatures. So it took me a week past midpatrol break. I got like three hours of sleep [in every twelve hours off] for [two] months. It was terrible, but I got it done."

Mark Manzer also completed his qualifications in one boomer patrol. Assigned to operate the diving planes (winglike structures mounted on the sail or bow, and stern, and used to control a submerged submarine's depth) during his watch periods, Manzer was able to take advantage of the mundane but fairly relaxed duty: "I was pretty lucky. It was four-section duty, and I was doing planes the whole time. I had it made—I had the six to noon, so you're doing the planes six to noon, and they always drilled in the afternoon, so what's the point in trying to go to sleep or anything. So I would just go hole up between the missile tubes and just study my ass off until after drills were over. I really had it nailed down."[12] As Macaluso added, "The motivation [for] doing it in one run, is in the boomer world, when you give your boat up and then you're away for three months, you forget it. So you get back to the boat three months later, it's like, '[Oh] shit . . .'" Each ballistic missile submarine was assigned two crews, a "Blue Crew" and a "Gold Crew." By alternating the crews in a fixed rotation, a boomer could be kept out at sea for a longer period of time overall, where one crew would be at sea while the other crew was training in Navy schools, in an off-crew building, or relishing precious time off at home. But because the off-crew did not have access to its submarine, it became an imperative for many sailors to qualify while they were still immersed in their natural training environment.

Fresh submariners assigned to new construction crews oftentimes took much longer to qualify. While a submarine was in the phase of life prior to commissioning, there was only so much realism the training could simulate. It took Garth Lascink close to a year on the USS *Mariano G. Vallejo*: "I was on new construction, so we could learn the systems and all that, but the word came out: 'You will not be qualified until this ship's operational.' So it took awhile, but in new construction, until we were commissioned, nobody was allowed to be qualified."

Garnering respect was not the only incentive to qualify; earning one's dolphins also paid dividends in the pocketbook. As Lascink remembered, "When I got out of sub school, I wanted to go to the fleet before I went back to 'C' school. I spent basically two years in school, between 'A' school, 'C' school, and sub school. So everybody wanted to go to a boat out of sub school [and] get qualified, cause then when you went back, you got sub pay. So if you don't go [to sea first], then you go [to] 'C' school, there's no sub pay. Going to our boat in June of '65 . . . it wasn't commissioned until December of '66—no sub pay, you know. So they made out like a bandit, cause here you are on there, but there was no sub pay cause you weren't qualified beforehand, whereas submariners could come there, and they'd be getting sub pay all the time."

Additional pay would also be available for qualified sailors who went to nuclear power school. As Nelson explained, "It took me about seven months to qualify on [the *Blueback*]. I was a nuke, and nobody likes a nuke on a diesel boat, but if you got qualified, you drew nuke pay [if] you went to nuke school. So it made it worthwhile to try and get off your ass and do something."

The whole qualification process was anything but a walk in the park. Sailors working on their qualifications generally devoted all their free time to study and training, and the learning curve was steep. The line of thinking behind immersing submariners in such an inundation of intensive training was to ultimately ensure that each sailor was completely comfortable with any and every job onboard the boat: "Everybody had to have an idea about everybody else's job. [The] theory in that is—if [someone] got hurt, you could step in and relieve them [immediately], regardless of what job it was. That's the reason they wanted everybody to know something about the whole boat."[13] While at sea, sailors could routinely stand watches outside of their regularly assigned station. As Bryan, an engineman, recalled, "Skeeter was the first-class electrician, I was the throttleman, and we was doing a battery charge. He was standing my watch in the engine room, and I was standing his watch in maneuvering. In order to qualify in his department, you better know everything there was about what you were supposed to know. He says, 'You start the engine, you sit down, fat, dumb, and happy, [and] every thirty minutes, you write something down in your log. You need to know *why*.' That's the way it was. I stood eight or ten watches doing battery charges, learning how to do a battery charge in maneuvering." The value of qualifying was especially pertinent during wartime, when the potential for casualties was high, and the responsibilities associated with relieving an injured or fallen comrade was not as simple as picking up his rifle from the battlefield and continuing to shoot. Inside a submarine, everyone's life depended on everyone else. As Bryan added about Skeeter, "He'd been on boats long enough [to know]; he was a World War II vet. He says, 'Suppose something happens to me back here. You got to know what's going on.'"

The only way to learn all the different technical aspects of a submarine required a certain intimacy with its mechanical and electronic systems, but unfamiliarity with the boat often resulted in little surprises for the unsuspecting green submariner. Everyone on the boat seemed to speak in a foreign language, which was nowhere more evident than in the boat-wide announcements that came over the 1MC, the main public address loudspeaker circuit that connected every compartment of a submarine.[14] As Macaluso remembered from the USS *Patrick Henry* (SSBN/SSN-599), "I didn't understand all the 1MC announcements underway, when you prepare to snorkel and what that meant. So I was back in the engine room. I was laying underneath the diesel at the time they went off. Had no ear protection; nobody bothered checking down there to see [if] anybody was down there. I heard the 1MC announcements, 'Prepare to snorkel . . . ' I didn't know what the hell that meant. I was just down there looking for valves and tracing lines, and that sucker went off and scared the living daylights out of me. I couldn't get out of that lower level quick enough. The air start was just like a bomb going off next to me."

On the USS *Barbel* (SS-580), Chris Stafford also got caught, literally: "I was crawling around the superstructure, tracing all the valves; I was way underneath the deck, and I got stuck. I couldn't move. And you're completely surrounded by steel, and what the heck you going to do now? If you really got stuck, the only way they could get you was cut you out. So you basically just have to relax, get real limber, and then kind of weasel your way out of it. But for a short period of time, I was stuck, and once your muscles start to tighten up, you're in a world of hurt. So you learn where you can get into and where you can get out of."

Furthermore, sailors had to pass two sets of qualifications. There was a standard boat qualification, incorporating all the basic important equipment and procedures on a submarine, and a duty or watch section qualification, which required detailed and intricate knowledge of specific equipment in a sailor's area of specialty.

Vrooman was required to qualify for a watch section first, so that he would be capable of standing watches as soon as possible. However, this delayed his overall qualification schedule, because he was now spending more time on watch, and much less time studying. But such a crash course was often necessary when there was a lack of qualified sailors onboard; the result of this shortage was that more senior enlisted men sometimes had to double up and stand port and starboard watches until the others qualified for at least a watch section.[15]

Walker had the unfortunate experience of having to learn the nuances of his rating without much guidance, and was forced to hone his skills on the job: "I was the only cook aboard. How do you like that? A striker being the only cook. We left for WESTPAC, we lost our Filipino cook—his daughter got sick. We got to [the] Philippines; we lost the other cook. His wife got in a car wreck, and so that left me, to cook for the next four months."[16]

Standard boat qualifications varied in difficulty by area. As Webb, the sonarman, explained, "Before I got off the boat, I was a second-class, and I was responsible for qualifying other non-qualified people in sonar, and after a few guys went through, I actually got to the point where I kind of felt sorry for enginemen. It was my own personal perception, but I thought it was a lot harder for an engineman to qualify than it was for an ET, or a sonarman, or a fire control technician. Cause all we had to do was learn how to fire an air slug out of the torpedo [tube], light off an engine and put it online, and run the sticks. And that was fairly simple compared to firing off sonar and making a contact, or firing off radar, or bringing up a radio set online. If you came through sonar and qualified, everyone that went through sonar qualified exactly the same way, whether you were in that section or not." However, the enginemen had to learn all the specific nuances of the engineering spaces (from starting the compressors and low-pressure blowers, to storing air in the air banks, to running the freshwater distillers) in addition to going through equally rigorous training in the other departments to get qualified. Carneau, one of our enginemen, recalled, "I went through with three different people—a second-class, a chief, and an officer. And I went through the boat three different times, with about a week in between. And you had to go through everything from firing a water slug to the sticks, the whole routine." But irrespective of perceived difficulty, the qualification process for any submariner was rigorous enough that everything had to be earned. As Collins aptly added, "There wasn't anybody sacred."

While qualifying at the helm, Collins wasn't exactly faced with his most difficult challenge, but the nervousness of being under assessment allowed a quartermaster to get the better of him: "When I was qualifying, I was trying to make an impression. I wanted to be a good corpsman; I didn't want to be a screw-up, like some of the guys, you know? So I'm reading everything I can find. [But] the one question I did not know the answer to . . . and I'm on the helm, I got this third-class quartermaster—he's checking me out on the helm, and I'm up there; I knew, 'What is your course?' I had all that cold. Smart me. [Then] the executive officer says, 'What are you steering?' I looked at this quartermaster, and he [whispers], 'A big black submarine!' [So]

I said, 'Big black submarine, sir!' Needless to say, the exec said, 'Sign him off and get him the hell off there!' So I got off the helm real easy." But the engineering spaces of the *Catfish* were not as easy. Collins continued, "I went through with a chief. The first time I went through, he says, 'You're kind of weak here, and you're kind of weak there. Catch up on it before you go see the engineering officer.' So I put another couple weeks in, tuned up on it, and I still got caught with some questions I had to scratch my head on."

But as difficult and taxing as boat qualifications could be, Collins did point to one invaluable resource a qualifying submariner could use to his advantage: "There wasn't a guy on the boat—if I went up to him and asked him to explain to me why [something] worked—there wasn't a guy there that wouldn't tell me. And they really were good about it." Qualified submariners eagerly helped their fellow shipmates-in-training, even if they weren't accorded the same respect yet: "You go onboard, you're 'seaman douche non-qual,' and you see all this crap around [you]: 'What's that? How does that work?' So he sits you down and tells you."[17]

2
Underway

The quintessential aspect of naval service is sea duty. Whether attracted by a romanticized desire for adventure in the age of sail, or pressed into conscripted service guarding convoys in the freezing and unforgiving terror of the North Atlantic, sailors past and present have always lived in an uneasy marriage with the sea. Both moments of unflinching serenity and indiscreet power have defined this imposed relationship. But for submariners, such a storybook experience was only infrequently visible. They lived, worked, ate, and slept in a windowless capsule, isolated from a mostly featureless environment. The sea, it often seemed, was there only in passing. As a result, every aspect of life onboard a submarine was extremely self-contained, from the routine to the unusual, on watch and off watch. But every once in awhile, a submariner could be caught off guard when the sea decided to reintroduce itself. It would just be a gentle reminder of who was really in charge, for the sailor has always been subservient to the sea.

Standing Watch

Undoubtedly, the type of submarine (diesel fleet, fast attack, or boomer) was the single most important factor dictating the wide range of daily experiences for the men who sailed them. But even onboard any individual submarine, it became quickly apparent that there was no such thing as a typical day out at sea, especially in an environment so prone to the unforeseen and unexpected. What one did on any given day depended on a multitude of variables concerning the submarine's particular mission, geographic location, and the sailor's assigned role and responsibilities.

Because fleet boats carried out a wide variety of missions, their schedules were equally varied. William M. Bryan Jr. was assigned to the USS *Thorn-*

back (SS-418), which was based out of Florida: "Like [in] Key West, we had daily ops. Leave either seven o'clock in the morning, get back four o'clock in the afternoon, or leave at nine o'clock in the morning, get back seven in the evening. So it depends on what coast you were on, how your ops went. First year I was on the boat, other than in the yards, we were daily ops. We didn't do 'five-days' until the second year, and the only 'five-days' we did after that was when we made the overseas run, [when] we're out for ninety-one days. Beyond that, it was five eight-hour days [a week]."

Robert W. Sumner's boat was also based out of Key West and operated on a similar schedule. But the daily routine changed when the USS *Sea Poacher* (SS-406) participated in antisubmarine warfare (ASW) exercises, during which the boat would play the part of prey for the surface fleet: "We would go out for two or three days, when the fleet would come down for ASW exercises. And then occasionally we'd go into Guantanamo on the weekend for a couple of days, and then come back out, operate with the fleet." Otherwise, the common "five-days" patrol many of the fleet boat veterans were familiar with was a Monday morning to Friday evening engagement. This schedule was also standard for many of the Pacific Fleet diesel boats, including Robert Walters's USS *Caiman* (SS-323) and Robert Austin Jackson's USS *Pomfret* (SS-391).

While on a defined patrol, daily schedules became more predictable, and ultimately, oftentimes dull. As Walters noted from the *Caiman*, "A lot of it depended on what you were doing. If you were on a patrol, you were out for forty-some odd days, and your typical day at sea was stand your watch, chow down, and then go watch a flick if you're offshore snorkeling. Or if you're not snorkeling, you'd go up and try to fix something if something's broke." When Sumner's *Sea Poacher* was finally deployed on a North Atlantic run, he quickly found himself settled into a routine: "You stood your watches, then if you didn't have anything to do, you watched movies, you eat, you go to sleep. Then get up and stand the watch again. We might have had one day a week where we had general cleanup, and we'd fold the bunks up and clean all the crap out of the corners."

The contrasts between the unusual and the routine remained unchanged even as the Navy transitioned to an all-nuclear submarine fleet. Garth Lascink echoed a similar experience from the USS *Mariano G. Vallejo* (SSBN-658): "The typical day depends on what you're doing; if you're out and you're doing sea trials, or you're doing some kind of special thing out there, then [those] days are a lot different than your normal 'boring' days; [but] once you get into that routine, actually it's pretty good, because you know what your routine is. You usually get sack time, or you do some studying."

Having served onboard both boomers and fast attacks, Charles Fredrick

Macaluso was able to offer a comparison of daily life aboard the two types of submarines:

> Every day it could be different. On an FBM, if you're out on deterrent patrol, you could spend weeks at a time . . . it's repetitive. Standing my watch was probably the most exciting part, and I just couldn't wait for the monotony to end, so if you didn't have after-watch drills, then I'd hit the rack or watch a movie, one of the two, right after a quick twenty-minute meal. Thus my nickname was "Rackaluso." And you could find me reading a book and trying to sleep [the] patrol away. But on an FBM patrol, it's kind of boring after a while. If I wasn't on watch, it was really dull. There's only so much card-playing I could do. You just kind of wait for it to end. You're thinking about family, when you're coming into port, or when you're coming for midpatrol break or some break, what you're going to do when you get into port.

However, Macaluso contrasted this experience with life onboard a fast attack, and showed how different the pace of life could be: "But if we were on a fast attack, and not a boomer, it was different day to day. You had evolutions and you had drills, more drills, and you had VIP tours going through, and just . . . things you're doing with other countries where you're not supposed to be, and they keep everybody kind of on their toes. Then it gets more exciting and time goes by quicker when you have variety from watch to watch."

But the time spent on each watch was often a less exciting story. For most sailors, the midwatch was the most detested, especially while in port. Not only was there not much excitement in the middle of the night, but when there was action taking place, as Richard G. Walker remembered, "It's the worst watch, [with] all the drunks coming on." And it was cold. On Alan L. Nolan's USS *Ethan Allen* (SSBN/SSN-608), "It was required to take coffee up to those guys during the midwatch."

The length of the watch also made a big difference. For many of the sailors, especially the older diesel boat veterans, watches were typically four hours on, eight hours off, in a twenty-four-hour-day cycle. With the exception of chipping paint or polishing brass, the fleet boat sailors didn't recall having many dull moments during the day.

But on many of the newer boats, the watch schedule was modified to a six-on, twelve-off pattern in an eighteen-hour cycle. The extended watch period made watches slightly less bearable, and the younger boomer sailors noted how repetitive and routine their watches could quickly become. As Macaluso remembered, "There were some times [when] time just dragged . . . and you send the messenger up to go make wake-ups. You just can't wait to get the hell off watch. Sometimes there could be *nothing* going on. No evolutions on this ship, nothing. You're just sitting there, you're not surfacing; you're not doing anything . . . in control room, [standing] chief of watch, just sitting there. When you're in a boomer, you're not out there doing crazy stuff, just at three, four knots, going through the water." One of our missile technicians, Michael A. Stephens, added, "The last one hour of watch, time . . . slows . . . down . . . [On missile] launcher watch, you're sitting there watching your panel, or you're supposed to be watching your panel, of lights that never changed . . . hopefully."

As a fellow missile technician, Lascink couldn't agree more, but tried to fashion entertainment to pass the time: "You know how we made it less dull? [The] rover, which is generally a missile tech, he's roving the compartment. We go down to lower level, and the sensor for water in the bilges is down there, and the horn—the funnel is right on top of the launcher guy's head. So he's up there, you can kind of see him [nodding off]. We get a glass [of water]; we go down there and put it right under that sensor for that bilge water alarm . . . [And now] they got a cone on their head from jumping out of that seat, [hitting] that horn up there!" Lascink brought up another short-lived tactic sailors on the *Mariano G. Vallejo* used, to make watch more exciting in the missile compartment: "We had a ex-Tampa policeman on our boat; he was a missile house torpedoman. So he had all these different codes the cops use: 'What's your 10–7,' 'We're 10–8 down here,' and all that. So we come up with a bright idea. We're going to use these codes back in the missile house. We had 35MC back there, just goes throughout the missile house. So anytime we're doing anything, we're giving codes. So nobody understands what the hell we're doing! [But] the officers somehow started hearing this stuff when they're passing through: 'What in the heck is going on in the missile house back there?' So then they come out with a rule for us that we could no longer use codes in the missile house because 'We can't tell what you guys are doing!'"[1]

But dull watches weren't by any means limited to the missile compartment. Sonar was also a potent sleeping pill for our two younger sonar technicians. As Mark A. Manzer recalled, "I remember turning that wheel in sonar stack, kind of falling asleep. The blue lights in sonar, you listen to that noise, man that puts you out. Just listening to that static, that white noise." Nolan added, "[I] got real good at doing that in my sleep."

Even though routine responsibilities were often handled as such, attention to detail was consistently expected from the sailors on watch, however dull and listless the duty might be. This was especially important on such advanced weapons and technological platforms as nuclear-powered submarines.

But given the repetitive nature of most watches, many submariners battled hard to stay focused. While deployed on a special operations mission aboard the USS *Guitarro* (SSN-665), Macaluso nearly got himself into trouble on one such occasion. Fortunately for him though, Macaluso's mistake was discovered as the *Guitarro* was executing the potentially compromising maneuver known as an underhull, which involved a close proximity approach from underneath a Soviet submarine of interest:

> I was standing AEF watches as the IC-man, and every hour we have logs we have to have signed. Every six hours, the oncoming duty officer walks through the boat. He's walking through the torpedo room, and being in the torpedo room, we'd been sitting down here, just relaxing, talking, shooting the shit, and just enjoying ourselves. And one of the things I'm supposed to be checking off on this list, is the security of that nuclear-tipped warhead over here. And . . . I had skipped two rounds. He came in, he saw my logs, and by rule, he should have called a security violation because I had not been keeping logs on a nuclear-tipped torpedo, except we were three minutes from doing an underhull on a Soviet submarine. So we were at ultra-quiet underway. And the last thing he was going to do was sound off a security violation when we're feet from doing an underhull. So I had somebody looking over my shoulder cause it kind of got blown off after that; I never heard anything afterwards. Everyone got tied up with the underhull and picture-taking, and yeah, I was pretty good at keeping logs after that![2]

Other types of watches were equally difficult to get through, but for different reasons. Although hardly misconstrued as boring, life in the engine room of a diesel submarine was often beyond unpleasant. With all the engines running, the engine room could reach temperatures normally reserved for the high desert: "It was about 120 degrees in the engine room. You're sweating like a pig. You get off watch. You take your sweaty dungarees and hang them up. You go to sleep and you wake up for your watch again, and you got cold, wet, slimy dungarees to put on. And then you start all over again. You don't change dungarees for at least a week."[3] And to say it was noisy is an understatement. Enginemen wore earplugs and earmuffs, but many of them were left with permanent hearing damage after a career of prolonged exposure to deafening decibel levels. And that was just on a regular basis.

There were a lot of other little disgusting surprises that could pop out of nowhere. As Gary W. Webb recalled from the USS *Sea Fox* (SS-402), "We were operating out of San Diego, and we were preparing to snorkel on engines 3 and 4. And 3 lit off fine, [but] 4 false-started, and puked a good gasp of raw diesel back into the boat. The closest I ever come to getting sick, was [from] that raw diesel smell. That is the most obnoxious smelling crap. It just permeated the whole interior of the ship." Sumner, an old hand in the engine room, recalled another related danger with equally unpleasant results: "If you didn't get the outboard exhaust open, and then you lifted the explosion covers, you couldn't see your hand in front of your face."

But with all the unpleasantness standing watch could bring, sailors were occasionally rewarded with an idyllic, breathtaking experience. Walters provided a much more relaxing anecdote from his watches on the *Caiman*: "When we're at sea on the diesel boats, I stood either sonar or ECM watches. Before that, I was standing lookout watches. And you get out there in the middle of the night, and . . . you're heading for Tahiti or some dang place, it was beautiful! The best watches I thought was the four to eights. You saw the sunrise, you saw the sunset, and you looked at the stars. The guy came up with his sextant, and talked about Betelgeuse and this and that and everything else. You look up there and there's a thousand stars . . . 'Which one you talking about, sir?'"[4]

Although such an experience was no longer commonplace on boomers, as they spent nearly the entirety of patrols submerged, there were a few exceptions. While the *Mariano G. Vallejo* was conducting sea trials off San Francisco, Lascink remembered one opportunity he received as the lookout planesman following an emergency blow. Executed on a submarine during an actual or simulated emergency, high pressure air is forced into all the ballast tanks, which empty immediately and simultaneously, expediting the submarine's ascent to the surface: "When you blow emergency, then you're up on the surface for a number of hours charging [the air banks], and you're out there at night . . . Man, there's nothing like being out at sea on a nice night . . . the phosphorus in the water, stars up there . . . beautiful out there."[5]

Boatkeeping

Regular cleaning and unplanned maintenance fell into the blurry gray area between on-watch and off-watch time. Both Chuck Macaluso and Mike Stephens vividly recalled the weekly ritual known as "Field Day." As Macaluso described it: "Saturday was the big day to look forward to. At least in the boomer fleet, Saturday was Field Day. Everybody got up, everybody cleaned up for six hours. It didn't matter what boat I was on, Saturday was the clean-up-ship day." Stephens added, "Security violation drill required once a week. It always happened just before Field Day—'Okay while everybody's up here, rub-a-dub-dub, clean up the sub.'"

Scheduled Field Days aside, there was another occasion when a submarine was required to be in pristine condition—when she played host to high-ranking visitors. Whenever any dignitary visited a submarine, "You'd scrub-scrub, clean that boat up, and then the day they were coming down, you'd better be off the boat, except for the duty sections and essential personnel. They didn't want anyone on the boat that didn't need to be there . . . 'Get off the boat if you don't have duty. If you have duty, stay out of our way; we're coming through with the VIP group.'"[6]

And then there were the freak accidents. As Macaluso recalled, "We were on the pier one time doing quarters when a sanitary line broke. First it broke at the pier and squirted everyone on the pier. Then the connection on the boat was one foot from the hatch going down the boat, and it broke free. Everything drained down the hatch into the boat. And of course, at the very bottom of the hatch, two feet away, is the CO's stateroom. He had the door open. It was interesting quarters that morning; officers were upset, CO was upset, we were cleaning up."

Quite obviously, housekeeping, or rather boatkeeping, was never something to really get excited about. Evert Charles Nelson befittingly summarized the general sentiment by remarking, "You know, everybody hates a Field Day," and remembered an instance when he asked his captain, "Why are we doing this? This vessel's clean!" The captain acknowledged Nelson's observation, but responded, "It gives them something to bitch about!"[7] Alan Nolan, a sonar technician, recalled one occasion when he became a Field Day legend onboard the USS *Ethan Allen*, "Because I knew how some of the guys were feeling, so we made up a fictitious contact on the sonar—recorded a suspicious noise level, and they secured Field Day so fast that everybody's head spun. And they never did get it started back up. Sonar was heroes that day."

Although this was a regular and familiar experience for the men who served after the mid-1970s, the narrative seemed completely foreign to Garth Lascink. In the Navy a mere decade earlier, he never participated in a Field Day. Neither had some of the older diesel boat veterans such as Bob Walters, Bill Bryan, and Fred A. Carneau, who remembered that in his day, "The relieving watch went in [and] looked over the compartment. If something's wrong, it was taken care of before they changed the watch. They cleaned every nook and cranny on that thing, the watch did."

But whether it was once a week or once every watch, cleaning was just a necessary part of life onboard. In rare instances though, this routine was bypassed, as it was during a special operations deployment on the USS *Guitarro*. Because water is an excellent medium for the transmission of sound, submarines would take every precaution necessary to limit the sounds they produced while on station, in order to protect the ultimate tactical advantage any submerged boat has: its stealth. But Macaluso noted the disastrous results when "We tried that, and we didn't Field Day for ten weeks. Oh my God, when it came time to Field Day and you actually turned the lights on when we came off that patrol, you had hairballs floating around everywhere. It was nasty, man. That was obvious we didn't clean up. But they didn't let us clean up because they were afraid we'd be making noise; we couldn't turn vacuum cleaners on."

Performing repair while underway was also a common theme, especially on the older diesel boats. As Carneau, a chief engineman, lamented, "In between the stuff that was broke down, which was always something . . . [If] it wasn't an oil separator, it was something. And them damn de-salters; those things never did work right."

The engine room was often a place for impromptu maintenance; with all that machinery, it was a likely target for Murphy's Law, never discriminating between the whims of man or nature. As another engineman, Bob Sumner, recalled from the USS *Sea Poacher*,

> We were in Portsmouth, England, taking on stores, and we left Portsmouth, out two or three days, and a couple of torpedomen decided to make some booze. They went and got a bunch of raisins and all this stuff, and put it in these big mustard jars. Back in torpedo room, they didn't have any place to store it. So we all decided we'll store it in the few lockers we had in the forward engine room. Week-and-a-half, two weeks [pass]; I'm looking at this stuff, and at some point in time, I decided this stuff has got to be bad. So I told the oiler [to] dump it down the bilges. So he did, and of course, the torpedomen realize that and they weren't happy at all. I had the four to eight watch, so we dumped it, and then went off watch. And then when I came back on watch, the next four to eight, [the] engineering officer comes back and said, "There's something wrong. We can't pump bilges. Would you go down and look at the screens?" So I sent the oiler down; of course by now the raisins are swollen up. The screens are just plugged solid with all these damn raisins, and we got to clean the suction screens out. He wanted to know where all the raisins came from, and of course we didn't have a clue!

The origin of Bryan's conundrum in the engine room of the USS *Thornback* was a little more unexpected:

> I was an engineman striker, and we were snorkeling in the Med and we took on shrimp in the cooler—the freshwater/saltwater cooler. We didn't have a spare strainer, and the old man shuts down the forward engine room, and [asks], "Can you fix it?" We were in maneuvers, and

> [the captain] was getting ready to shoot. He says, "I want that engine on the line when we come up." We were about fifty or sixty feet [down]; you got to put pressure in the boat if you're going to open that valve to sea. So we close those two hatches, get pressure in the engine room, and take the cap off this sucker. The chief looks at me and says, "You know anything about cleaning that strainer?"
>
> "No . . . I'm a seaman!"
>
> "How do we know we got enough pressure in here?"
>
> "Well, [when] we don't have any water coming in!"
>
> [So] we cleaned that strainer. But the only thing you can do is rod [the shrimp] out. And the second that you hit that first one, a fountain of water [would spray up] until you got a little more pressure in the boat. As you rod each one out, you got to add a little more pressure. That was a real experience, and that turned me from a seaman into an engineman!

On these older diesel fleet boats, veterans like Sumner, Walters, and Bryan, noted that if it "Broke on your watch, you fixed it."[8] Gary Webb, an experienced sonarman, pointed out how "If a piece of equipment broke down, we fixed it—whatever it took. I can recall one time when I was up for about forty hours straight, working on the active sonar. [Then] when you came to port, that's when all the [regular] maintenance took place."

Paralleling Field Days on most nuclear-powered submarines, repair and maintenance were left to the sailors off watch. As Macaluso noted, "When you were on watch, you weren't fixing things. You were watching the ship. If something broke, you woke somebody up; they came up and worked on it, [or] the off-going watch would be the one [fixing it]. If I had something break in Control, the IC-man still needed to make his rounds. [So] the off-going IC-man had to go fix it, troubleshoot it." David Meade Vrooman, the electrician's mate, added, "When we had something break down, the off-duty electrician would work on it, and when they came to relieve you on watch, if it [still] wasn't fixed, then you go fix it." Lascink, a missile technician, noted that "We had some areas of expertise in our division, so if the particular piece went down, [and] it was your expertise, when you're off watch, you were out there working on it." But it was also possible that "If you happened to be on watch, [and] you were the guy who knew how to fix it, somebody would relieve you, and then you'd get off watch."[9]

But whether cleaning and repairs happened on watch or off watch, the distinction was ultimately academic. Submarines still had to be scrubbed and fixed. Carneau epitomized the idea of ship-shape maintenance by quoting the mantra of one of his engineering officers: "If it's broke, fix it. If it's not broke, fix it anyhow."

Off Watch

Even though life onboard could quickly become repetitive, sailors had many opportunities to find something new to occupy themselves with, during their free time. Many of them would dabble in and pick up other skills that were outside their area of specialty. Although rated as a fire control technician, Bob Walters often "Tried to learn how to listen to the radio, but the spooks were there and they kept you out. I also did charts, because the quartermaster was too lazy. But if you wanted something to do, you could do it." Normally working as an engineman, Bob Sumner counted himself among those who enjoyed listening to sonar when they weren't standing watch. And as Gary Webb noted, "When we went to sea, we stood our watches, and that was it. We stood four on, had eight off, and those eight off—if you were qualified—that was your time; you did whatever you wanted to."

Onboard any submarine, the off-watch time for a nonqualified sailor was starkly different. If a submariner was still working toward his dolphins, he was subject to a whole host of involuntary work: "It also depended [on] if you were qualified or non-qualified. If you're a non-qual, as soon as you got off your watch, and had maybe something to eat, you'd work on qualifications, cause until you got qualified, you were scum, and the trick was to get qualified as fast as possible so you could actually do something and have some fun."[10] After qualifying, one could finally "Watch a movie or read a book, without somebody giving you shit."[11]

Reminiscing from his days as a fresh submariner, Walters recalled how "Another thing that non-quals had to do was mess cook. We were up at five o'clock and maybe able to hit the rack around ten in the evening, with no breaks in between, serving soupdowns, three meals, and learning to keep your mouth shut . . . because you did take a lot of crap, and if you start answering back, you just might have to mess cook for a month." Meals onboard most submarines were served four times a day: the three main meals and a fourth meal known as the soupdown, usually comprising of light deli fare and leftovers from earlier in the day.[12]

Mess cooking was a common experience that elicited a wide range of sentiments. Generally not a fond memory of most sailors, mess cooking duties encompassed the dregs of meal preparation: washing dishes and peeling potatoes. But on the USS *Pomfret*, Bob Jackson recalled the head cook, who "If he liked you as a mess cook, you didn't have to worry about anything. He took care of you. The whole time I was on mess cooking, he had nothing but good words. In fact when my shift was done, he asked me if I wanted to be a cook. He liked the work I did."[13] Mark Manzer remembered a different side of the story. While the galley on the USS *Sam Houston* (SSBN/SSN-609) was out of commission and under repair, Manzer was dispatched to mess cook on the submarine tender tied up alongside. Specifically designed as auxiliary ships to support and service submarines, these tenders were relied upon to provide any requisite logistical replenishment. Closer inspection of some facilities onboard though, produced disturbing observations: "I remember my first patrol, in Guam; they told me I was going to mess cook, got me up at four o'clock the next morning, sent me up to the tender. It wasn't fun. The galley was crawling with cockroaches and everything; it was nasty."

However, for submarine sailors who didn't have to mess cook, chowtime was often the most anticipated part of the day: "You looked forward to a good meal. You actually get to talk to people you hadn't seen."[14] Because meals offered such a different change to the pace of life onboard, Mike Stephens noted how he looked forward to "Even a mediocre meal."

Although infrequent, logistical limitations would occasionally affect the quality of the food onboard. Chuck Macaluso pointed to a deployment where breakfast became difficult to bear after "We ran out of all this fresh stuff the first week underway." For some of the diesel boat veterans in the 1950s, eggs were the one culinary item to be avoided. As Bill Bryan recalled, "You got 1945 eggs, frozen. You get ready to put it on the grill; you got to have the grill hot, cause when you cracked that sucker, if it rolled two times, it turned green. If it laid out, [the] color stayed. If you cracked that sucker in a bowl, it was green before it hit the grill!"[15] Yes, the Navy was attempting to not waste extra food left over from the war, but provisioning decade-old eggs seemed a bit excessive. As Walters added, "We had eggs from '44–'45 and they were in these cartons of [twelve] dozen. And [while] I was mess cooking, [they said], 'Okay Walters, will you take those up and throw them over the side?' Very well. So I got them through the hatch, and I had help getting them up to the conning tower, and I had help getting them up to the bridge . . . and 'Permission to throw them over the side.' Sure [enough], the boat pitched and I slipped, and the eggs went all over the goddamn deck!"[16]

In the late 1970s, the Navy tested a short-lived experiment with its supply of coffee onboard submarines, substituting ground coffee with the instant Taster's Choice. It would have been mildly put to say this move turned out to be extremely unpopular with the sailors: "They made us go to sea with instant coffee. They were trying to make something new; it would be less space [for storage]. Fortunately after that, we got back to our regular coffee, but can you imagine going to sea with nothing but instant coffee?"[17]

But overall, with the aforementioned exceptions aside, the food quality onboard submarines was considered to be the best in the military. It was, of sorts, compensation for some of the hardships the men had to endure while isolated from the outside world. Jackson summarized a unanimous consensus in seven simple words: "We ate good. We ate real good." For many of the veterans, the first time they had lobster was onboard a submarine. Other commonly featured foods included steak, ham, and turkey, delicacies prepared in such a fashion that sailors would be hard-pressed to find anything close on a destroyer or aircraft carrier. And all this food, of course, was served on fine china.[18] Also, whenever possible, the cooks onboard would prepare local specialties. As Alan Nolan recalled, "When we were in Bangor, at the end of every duty day, we'd throw our crab pots over the side, and every night for the movie, we'd have fresh crab. The cook would cook whatever we brought in."

Some of the food onboard was even created, however inadvertently, with a unique dash of submarine experience. As Macaluso recalled, "I loved it when you get those pans of cake they cook. The cake would be thick at one end and [thin] at the other end, depending [on] the ascent of the boat." As a cook onboard the USS *Capitaine* (AGSS-336), R. G. Walker fondly remembered his own cake-baking adventure: "We're going to dive. Just to the critical point, and all of a sudden this guy loses the angle and we start going down real steep. The captain had to go in and relieve the diving officer and brought her back up. So I open up the oven, [and] all the cake had sagged to one end!"

At times, the meals themselves took on a special significance and were integrated into a customary part of routine onboard. While Macaluso was stationed on the USS *Kentucky* (SSBN-737), "Every meal you had before you pulled into port was a pizza meal. Didn't matter whether you were pulling into port to pick somebody up, or pick up an inspection team. We're coming into port, the night before, it was pizza. And each division onboard would take turns making pizzas for the ship; that was fun." Pizza was definitely one of the most popular meals among the veterans who were onboard submarines that served it. But as many older diesel boat veterans quizzically remarked, "We didn't know what pizza was!"[19] On the USS *Ethan Allen*, pizza was served every Saturday night; however, as Nolan recalled, the dinner that everyone really looked forward to was served on Halfway Night, when "All the chiefs onboard would get together and do a Mongolian barbeque for the crew, and that was a delight." Other themed nights were a bit more unique. On the USS *Mariano G. Vallejo*, "Italian Night" was combined with "topless waiter service," when the crew would be served spaghetti by shirtless mess cooks.

Halfway Night was essentially a holiday, celebrated to mark the halfway point through a submarine's deployment. As Macaluso recalled, "We'd have a contest for volunteering people onboard to do things on Halfway Night, like the XO would get volunteered to compact the trash for six hours, whoever got the most votes. Or you'd get the CO in there doing the dishes. So that was fun to see the roles reversed like that occasionally, cause they were willing to play along." And although fine cuisine was always a hallmark of the festivities, sometimes not everything went according to plan. While cooking for the crew as a chief, Macaluso remembered how "We had a bug infestation onboard, and they were getting in all the rice and the grains. I was asking the cook as I'm boiling the rice up, 'How many bugs per pot are you allowed to have before you can't serve it?' Because they were all floating up black, floating up to the top, and you're just spooning them off and serving this stuff out. But it was a fun Halfway Night!"

Indeed, bug infestations certainly weren't limited to surface ships, and even war patrols did not receive an exemption from nature's inconveniences. Walker continued with an anecdote from cooking on the *Capitaine*:

> We were operating in Vietnam, and we went to some island. The captain went ashore with a bunch of other people, gone all day, and then they came back and they threw this great big hundred-pound bag of rice up on deck. So we're getting ready [to] get going, and they're starting the engines up. He's walking up the forward deck to climb up to the conning tower and go in that way. He looks back just as I'm starting to shove the bag of rice over the side. He screams at me . . .
>
> "What's wrong, sir?"
>
> "That was a present to me and I want rice every meal!"
>
> "Well, sir, this has probably got bugs in it. It'll contaminate the submarine!"
>
> "I don't give a damn; get that down below! I want rice every meal!" [For] two weeks, we had bugs all over that submarine . . . everywhere. Then it kept getting worse and worse. Every meal, he had rice and we left every bug in it, and if we could find any other bugs crawling around, we'd put it in the rice. And he never complained once. He never complained. That's the only credit I can give the guy. And the thing is, all the officers . . . whatever you took you had to eat, and everybody had to take something of everything. I mean that rice . . . about every tablespoon had two or three bugs in it. You just look at it and you say "Ooh God." I'm sure the other officers hated our guts!

But under normal circumstances, as one of the special privileges provided to a submariner, good food onboard elicited much excitement and fond memories from the veterans. And for many of the men, especially the older veterans, one of the greatest privileges they received was an open galley, allowing them to prepare food for themselves whenever they wanted: "The only thing the cook wanted—was [to] not leave a mess."[20] Sumner added, "And let him know what you took, so he didn't rely on it for some other meal." But for some of the younger veterans like Macaluso, there were more restrictions:

"We only did that in the yards when we'd go in the chill box at midnight. They didn't allow us to do that underway though."

Another fun and memorable experience that changed over time was found in loading provisions onboard before a submarine set out to sea. Cans, crates, and boxes of food were passed along a human chain, from sailor to sailor, down and through hatches, passageways, and corridors. On a boomer like the *Mariano G. Vallejo*, the point of entry was the hatch above the auxiliary machinery room (AMR): "Everything came down through AMR number 1, and then went forward. [But] peanuts!? [Stuck] them in one of the fifteen bunks back in the missile house, and a *lot* of peanuts went into the bunks back in there."[21]

Food storage created its own omnipresence, inseparable from life onboard a submarine, especially on the older, more cramped diesel boats. Foods that could withstand high temperatures, such as coffee, flour, and sugar, went into the engine room and aft machinery spaces, where the thermometer could easily pass 130 degrees with all the diesels running. Fruits and vegetables that required cooler temperatures to prevent spoiling were stored all the way forward in the torpedo room once the limited refrigeration space was used up. But the remaining containers of food were lined up on top of the compartment decks and covered with a tarp or floor mats. This made what was already the formidable challenge of squeezing through narrow passageways even more difficult for even an average-sized sailor. Now with the overhead clearance decreased by as much as a foot in some compartments, submariners found themselves chronically hunched over—out of necessity—until they literally ate their way back down to the deck.

Beginning in the late 1970s, the experience of sailors passing containers of food along slowly disappeared onboard *Ohio*-class boomers. As Macaluso recalled, "They pulled the entire hatch out, and they load a pallet down. It comes into the boat, it rolls out on skids, and goes into the freezer, and never gets touched. The forward hatch, they just pull it right out, they put it out on the dock, and you got this huge hole with like four or five ladders going down into the boat. Or they could just load a circular staircase." These food pallets were fully loaded eight-foot-tall pantry cabinets that were lowered by crane into the submarine, via a logistics escape trunk. Six feet in diameter, this removable escape trunk and the "bomb bay doors" on each deck below the trunk were designed to facilitate equipment removal and replacement, but also made the loading of provisions a more efficient process.

Although mealtime was the most consistently reliable break in the tedium of everyday life aboard a boat on patrol, submariners passed the time with various other forms of entertainment. Games, contests, and movies were interspersed with more creative ventures, many of which were fashioned as an integral part of the submarine experience.

Chess was one of the most popular games onboard, as was a version of backgammon known as "acey-deucey." Card tournaments involving games like bridge, hearts, spades, pinochle, and cribbage were also a common pastime. And then there were the poker parties: "That's big time stuff, you know; you're not supposed to have it. Those guys were . . . some of them were crazy, cause they could lose a whole patrol's salary down there in a matter of just a few hours . . . two months worth of pay."[22]

High-stakes competition also extended beyond an individual submarine. Although friendly rivalries between crews from different boats could easily take the form of traditional recreation, Garth Lascink offered an anecdote from liberty in Guam that could hardly be construed as typical:

> You went over [to] Beer Can Beach and had some San Miguel that tasted like dog or panther pee. We're down there, we got a guy on our boat, a big, old torpedoman—he'd eat lizards that were running around on the rafters in this place. So we bet this other boat over there that he would eat a lizard. All of a sudden, it looked like a poker game. There's money out on this table in a big old heap there:
>
> "Oh, he won't eat . . ."
>
> "Yes he will!"
>
> [And] everybody's funding everybody else's money in there. So [the torpedoman] grabs this gecko or lizard, and he swallows this thing. And of course, we pick up all the money. We says, "Okay, we're going!" So we head back to the boat; we're about halfway between Beer Can Beach and the tender *Proteus*, and he barfs this thing up. And it starts running! He says, "Goddammit! I ate you once; I'll eat you again!" He steps on it, picks him up, swallows him again. And everybody's [getting nauseous], but he wasn't going to let that thing run away![23]

Beard- and mustache-growing contests were also commonly held in earlier decades, but as Macaluso observed, "I joined in '79 and a lot of people had beards then, and nobody cared. It seemed like as time went on, all the way into the '90s, it had become politically incorrect to have these beard-growing contests underway, so [there] were very few in between; some COs would allow that, but not very many, cause they'd have riders in and out through a patrol and they just wanted the crew to look all trim and [in] shape." Along the same lines of political incorrectness, Macaluso recalled how, "People would dress up as women onboard, to see who would get the best [reviews]."

Movies were a mixed bag: "If you just left port and had some new movies, that was good; if you'd been out for awhile and you'd seen the movies ten times, that wasn't very good."[24] One common method to acquire new movies while underway was to trade with other ships: "You had movies, and you'd seen all these movies. So you get alongside; somebody says, 'Hey, let's trade some movies! Oh yeah, we got some good ones!' [But] everybody's getting rid of their worst movies—is what's happening with this trade deal that goes on. And you're saying, 'Oh man, got new movies!' [Then you watch them] and you go, 'God, no wonder they got rid of these things.'"[25] Elbert H. Collins rhetorically lamented, "You ever try to get rid of a movie and the damn thing keeps coming back? *Body Stenches from Outer Space* . . . I've watched that sucker about twelve or fourteen times. I never want to see it again! They traded it out and it comes right back to you. How the hell it gets back, I don't know."

And with all the bad movies robustly circulating, submariners relied on some ingenuity to cope. On the *Ethan Allen*, Nolan described the formation of "The Gagger-Watchers Club—you had to watch five of these gaggers, and when you watched it, somebody else would sign your gagger card; once you got five, you were 'qualified.'" Lascink noted how some sailors took it upon themselves to improve the quality of certain movies: "We turned the sound down, and [replaced it with] comments from all these guys watching. Some of those bad movies [turned out] pretty decent; these really terrible movies, but somebody [would] talk for the woman or the guy in the [movie]." And when all else failed, sailors could always run the movies backward, in reverse, for some measure of amusement.

But even though it was accepted that the movies circulating among the fleet were generally of poor quality, some ships had to be persuaded to engage in trade. As Sumner recalled from the USS *Sea Poacher*, "We were tied up next to a destroyer in Portsmouth, England. We were getting ready to go up north, and we had two or three movies that we'd seen about ten times, and we wanted to trade with the destroyer. And they wouldn't trade with us. So at night, they'd always go back and sit in the fantail—watch [their] movies. [One] evening, we said, 'The hell with you guys,' went and pressurized the sanitary tank, and then just vented it, right out! They traded the next day."

On the *Capitaine*, Walker recalled how the exchange of movies was prevented by natural phenomena:

> We were in San Diego; I had weekend duty, so we were watching movie after movie after movie. And we watched Albert Hitchcock's *The Birds*, and [afterward], there's a third-class radioman—they're going to send him over to another boat to exchange movies. So they send him up—

> goes out the hatch, and he drops the movies [back] down the hatch. He pulls the hatch shut, locks it, and he says,
>
> "I'm not going out! I'm not going out!"
>
> "What's the problem?"
>
> "There's birds!"
>
> There were! You go up, and there was literally thousands of birds and they're everywhere, out [on] the boats. It was so surreal because we just watched that movie. I looked down and I said, "I'm not going up there [either]!"

But quite often, sailors would simply showcase their talents to pass the time. On the USS *Plunger* (SSN-595), Dave Vrooman recalled hanging out in the torpedo room in his spare time, listening to a torpedoman who was exceptionally skilled on the banjo. And Bryan took note of two brilliant cartoonists that had an awestruck and devoted following on the USS *Thornback*.

There were also more ingenious forms of entertainment, invented to take advantage of the facilities onboard, especially in the missile compartments of boomers. Inside the largest single compartment on a ballistic missile submarine, several long passageways snaked in between two rows of missile tubes that were painted in various shades of brown. As these tubes resembled tree trunks, the compartment has often been referred to as "Sherwood Forest," and in reality, it was administered by an ad hoc parks and recreation department.[26] Macaluso counted himself among a cadre of crewmembers on the *Kentucky* that designed and raced miniature cars down the passageways of the missile compartment, showing off their engineering skills: "We'd just keep an up-angle on the boat, and each division would make their own little car out of parts they found onboard." The same compartment was also the perfect setting for an improvised theme park ride. All one needed was a blanket or gunnysack during "angles and dangles," a series of extreme maneuvers and twists and turns a submarine routinely executed to test the integrity of the mechanical systems onboard.

The theme park could certainly be chalked up as a creative way to take advantage of the submarine's operations, but the startup farm onboard the USS *Thomas Jefferson* (SSBN-618) probably wasn't officially sanctioned by the Navy: "Somebody took three eggs, marked 'One Dot,' 'Two Dots,' and 'Three Dots,' and they actually incubated the damn birds on patrol. And they had these three chickens, One Dot, Two Dot, Three Dot, onboard the boat, back in Sherwood Forest, running around!"[27]

One occasional pleasure that all sailors particularly enjoyed was swim call. Lascink recalled, "Captain says, 'Hey, we're off Acapulco; we're having swim call.' Man, the whole boat's roaring. Go up topside, up there, and everybody's looking around, saying,

'Where's Acapulco?'

'One hundred miles that way . . . '

So then there's all these sailors out there in just their skivvies, diving into the water out there. Back near the after part, there were some things you could crawl up [on]. You wanted to catch it with a swell though." On the older diesel boats, the submarine was flooded down or the bow planes were folded out, so that the sailors could easily step off into the water.

But one aspect that was common to all swim calls was the shark watch. As Walters remembered, "We always had some guy standing up there with a M1, for shark watch. And the CO said,

'OK, we're going to secure swim call . . . pump two rounds off.'

POM! POM!

'Shark!'

[And everybody's] walking on the water." Lascink added, "Our CO made a mistake of having the shark watch practice first. So you know the old metal cans you have for oil or for detergent . . . throw them out there and these guys were shooting at these things. Hell, they were five feet away from this can trying to shoot this thing. Everybody's looking and [saying], 'If there's a shark, let us know, cause we'll be out of the water before you can get that gun [in] your hand, cause you're not going to hit it! You can't hit the can out there!'"

Because swim calls proved to be a rarity, finding ways to stay fit became more of a challenge. Due to the obvious space limitations, submariners on fleet boats or even fast attacks were resigned to doing push-ups on the deck, or pull-ups on a bar wedged across the torpedo racks in the torpedo room. Sailors on ballistic missile submarines were a bit more fortunate. Because of their sheer size, many boomers would often have room onboard to carry exercise equipment, such as treadmills, stair-steppers, and weights. Going for a quick jog around the missile compartment was another option. And sometimes, crews would launch their own fitness competitions while underway, taking advantage of a luxury not found on other types of submarines.

The admittedly arduous realm of mental training also benefited from some lighthearted creativity. On Lascink's boat, the *Mariano G. Vallejo*, the crew took a standard trivia game show format and modified it to help facilitate training onboard. Known as the "Polaris Bowl," the weapons compartment edition featured teams of three, comprising of an electronics technician, a fire control technician, and a torpedoman, competing weekly for bragging rights. The crew even fashioned a buzzer box that could allow the contestants to ring in, and demonstrate their extensive knowledge about the launcher, the missiles, fire control, and other aspects of the submarine's weapons systems.

The crossover of training and recreation manifested itself again with the popular "trim parties," during which a group of sailors would all run to one end of the submarine, causing the boat to lose balance or trim, from the sudden shifting of weight. In order to rebalance the submarine, the trim tanks at the opposite end of the boat would have to be filled with water. Undeterred, the men would then run to the other end in an effort to keep the watch in the control room one step behind. Webb recalled his participation in enhancing the training experience of a new officer, a lieutenant junior-grade ("JG"): "We had a JG who was trying to qualify. We dove the boat and he was the diving officer; he just had a hell of a time, because we had about fifteen guys going forward [and aft]." Although trim parties were often the spontaneous aftermath of a group of bored submariners with one bright idea, they were even on occasion officially organized: "There would be like twenty of us sitting on the mess decks doing nothing, and the skipper would come in and say, 'Let's have a trim party!' So you know when the skipper's leading it, that's got to be fun!"[28] But ultimately, as Nolan justified, it was "Just good training for the whole control room party."

Aside from meals and recreational pursuits, the remainder of the sailors' downtime was usually spent sleeping. But the crew's berthing situation varied from boat to boat and mission to mission. Very frequently, the lower-ranking enlisted men would be required to "hot bunk" or "hot rack," in other words, share beds simply because there were not enough accommodations for the number of men aboard. Usually, three men would be assigned to two bunks, and would rotate in and out based on their watch shifts. But as sailors like Webb incredulously wondered, "I didn't have a problem with it, [but] I couldn't understand why they had to assign me a boat and say that they needed people like me on it, and not have a place for me to sleep!" More fortunate sailors like Walters and Sumner never had to share bunks: "Everybody on the *Sea Poacher* had their own rack, except for when we went up north and took three spooks from England, and they had to sleep in the wardroom."[29] Spooks were intelligence agents who were assigned to submarines. Often associated with the National Security Agency (NSA) or the Central Intelligence Agency (CIA), they were in charge of a boat's intelligence-gathering operations. Because they were privy to top-secret information and often kept a distance from the other crewmembers, they weren't always accepted as part of a submarine's formal crew.[30]

So more often than not, it was under special circumstances that a submarine carried more crewmembers than it had bunks. As Lascink recalled from the *Mariano G. Vallejo*, "We all had our own bunks once we started operating, but during sea trials [and] shakedown, it was always hot bunking. For one thing, we had fifteen bunks missing from the missile house. Everybody's down below, sleeping on flash covers, basically in your dungarees with a blanket. So we hot bunked quite a bit until we went on patrol, cause you had yardbirds on there, we had partial two crews, you had all kinds of people crawling everywhere. Then after that, everybody had a bunk."[31] Macaluso encountered the extreme end of hot-bunking during the USS *Guitarro*'s deployment from August to November of 1989. Comprising the additional complement of personnel on the special operations mission, these "riders" included anyone not part of the permanent crew onboard, and their presence forced many others to accommodate: "When I went underway on the *Guitarro* with the spooks onboard, there were so many riders, that everybody E-6 and below was hot-racking. For three months, we hot-racked underway, until we pulled into port with the spooks and got all [of] them off and their equipment."

For the unfortunate Webb, hot bunking was just routine: "I spent the first three months with no [assigned] place to sleep. They had these flash covers on all the mattresses, and you could sleep wherever you wanted to, whenever you wanted to, but you don't ever open the flash cover. You had your own blanket, but you lay on that sticky, sweaty flash cover. And if you got in the wrong bunk, the guy—half-hour after you got to sleep—would come wake you up and say, 'Get out of my rack!' [But] we run from three to six [crewmembers] over, all the time."

The lack of storage space for food meant that space for sailors' personal belongings was at an even greater premium. For sailors who had assigned bunks, the mattress racks would lift up to expose precious real estate for a few changes of clothes, a book or two, and maybe a pack of smokes or a bottle of soda, in addition to some personal effects, such as letters from home, photographs of loved ones, and some small souvenirs from ports they visited. But sailors without assigned berthing lived out of their sea bags, stuffing them to the seam with whatever would fit. And finding several consecutive unused cubic feet of space onboard to store the sea bag was an equally mind-boggling challenge.

On occasion, though, a little creativity allowed sailors to overcome the problem of finite space. Armed with ingenuity and ambition, Walters made a valiant effort to bring home his piece of salvaged treasure by stashing it in a crawl space under the topside deck of the USS *Caiman*. But because it was outside the pressure hull and exposed to the ocean pressure, Walters's plan was ultimately thwarted:

> I've always been a junkie. They hauled a new piece of test gear aboard, and it was in one of these metal-covered wooden boxes with a locking top, watertight. [I said], "That's a neat trunk! I'd better get that home!"

> But the only place I could put it would be under the deck. And I was lead seaman, so what the hell! We went out a couple days later, and I hadn't had a chance to get the thing ashore. We were down a hundred feet or so and everything's fine; then [the] captain says, "Let's take it to 410." We went down about 325, and it goes "BOOM!"
>
> "What was THAT!?"
>
> "Well . . . I think it might have been my trunk . . ."
>
> [When we] went up, here's this thing; it's all caved in. But it was a good box!

A more successful sailor on the *Plunger* demonstrated that with meticulous (and covert) planning, no ambition was out of reach. As Vrooman recalled, "We're coming back from Pearl Harbor to go in the yards in Bremerton. Since we're going to be gone more than six months, everybody got their stuff shipped back, except for this one seaman. After we're out at sea for a couple of weeks, we found out that he'd taken his motorcycle all apart and stored it in one of the showers! We only had two showers!"

Showers were extremely limited onboard older boats for two primary reasons. First, the showers were frequently used for storage, oftentimes for food. But even if the showers were vacant, a diesel boat did not have the capacity to distill enough fresh water in sufficient quantities for everyone onboard to take a shower. Running the distillers required a large energy input, and generated an almost unbearable amount of heat. As a result, a shower once a week was a luxury, once every two weeks was normal, and never at all was common. Fleet boat sailors affectionately awarded their submarines with the nickname "pig boats." When reverse osmosis technology was introduced as a method of desalination onboard nuclear submarines, this unpleasant aspect of life eventually disappeared. The relatively much-lower energy requirement needed to force seawater through a filtration membrane (as opposed to bringing it to a boil) removed the limitations on how much fresh water could be produced. Having a nuclear reactor onboard to generate an essentially unlimited amount of energy toward the facilitation of creature comforts (fresh water, air conditioning) could not be understated.

But at the end of the deployment or patrol, what everyone looked forward to was just to be able to go home. The anticipation of stepping on dry land and of seeing friends and family again was no different than that of any other seafarer. As Sumner recalled, "We could always tell when we were heading home, because we'd crank up all four engines, go as fast as you could." Similarly, on one of the *Caiman*'s return trips back to her homeport of Yokosuka, "We're supposed to be doing ten knots, [but instead], we were doing about fifteen."[32]

Discipline and Order

Like every other branch of the military, discipline among the ranks was maintained and enforced. In the submarine service, major discipline issues rarely made headlines, although they were certainly not unheard of. If serious discipline problems with submariners arose, "Your section leader—he took you aside and talked to you, and if you didn't get squared away, you were gone."[33] Fred Carneau succinctly added, "You just had one shot at it."

But more often than not, officers actually relied on their chiefs to maintain discipline among the enlisted crew, simply because these so-called sea daddies had more effective leverage. Chiefs had gone through the same experiences the younger sailors now dealt with, and this connection generated a tremendous amount of respect from the younger enlisted men. As Bob Walters recalled, "I had a sea daddy that saved my ass. I met a young lady at Hunters Point, at one of the dances, and I came back just in time for muster. And this chief said,

> 'Walters, we got a job for you. Rewire the torpedo tubes.'
> 'But that's going to take the rest of the time!'
> 'Yes, it will, won't it?'

[But] he saved my butt . . . really did."

And the chiefs were fair. As Walters continued, "I had this one bunk in the main passageway in the after battery, middle inboard, top bunk. [This] big heavy-duty second-class engineman said, 'I want that bunk!' I took the one underneath; I didn't care. Anyhow, underway, the fuel ballast tank operating gear was up there, and it leaked. And all of a sudden, he wanted my bunk. He wanted it back. [But the] chief of the boat told him, 'You picked it, you got it!' So I kept my dry little bunk, [and] he kept wiping the shit off!"

When it came to disputes between officers and enlisted sailors, good chiefs always strived to strike a balance between the sailors' concerns and the officers' position of authority.

R. G. Walker noted how one young and arrogant lieutenant "Would never ask anybody nicely; [instead] he ordered them or intimidated. He was always having the lookouts go down and get him hot chocolate. So the lookouts went to the chief of the boat, cause [the lieutenant] did this all the time, three or four times every watch. They got tired of it and they said, 'Why doesn't he get the stewards to do this? We're not his servants!' [But the] chief of the boat says, 'Oh, just shut up and do what he tells you to.'"

Generally though, as Bob Sumner recalled, "We never had any captain's masts, but guys get restricted for a week, or two weeks. I think they spent a lot of time restricting them." A long-standing naval tradition, captain's masts usually involved nonjudicial punishment meted out by a commanding officer to enforce discipline. But in essence, as Sumner alluded to, submariners were prone to mischief, not murder.

And oftentimes, submarine mischief was fueled by alcohol.[34] In one typical but memorable incident in Yokosuka, Christopher Stafford recounted:

> We had an engineman who was an alcoholic. He had been kicked out of the Navy once. He'd been on the boats, got kicked out for being an alcoholic, and then he got himself sober enough to get back on the boats. [So] he was out drinking, and he decided he needed a pet chicken. He found a chicken for an American dollar. But then he had to get a cage for the chicken. And the cage cost him twenty-five dollars! So he wanted to bring the chicken back to the boat. At the same time, he goes, "Well, geez, we got to have a party for my chicken!" So he brings a case of champagne along with him. I'm sleeping, and about two o'clock in the morning, I hear all this commotion. And I wake up, [and] this guy's got the chicken in the mess hall, with the cage, and everybody's drinking champagne! Somebody wakes up the corpsman, and the corpsman's freaking out: "Can't have a chicken in the mess hall!" So they move them down to the engine room, and then they kick the chicken off the boat. Then the officer of the day wakes up, and [he sees] everybody drinking champagne in the crew's mess, and he gets all upset about that. About an hour later, they finally get the chicken off the boat, get all the champagne off the boat, and get the engineman sobered up. And the next day, [they] put out the word: "No more animals onboard the boat!"

In twenty-two years of service, Chuck Macaluso remembered only rare instances that resulted in serious disciplinary ramifications: "One was between a cook and a lieutenant, went into a fistfight. That was probably like the tenth week underway; so everybody's getting on each other's nerves, and they got in an argument and took it out on each other, lasted like thirty seconds. And then [another] thing I saw was, a big old cook, got pissed off at somebody, came back on the boat and went and pulled out a butcher knife and was going to stab somebody in the mess decks, a machinist's mate he got in an argument with; took like twenty people to calm him down so the corpsman could sedate him."

An extreme example of the Navy's disciplinary problems happened onboard the USS *Thomas Jefferson*. After the dust settled, as Mike Stephens recalled, what resulted was "The great drug bust of 1976, where we lost nineteen people." Originally, a staggering thirty-seven sailors had been segregated from a crew of 120 and investigated for suspected marijuana use. Two NCIS agents in long trench coats had conducted the raid as the *Thomas Jefferson* pulled into port at Bangor, Washington.[35] During the inquiry, sailors who normally worked with nuclear weapons were temporarily reassigned other duties while under investigation; in the end, the nineteen that were taken to mast were removed from the submarine service. But this episode on the *Thomas Jefferson* was just one instance of rampant drug use in the Navy, and was inherently tied in with the counterculture movement permeating greater society during the 1970s. For the most part though, this was just a transient problem as the upheaval in society failed to leave the military untouched.

But most of the disciplinary issues involving submarine sailors occurred on shore, as Macaluso pointed to a flurry of troublemaking during his first midpatrol break in Guam:

> We went to the base club, and we were there about twenty minutes, [when] one of the guys put some pool sticks through a video game [machine]. They threw us out of the club. [Then] we had one of our Nav ETs come back onboard drunk and the topside watch was a sonarman [who] wanted to screw with him. The ET didn't like it and went over and started choking him. So as he was choking him, [the sonarman] got on the 1MC and . . . you could hear him gargling on the 1MC below decks. We had a security violation at two in the morning, so everybody came up and relieved him. And about an hour later, a machinist's mate came down, [threw] binoculars over the side, and punched the duty officer cause he was drunk. He went to captain's mast and got reduced in rank. Plus, somebody put their foot through the CO's car, and busted the windshield on the duty van. Now all this stuff happened the third night in, and we're getting underway the next day. The next morning at quarters, the CO's going through this whole list of things that happened. And he goes, "And you might have heard that Reagan was shot last night. But that's not the big news. Big news is . . . we're not allowed in Guam anymore. I've been asked not to bring the boat back."[36]

However rare captain's masts were, they were still used to sanction repeat troublemakers and to send a message to other sailors. But such punishment was not always a deterrent, and a situation could quickly deteriorate if other enforcement entities, such as Military Police (MPs), got involved. As Walker recalled,

> We had two guys get captain's mast [twice]. They stole a bus in Vietnam. We could see a firefight going on, all these explosions at nighttime. So

they took this bus, were driving down this road trying to get to this firefight so they could see what was going on. Anyway, the MPs finally caught them and arrested them and threw them in jail.

[And then] we're the first submarine to visit this port in Japan since World War II, so everybody had to be on their good behavior. For some reason, all the anti-[war] protestors from Tokyo found out we were there. So anyway, we got word of it and they sent word out to town to get everybody aboard. Of course, these same two guys were someplace—couldn't be found. They come out and these protestors start chasing them around town. So these guys are running into basements, into houses, getting away. They finally got away from [the protestors]. [But] we were moored out; they provided us with a ferry to get in and out, so [these two] said, "Well, we're going to have to swim it," and they go to the beach and they found these boats. They grabbed a boat, paddled out, and sank; swam back to shore, grabbed another boat, paddled out, sank; went back, got a third boat, paddled out, sank! So they swam for the boat. The topside watches, we had two of them cause we were afraid of the protestors trying to board; they spotted them and made a big thing: "People approaching the submarine!" [At] that point, you need about ten guys on topside, shining lights on them, seeing who they were. Next day, the mayor of the town came aboard, saying they ruined these three fishing boats. Well, they pulled the plugs out the bottom [to] let the water drain out apparently, but of course, these guys had no idea. They sank these three boats, so they had a captain's mast about that.

One of the regular offenses unique to the Navy was missing movement, or not being onboard when the ship or submarine departed. Chuck Nelson recalled a first-class quartermaster who failed to report back in time: "We're getting underway, I'll say seven o'clock in the morning, [and] he's not there. So they wait a few minutes, and he's not there, so underway we get. We're out, pretty much close to the ocean—we get this radio message. This tugboat picked him up; he hired a tugboat to take him out. He says, 'Captain, could you loan [me] fifty dollars? I'll pay you back!' So anyway, they paid the tugboat some money, and [the captain] took him to mast." Even in this predicament, the sailor's punishment was quite lenient, as Nelson explained, "He got a thirty-day suspended bust when we're going to be at sea for two months."

But one's fate to some extent depended on sheer luck. Following a port call in Bangkok, Thailand, Walker recounted an incident in which a first-class failed to make it back onboard the USS *Capitaine*: "We had muster, [and] everybody's hung over; we're standing there, getting ready to pull out. They said, 'Where's this guy at? Somebody go down below and search the submarine!'

Not aboard. 'We'll give him another hour.' No first-class. So we're going to have to leave him, cranked up the engines, put four engines on-line. Meanwhile, this guy is in one of those little boats, had this long canoe-type thing, big propeller-type thing, chasing us. We're pulling out away from him; he's waving at us, [and] finally [we] disappeared. So he turned around, went back, and turned himself into the embassy, and of course they arrested him, the Marines did, and flew him back to Tokyo, put him in the brig. So we had to pick him up when we got to Yokosuka. He got busted."

One common punishment for serious offenders was a reduction in rate, a demotion, essentially. As a result, problem sailors often would never permanently advance in rate, even though they managed to stay in the Navy. Carneau described one such sailor who was "Very qualified. In fact, he knew more about the boat than the old skipper did. He was chief in four different rates. He was a signalman, he was a quartermaster, he was an engineman, and he was an electrician. And the last time I saw him, he was seaman second-class. He only went ashore every three or four months, and when he did, they used to send the shore patrol out to follow him around. As soon as he got in trouble—he'd normally get into a fight—they'd haul him back and bust him. When he was sober, he knew more about that boat than anybody aboard. And you could ask him a question on *anything*, and he knew about it. He was really qualified, but he was the biggest mess you ever saw when he went ashore."

Bill Bryan's captain tried to save another troubled sailor from himself: "When the commander left, he finally took this second-class off with him. When he'd go ashore . . . we went to Havana, and the old man went in after him. [The captain] said, 'You'll never keep that second-class if I don't take you off the boats. You're going to lose a stripe. You lose a stripe, you're out of the Navy, boy! You only got two more years.' So we all got him back to the boat. He had already been to chief, twice. And he was going back up the line [for] the third time."

Lurking Dangers

But ultimately, life onboard a submarine is defined by more than just the routine and boredom of standing watch. One of the least understood aspects of the submarine service is the risky nature of duty onboard. And even though an active, shooting war would certainly multiply the dangers for any crew, they didn't need any additional reminders about the risk inherent in submerging an enclosed steel hull for weeks in the unforgiving sea. The whimsical forces of nature combined with the unrelenting ocean pressure bring to bear a true test of the best in mechanical and nautical engineering. As such, submarine disasters resulting from a failure in engineering have been equally, if not more, publicized than those that were a consequence of enemy action. And due to the dangerous nature of their jobs, submariners were paid more than their counterpart sailors in the surface fleet. Originally classified as "hazardous duty pay," and then later changed to the more specific "sub pay," this wage incentive was intended to compensate the men for the dangers and uncertainties they faced.[37]

On occasion, some submariners were actually asked to take certain risks. Bill Bryan remembered how "We had a fuel valve stuck open, and we were dribbling fuel and leaving a track in the Med. The old man says, 'We need somebody to volunteer to go up [topside] and fix that valve.' The throttleman says, 'We'll go!' I says, 'What's this 'we' crap!?' So we go up, and they wouldn't let us go out the engine room hatch, cause it was still awash. We did fix the leak. [When] we get back down, the old man says, 'You know, if it's wartime, you get a ribbon for it. Because if we had to dive, we would've left you up there . . . ' [The throttleman's] eyes got about that big around, and I [about] turned white!" But for the most part, dangerous situations just lurked in the seas, idle and waiting to pounce upon a careless or unlucky submariner.

In what was the most publicized pre–Cold War submarine accident and rescue, the USS *Squalus* (SS-192) sank on May 23, 1939, after the main induction valve, through which outside air enters the diesel engines, failed to close, flooding several of the aft compartments. Twenty-six of her crewmembers were trapped in the flooded compartments and perished. The remaining thirty-three were eventually rescued after a long and exhausting effort by Navy divers, using a rescue chamber that had been developed in the wake of the earlier USS *S-4* (SS-109) disaster, when primitive efforts had failed to rescue several men trapped onboard this sunken submarine.[38] Because the water in which the *Squalus* (and *S-4*) sank was relatively shallow and not any deeper than the submarine's crush depth, rescue was possible—an unusual circumstance in most submarine accidents because the vast majority of the ocean floor lies beyond the ability of a submarine's steel hull to withstand the crushing ocean pressure. Garth Lascink didn't mince words when he noted, "You do realize, as soon as you go out the harbor in Guam, the bottom of the ocean is about 20,000 feet down."[39] Collie Collins described how this awareness manifested onboard the boat: "Everybody could be screwing around, having a good time, when you go over the [Mariana] Trench. Before you get to the Trench, that fathometer [is] going: '*pling*-pling, *pling*-pling,' and everybody's having a good time. And all of a sudden you hear, '*pling* . . .' Man, you could hear a pin drop on a rug. No more screwing around here; we're down to the serious stuff."

Even with all the precautions, many of our veterans could still plainly recall separate instances when their respective boats came perilously close to the marketed crush depth. Whether it was a result of carelessness or just bad luck, such incidents were not uncommon. Inexperience on submarines was also a contributing factor, as was the case with one officer who came onboard from a "tin can," or destroyer:

> We had a new officer, and he was trying to get qualified. I was on the trim manifold, and the old man asked me if the trim manifold was proper. I said,
>
> "No, sir."
>
> "What's the problem?"
>
> "We're heavy aft."
>
> [But the new officer] says, "We're not heavy aft!" [So] the old man says, "Dive it then! But if you're wrong, everybody grab their britches!" And it was about 7,000 pounds heavy. We took it down, and the stern went [straight down]. And I can remember the torpedoman in that aft room saying "500 feet!" and the electrician has already taken the sticks, and he's . . . flank speed forward; we've already blown everything, and we're slowing down. When that stern gets at 600 feet, that's crush depth for that sucker. [But] it doesn't . . . and you go back up, and you finally flatten out and everybody [breathes a sigh of relief]. When we finally got it settled down, and we were at about 150 feet, the old man looked at [the new officer] and says, "Where's your math? If you can't do that in your head, go back to the tin can you came off of." Those who didn't panic all did their job. The one or two that panicked, they disappeared. We never saw them again. Everybody else on that boat did something to bring it back.[40]

On another occasion, Gary Webb and the USS *Sea Fox* experienced a mishap while practicing deep dives: "We had done about six of them, and we're [about] to do another one; the engineman did something with the sticks back in maneuvering, and we lost all power on the way down. First of all, you don't ever want to put the helm or the planes in manual—you crank forever. But we [finally] got it turned around at about 570 feet [down]. Crush depth is 600 . . . It creaks and pops and makes all kinds of weird noises."

But it was Fred Carneau who came closest to the tragic number: "The only time I ever got excited was when we got a cable caught in the main induction. We had just dove, and the guy in the engine room didn't shut the outboard fast enough, so it flooded an engine, and also half-flooded the engine room, and we started down backwards about 60 degrees. The stern was at 600 feet . . . on a 400-foot test [depth] boat. Boy, you don't think that didn't get my attention . . . And that kind of shook me up a little; that's when the frames and the boat starts popping. After it stopped, and we started back up, oh, it's just a sigh of relief!" For these submariners, this was the real deal. It was certainly nothing like what they had seen in the old World War II movies, and certainly beyond what they had bargained for. But, as Carneau added, "It's enough to make a believer out of you."

Collision at sea was another commonly feared danger. Usually career-ending for the captain, and perhaps for others found negligent by a court of inquiry, running into another vessel has long been considered the most despised, consequential, and embarrassing incident that could befall any ship, because it reflects poorly on the seafaring ability of the crew. And due to the very nature of a submarine, the risks of collision are heightened because the boat is unable to consistently maintain a visual reading of its surrounding environment; the only exception is when a submarine happens to be operating on the surface, or at periscope depth. But aside from these special circumstances, a submarine is solely dependent on sonar for object detection.

But sometimes, even having a visual reference was not enough to prevent a collision. As Bob Jackson remembered:

> The *Pomfret* hit a destroyer, and I was on it. We hit it broadside, both scopes up and the snorkel [mast]. It took us over, just like that, and the first thing you heard was the diving alarm. The second thing you heard was [the] collision alarm. Well, you were so damn far over [already]. I was on trim manifold, and I was hanging on to everything I could. It happened so fast, and we didn't know what we hit [at the time]. Both scopes up and they didn't see . . . and [the destroyer] was dead in the water! [The destroyer] had asked us . . . they had a bunch of ROTC or junior officers on there, and they wanted to see the boat snorkel, [and we] snorkeled right into them! Then we surfaced, and both scopes were bent completely over, and the snorkel mast was destroyed. And so we went back into San Diego. I think at that time, the quote was $78,000 damage. Today, it would've been in the millions.

In a very widely publicized accident, the USS *George Washington* (SSBN-598) surfaced underneath a Japanese freighter in April 1981, sinking the freighter in twenty minutes and killing two of the merchant's crewmembers.[41] The *George Washington* suffered damage to her sail, and induced a ripple effect through the submarine service. As Chuck Macaluso recalled, "My very first patrol, we were due . . . a couple weeks out from coming in, [and] we got word that the [*Washington*] had surfaced under a Japanese freighter and sank it. So she was in port; we got extended two weeks. When we came in two weeks later, she was in drydock—had her entire sail covered. The entire crew was briefed: 'You can't talk to anybody off the [*Washington*]; you can't ask them any questions, etc.' We were not happy with [them]. We didn't want to get extended two weeks. Two weeks don't sound long, but when you're looking forward to coming in this date, and you get extended, waiting for someone else . . . We were waiting for [another boomer] to come out of drydock to finally relieve the *Washington*, who couldn't be on station."[42]

Although the *George Washington* collision resulted in disastrous consequences, she was by no means the only submarine to have risked being in that position. Both Lascink and Mike Stephens recalled having come dangerously close to freighters while submerged: "That's what's amazing—all this sonar gear, but you can [still] come up . . . When you start hearing those screws through the hull, you don't need any earphones on. You're going, 'Holy crap!'"[43] Stephens described the lead-up to his own encounter on the USS *Tennessee* (SSBN-734): "We were hovering at missile launch depth, and then all of a sudden, we lost depth control. We watched the depth gauge go up. We're at 100 feet now; scopes are going up. Then you heard the sound go by."

But the truth of the matter was, if something catastrophic happened to a submarine while it was submerged, escape was very unlikely. One interesting devolution that took place as newer submarines were rolled out was in the number of watertight compartments integrated into the new designs. Made infamous by the *Titanic* disaster, the idea behind having watertight compartments was that if one (or a few) flooded, the ship would still be able to remain afloat. The flooding would be contained within the damaged compartments and would not spread to the undamaged ones, allowing the ship to maintain its buoyancy. World War II–era fleet boats had nine such compartments, conning tower included. The USS *Blueback* (SS-581) had only three, and the current mainstay of the Navy's attack submarine fleet, the *Los Angeles* class, features only two watertight compartments. Suffice to say, if one of the newer submarines suffered a completely flooded compartment, she wouldn't be surfacing under her own power. But even partial flooding is serious cause for concern, especially in a submerged state where neutral (not positive) buoyancy is maintained. Although a submarine would likely survive some extra water amidships, the additional weight of an incompletely flooded compartment at either extreme end could be enough to act as a lever arm and unbalance the boat at an angle from which it could not recover.

Then there was the matter of deployable safety features for an emergency situation; or, rather, what were ostensibly deployable features, a selection that ranged from potentially useful to downright ironic. One such feature was the rescue buoy, a device that would mark the submarine's position in the event it was disabled underwater, and make it easier for rescuers to locate. Intended as a harmless safeguard, the buoys were instead removed or disabled by the

Navy, which feared that its accidental deployment could unknowingly reveal the submarine's position to snooping Soviet surveillance. However minuscule the chances of an accidental deployment were, the consequences, especially if the buoys revealed a boomer and its nuclear arsenal, could be disproportionate.[44] As Lascink acknowledged, "The last thing you want is to be going around in a patrol area with that thing up on the top." Macaluso noted how on the USS *Patrick Henry* (SSBN/SSN-599), "The buoys were welded shut. So there's no way you're going to sink and send a buoy to the surface and let people know where you're at, because they were welded. That was just normal operating." Other standard procedures involving the security of deck peripherals included welding down the retractable deck cleats, removing deck and mooring lines to shore or to tender, and installing hatch covers. As Bob Sumner summarized, "Anything that could come loose was taken off."

One curious preparation noted by the older veterans was the attachment of a steel plate to the inside of the escape trunk prior to a deployment. As Bob Walters noted, "When the *Caiman* went on patrol, we had a plate, bolted to the bottom of the escape trunk; ergo, if we went down, sayonara." Dave Vrooman observed similar preparations on the USS *Plunger*: "They welded the trunk shut. The only way we could get out was through the top of the conning tower." Although no one was able to pinpoint the reason as to why the trunks were blocked and sealed, they noted that this was not done for routine operations, only on patrol deployments. However, this effectively ensured that "You really didn't have any escape trunk."[45] On the other hand, the surprised boomer sailors noted that this modification was never installed on ballistic missile submarines.

But taking the prize for the most ironic (and useless) safety preparation was the lifeboat. As Macaluso recalled from the *Patrick Henry*, "As I'm learning about damage control, in the forward escape trunk, they had a lifeboat. I go,

> 'Why do we have a lifeboat?'
>
> 'Well, that's really for the senators and mothers . . . Cause we're never going to be using this lifeboat, not where we're operating—there's nobody going out the hatch.'"

Bryan also observed this out-of-place novelty on his submarine: "I was lead seaman on the USS *Thornback*, for just over a year, and every six months, you had to change all the food in that [lifeboat], all the radios, everything in them. I said, 'When do you use it? What am I changing all this junk for?' Chief of the boat [said], 'Rules of the road! The Navy says you got to do it.' He says, 'Just think about this sucker. It ain't going through that [hatch].' More I thought about that, he's right. That life raft, as small of a bundle as it was, for eight or nine men, there ain't no way it was going to go through that thirty-six-inch [hatch]. He says, 'I'm glad that you're qualified.' I said, 'You know,

I'm not quite as dumb as I look somedays. But that sap-sucker, unless you cut it up, it ain't going out that hole!'"[46]

Even everyday routines could have disastrous consequences if not handled properly. On the USS *Sea Poacher*, a seemingly harmless act by one of the spooks showed that ignorance could come with a steep price tag. Sumner, a seasoned engineman, explained:

> We were up in the North Atlantic, and we had the spooks after we left England. We would go in during the daytime and watch the operations [of] the Soviets, and at night you'd go back out to charge the batteries. And one thing that's kind of unique on a diesel boat is, when you're charging batteries, you have to have all the hatches open throughout the whole boat so that the air flows. The intake came down and dumped in the forward engine room, then it was sucked forward through the hatches and down into the battery wells across the batteries, because the batteries are creating tremendous [amounts of] hydrogen while you're charging. And then that air, that hydrogen is pulled back through the piping into the engines and it's burned. We were charging batteries on two engines and one of these spooks shut the hatch between the forward engine room and after battery, and of course it immediately pulled a vacuum on the boat. Now you can't get that hatch open; the hydrogen is building quick—3.5 percent is like TNT. And so immediately everything ceases. Everybody just stops. Nobody walks around; if you got shoes on, you take them off in case you might spark something. It's a real bear to get that hatch open cause of that vacuum, and it takes a little while, but eventually we got it open and we had to bleed air into the boat through the air tanks. It's really a dangerous situation, and I think anybody who was on diesel boats probably [has] gone through that one time or another.[47]

In addition to the vulnerable state a battery charge could leave the submarine in, a common danger involving the batteries was that any contact with seawater would generate poisonous chlorine gas. This could quickly become fatal because a submerged submarine had no way to ventilate with outside air. As a result, in the event of a leak (which was surprisingly frequent), securing the battery wells was a first order of priority. Herbert A. Herman remembered an incident on the USS *Dace* (SSN-607), where "We dove, and the safety tank that vents into the torpedo room amidships—the vent didn't close properly, and water got in there. That's close to the batteries—we were scrambling." On the *Sea Fox*, a terrified Webb "Woke up to this water falling in front of my face. We were running on the surface, and we took a shot of water down the main induction. That gets you real nervous real fast. [For the] guys in the after battery, the first thing that goes through your mind is . . . you don't want that salt water in the battery well."

These everyday dangers were also present pier-side. While undergoing refit at Kings Bay, Georgia, the USS *Kentucky* fell victim to a careless mistake during replenishment. As Macaluso recalled:

> I was duty chief that day; we're in the wardroom, it's about 1600 in the afternoon, and we're having the end-of-[day] report with the captain, the duty officer, and the chief running all the repairs from ashore. And the below-deck watch comes over and says, "Chief, topside just reported a draft change of three inches back aft." This is a Trident submarine. You just don't see draft changes occur very quickly. Three inches in an hour is kind of . . . significant. It was the first time I saw the captain run. This is a really overweight captain. And he didn't run for anything. He could barely get from the stateroom down to the wardroom, about a level apart. And he went running back aft. We had a machinist's mate who was doing a freshwater load from the pier; [he left] the valve open, just kept it running, and the tanks filled. When the tanks fill, they overflow. They overflow directly into the missile compartment lower bilge. First bilge fills, flows into the second; second to the third. These bilges are eight feet deep, and we filled ten of them with water. It's still filling, and we start popping those decks up in lower level missile compartment, and one after another—bilges were full of water . . . oh my God. And that's a small [freshwater] line. [But] after running for about three hours, left unattended, that was scary.

Sailors perceive it to be universally true that any water coming into a boat always comes in too fast, be it intentional or otherwise. In another similar pier-side incident, Chris Stafford remembered:

> In the shipyard, we had a lot of the freshwater/saltwater coolers ripped out. You got a six-inch [diameter] line that goes through [for] seawater; you've got a hull valve and a backup valve. All the piping beyond that was gone. We were floating in the harbor. We wanted to clean out the bilges, 25 feet below the surface. So we popped open the backup [valve] and the hull valve, just to let a little bit of water in, to clean out the bilges. It was like a fire hose coming out! It shot all the way across, from one side of the engine room to the other. We were right there on the valve; we knew it was going to happen. We just didn't realize how much water was going to come out so fast. You look at that and you go, "Holy smoke!" But

> till you actually see it in person, when you see the solid wall of water coming out a pipe, you really don't realize how much water comes in. If you had a big leak, you'd be in a world of hurt.[48]

And therefore, even an innocuous amount of water would be sufficient to startle any sailor. On the *Plunger*, Vrooman recalled how one sailor was preparing to "Launch a smoke out the after signal ejector. Either the valve was leaking or they never drained it from the last time [it was used], but when the forward IC-man reached up and opened that breech to put the signal in there, and the water [came] out . . . I never saw somebody scared so much in my life."

Although the potential for a serious accident was fairly small, it was not uncommon for submarines to routinely experience minor leaks, especially through the myriad valves and piping that snaked through the interior of the hull, and were subjected to the ocean pressure outside. It was more unusual though, for the leaks to cause significant flooding to the extent of endangering the submarine. However, several of our volunteers experienced this battle first-hand. The *Sea Poacher* had just completed a North Atlantic run, and was now engaged in daily and weekly operations out of her homeport of Key West. Sumner was on watch in the forward engine room during one such local maneuver: "We were down 200 feet, and just inside the engine room, in front of number one engine, in front of [the] hatch, just to the right . . . a pipe split. About an inch-and-a-half-long split, right in the pipe. You talk about water coming in . . . of course, you immediately sound alarms [for] flooding. And the [watertight] hatches slam on you real quick. So you get out the old lead plates, and put it over [the split pipe], and then you band it. We got it stopped, but . . . water comes in pretty quick."[49] Although these sailors had trained over and over for such scenarios, these incidents still came as a surprise to everybody involved, because it was unpredictable as to when and where a pipe or valve would fail. However, there were other instances of flooding that unquestionably made sailors warier, especially because they knew the Navy knowingly gambled on fleet maintenance.

Macaluso described a telling experience in late 1981 onboard the *Patrick Henry*, which revealed some uncomfortable aspects of the Navy's maintenance program. Standing watch as an electronics technician, he began:

> We got rid of our missiles, and now we were [a] slow [attack submarine], doing ops out of Hawaii. We went out to sea. And I must have done this a million times. I'm sitting in the nav center and I got the headphones on and I'm in the back corner. We're ventilating and I'm looking through a window into the fan room through another door in there into the low-pressure blower room, and the point was, I've been told for

> two years now: "See if you see any water coming down." When you've done this a hundred times and you've never seen any water coming through two scratched-up windows, the first time I saw water coming through there . . . I'm sitting there on the headphones, I'm half asleep, I start looking through the lights . . . "Is that water coming through!?"
>
> And over the headphones I hear Radio report that they've got water coming in the lower level, grounding out all the radio gear. And then that's when I got on the headphones and then I report that "Control, we got flooding in the low-pressure blower room," and the boat takes an up angle; the front end of the nav center door opens up, a wave of water comes at me and I'm in the back of nav center, and I got this electronic equipment wrapped around me. It splashes up against [this] equipment. I'm wondering if I'm going to get electrocuted . . . I don't know . . .
>
> You're not supposed to see water around all this equipment, and we ended up getting to the surface and doing a bucket brigade. I think we took on about 1,500 gallons of water on the boat, and it was a bucket brigade, from the low-pressure blower room down to the toilets, down the shitter, back and forth. That's how we got rid of it. We ended up not coming in [to port] and I think the captain ended up reporting something less than what it really was, so they could keep the boat out [at] sea . . . That's the first time I saw water on the boat and I've never seen water coming in on a boat like that.

For the veterans listening to Macaluso's story, the most surprising aspect of the whole incident was not the amount of water the boat took on, but the fact that the *Patrick Henry* had to utilize a bucket brigade to dispose of the water, that the flooding didn't automatically drain to the bilges. This prompted Macaluso to deliver a shocking verdict on the state of his submarine: "A lot of our pumps weren't working. We were an older boat and we weren't well maintained after we became a non-FBM . . . Yeah, that was kind of freaky."[50]

The US Navy's submarine fleet was supposed to meet the most stringent maintenance benchmarks after the USS *Thresher* (SSN-593) was lost at sea with all hands onboard in 1963. The *Thresher* disaster prompted the Navy to institute SUBSAFE, a construction and maintenance program designed to certify all submarines as adequately prepared for the prevention of, and recovery from, a flooding casualty. This was an attempt to ensure that what was arguably a preventable catastrophe would never happen again. But throughout the passing decades, it became apparent that these strict requirements in the upkeep and maintenance of the Navy's submarines were not always met.[51]

On April 10, 1963, the *Thresher* was making a routine test dive in deep water off the coast of Massachusetts when what has been concluded as the most likely source of mechanical failure, a pipe joint, split and sprung a leak that was equivalent to opening a fire hose inside the submarine. The other likely problem was the loss of propulsion. It is not definitively known which came first. As the flooding increased, the water could have shorted out electrical circuits and initiated an automatic emergency shutdown of the nuclear reactor. Or, in the other scenario, an initial loss of propulsion started the *Thresher* on her descent, where the increasing ocean pressure caused the pipe to rupture. In either case, with the reactor shut down, an emergency blow was attempted to gain positive buoyancy. However, the valves feeding the high-pressure air into the ballast tanks likely iced over, and the rate of flooding by this point was too much to overcome. Weighed down by the intake of seawater, the *Thresher* slowly sank past its crush depth, where it imploded in a split second.[52]

This disaster hit the entire submarine community hard, and its ramifications resonated for a long time. As Chuck Nelson recalled, "We heard on the six o'clock news over in Hawaii. And everybody was kind of quiet after that. The bad thing about that . . . the next morning, we were leaving for WESTPAC. So you got a bunch of families that just heard this happen. I can just imagine: 'Why don't you just skip it today, don't go . . .'" Lascink added, "You think about it on your first dive, first time you take a new boat down, but at least you go down in hundred-foot increments. Once you've been down a few times, that's okay. You don't think about it that much, unless you're doing some weird stuff down there—you're going down backwards and the meter starts clanking around, then you start thinking about it, but you know, when you're young, you don't think it's going to happen to you . . . I'm sure the Marine sitting in that foxhole doesn't think it's going to happen to him either."

A few years after the *Thresher* disaster, Herman was transferred to the *Dace*, a sister ship of the *Thresher*: "You have it in the back of your head . . . You think about it, and you think about it, and nobody [then] knew what happened . . . And I remember, one time I sat there and I figured it out: [If] they had a four-inch salt water circulation valve blow out . . . all that water pouring through that four-inch hole would exactly . . . if they blew the ship's surface air, the emergency blow, it would just make up for the water coming in. So they didn't have a chance."

But for Collins, the *Thresher* tragedy was a bit more personal:

> I was in the hospital. I was trying to get duty on the West Coast, cause I had been on the East Coast for about four, five years, and I wanted to get back on the other side, so I was real tickled when they told me I had an ulcer. So I was in the hospital; I had done the tube down the throat, the whole ten yards, had been there about two weeks, and I only had two

weeks to go. I'm treading gently, I'm staying out of sight, don't want to rock the boat, let's do it and I can get the hell out of here. Then . . . Rickover sent some of his cronies down through the hospital. They needed nuclear-trained corpsmen real quick. And [they] came through; they're shaking everybody out, and I'm thinking, "Okay, they're going to take all those guys, those guys are okay," and they came up to me, and he says,

"You're going."

"I got an ulcer! I can't go back to the boats!"

"Oh yes, we need you . . ."

I'm thinking, "Oh Christ . . ." So I had to get out of the hospital, go check out, got ready to go. That night, there was a big thunderstorm, big typhoon crap came through; I couldn't get out on the aircraft that night, couldn't make that plane, couldn't execute the orders. I went back; I said, "I can't go to Portsmouth," and they said, "Well, you don't have to now . . ." The *Thresher*, which I had orders to, went down that day . . . and God, I'd kiss somebody's ass.

The ramifications of this disaster lingered for Collins. Following his recovery, he was assigned to the submarine tender USS *Proteus* (AS-19). Onboard, he discovered that "They actually had tapes on the *Proteus* of the whole [*Thresher*] situation. They were taping all this. And you sit there and listen to it, and the part that got to me was . . . who took my place. They evidently grabbed a corpsman right out of the shipyard [and] stuck him on the boat. So some kid . . . went aboard, probably his way [of] 'I get sea pay today.' Like all corpsmen, if you're going to get [an opportunity], go for it."[53]

But a mere five years later, calamity struck the submarine service again. The USS *Scorpion* (SSN-589) had been slated to return to her homeport of Norfolk, Virginia, on May 27, 1968, after a three-month deployment to the Mediterranean. One hour elapsed from her scheduled arrival time. Then another hour passed. When it became apparent that the submarine was uncharacteristically overdue, and attempts to establish any communication had failed, the Navy launched what was arguably its most massive search operation ever. In the end, some five months later, her wreckage was discovered at the bottom of the Atlantic, southwest of the Azores. Although no definitive conclusion has ever been reached, many theories for her sinking have been advanced and debated. These hypotheses range from an explosion caused by a faulty torpedo, to an implosion of the *Scorpion* as she uncontrollably passed crush depth, disabled perhaps as a result of a storage battery explosion onboard, or by another unlucky event that finally finished off a submarine with a problematic history of maintenance shortcomings.[54]

Once again, the submarine community was deeply affected. Even though our volunteers did not have personal connections to the *Scorpion*, many of them still found a way to relate on the most personal level possible. Carneau referred back to a friend who was a plankowner of the *Scorpion*, a member of her commissioning crew, but had transferred from the boat and was serving as a shore-based instructor at the time of the disaster: "Then the *Scorpion* went down, and he just . . . 'Well, I think I've crowded my luck,' and he got out of the Navy." Lascink also recalled knowing someone associated with the *Scorpion*—a sailor who was assigned to the *Scorpion* while they were in sub school together. Although four years elapsed between their encounter and the disaster, Lascink recalled, "I thought about him at the time." Walters noted,

> Anytime you hear of a submarine tragedy, you pay more attention. I was on a date, and I heard about the [*Stickleback*], pulled over to the side of the road and listened to the radio, and she said,
>
> "What are you doing!?"
>
> "Submarine went down . . ."
>
> "So!?"
>
> I looked at her, shook my head, and that was the last time I went out with her. When the *Thresher* went down, you turned on the radio and listened to it, and when the *Scorpion* went down, you turned on the radio and listened to it. When the *Kursk* went down, you pay attention, because you're part of that group. The Russians were "quote, our enemy," but hey, there were ninety to a hundred guys on that boat—went through the same crap that you did . . . they're submariners.[55]

And as Stephens reminded everyone, "It could be us . . . it could be one of us."

Social Setting

Admittedly a tight-knit group of men by nature, submariners seemed to have little room to differentiate socially; however, there were certain aspects of submarine life that inevitably segregated the crew at different times, with various factors coming into play depending on whether the submarine was in port, or underway at sea.

Onboard the USS *Mariano G. Vallejo*, Garth Lascink noticed a separation between many nuclear-trained sailors, or "nukes," and everyone else:

> Most of the nukes were in a land of their own back there. So everybody forward, all the enginemen through AMR1 forward to the torpedo room, all those guys, all hung out [together]. You knew everybody there

> and you were going out with any and everybody there. [But] just a few of the nukes back there would be part of the group that was with the rest of these guys. We used to comment, "Well, I wonder how the hell they became a nuke, because they're almost normal!" I mean, some of those guys back there are a little bit strange. They had their own little clique back in there—most of the nukes hang out together, except for a couple of them who are just crazy, and they would come up with us in the forward part; anything forward of the reactor compartment, it was all homogeneous—sonarmen, torpedomen, and [everyone else].[56]

However, Alan Nolan attributed part of this separation between the nukes and the rest of the crew to the fact that "On liberty, you probably saw that division [even] more, because those guys couldn't get off the boat for hours, after we were already out in town. The duty sections tended to hang out together a lot."[57] And while underway, it was an apparent fact, though not readily obvious, that the watch sections hung out together: "A certain section would be sleeping, a certain section would be in the mess hall, and the other section would be on watch."[58]

Another inadvertent source of segregation was found between single and married men, although this was mostly limited to the time the submarines were in port: "When you come into port, usually married guys—they're going home to their family. So single guys usually hung out together."[59] This was especially evident when the single men used to live together, either in barracks on base, or in their quarters on the boat. In San Diego during the early 1960s, Gary Webb noted how the USS *Sea Fox* "Tied up alongside a tender that was out in the middle of the harbor, in the middle of San Diego Bay. Squadron 3 tied up to the *Sperry* and [Squadron] 5 tied up to the *Nereus*. And that's where you lived, [on the boats]. If you wanted to go to town, you had to get into your dress uniform, and go across the gangway [to] the *Sperry* or *Nereus*, and either take a water taxi or liberty boat to the dock at San Diego. You're talking about an hour, two-hour job just to get to San Diego, even though it was close. It was definitely a different lifestyle." The amount of time spent in port was also a consideration: "If you're staying in port for a few weeks, then it would start to break up more. Cause then the guys who had families would be with their families. You were split automatically, cause they didn't stay on the boat; they didn't come back to the boat every night."[60] At Pearl Harbor, most of the married men lived in Pearl City, so the distinction there split along the lines of those who lived in Pearl City and those who didn't. This dichotomy was found in Key West as well, where most married men lived with their families in Navy housing.

Getting married while in the service was subject to several conditions, not all of which were easily met. Most of the junior sailors had to first receive permission from their commanding officer. As a petty officer third-class, Chuck Macaluso had to obtain a request chit. And sometimes, permission was not as straightforward as simply asking and receiving. Bob Walters recalled a second-class radioman who had to "Jump all kinds of hoops to get married." Bill Bryan was even denied permission while he was a seaman on the USS *Thornback*: "I had to wait till I made E-4. The reason the old man slowed several of us down is [because] we had almost the whole seaman gang married at one time. When we were in the yards, we got seventeen [seamen], and out of that seventeen people, nine of them were married already. They were coming from reserves and they were already married. The old man just finally said, 'Whoa! Our seaman gang can't be all married and go home at the same time, gentlemen! This sucker has to be cleaned!'"

Whether or not sailors were married also correlated to the type of submarine they served on. On boomers, it was not unusual to see close to half of a crew married. But on fleet boats like Walters's USS *Caiman*, "The only married guys I knew were first-class and chiefs, and they had war-patrol pins. The rest of us were single-jingles." And as Nolan added, "The single life is excellent for the fast attack sailor. These guys are partying everywhere."

But at the same time, even with the high ratio of married men onboard boomers, the divorce rate was also off the charts. As Lascink recalled, "We had lots of guys getting a divorce. I heard the divorce rate was close to fifty percent; I know a lot of guys that got divorced." And even though fast attacks generally had a lower percentage of married men onboard, the divorce rates were often higher. Macaluso remembered how "Every time we got back to sea, somebody's getting a divorce because they'd be gone for months . . . It was [worse] on the fast attacks than the boomers. It was more predictable on the boomers, and they weren't away from homeport like they used to [be], have to fly to Guam or Scotland. They were actually home longer. When the guys go out on patrols on the boomers, they're only gone for two months. It's just seventy days, and they're back the rest of the time. [And] they only go twice a year." The crewmembers of boomers that were forward-deployed in Apra Harbor, Guam, Holy Loch, Scotland, or Rota, Spain, would typically spend slightly more than three months away from home, even though patrol durations were the same. The three months accounted for the one day it took to relocate whole crews overseas, from stateside to their bases halfway around the world, in addition to two or three days of crew turnover and transition on the submarine, and approximately twenty-five days of refit, during which preventative maintenance and repairs were performed, and stores were loaded. Even then, the time they spent away from home was usually still shorter and far more predictable than the deployments fast attack sailors faced.

Through twenty-two years of service and onboard five different submarines, Macaluso saw three distinct groups develop: "The officers just hung out underway; they had their own officers' wardroom, [so] they hung out together. The chiefs had their chief [quarters]—they had a goat locker onboard; in the five boats I was on, there was a goat locker. In fact, the junior enlisted guys weren't even allowed to go into the goat locker unless you knocked and asked permission to enter. And then you had the rest of the crew. So there were kind of three groups underway, but [with regard to] the different ratings in those groups, it didn't matter. A ET or an MT or a sonar tech or a quartermaster—it was all the same, within the junior enlisted, or the chiefs, or the officers, cause they did have separate areas that they hung out." The revelation that these chiefs formed a separate social group came as a surprise to some of the older diesel boat veterans, who did not recall seeing any differentiation among the enlisted ranks: "[Our] chiefs eat [and] mix, right there with the guys."[61] There were also other exceptions. On R. G. Walker's USS *Capitaine*, he noted that "Generally, third-class and below hung out together; second-class and above, and [sometimes] third-class, would run around together." But this separation didn't always hold, especially while underway. Although chiefs would only on occasion spend time ashore with sailors of lower rank, social dynamics on the boat were much more integrated. As Walker continued, "The chiefs integrated with the crew too. We ate at the same tables; I know some boats had special tables, but ours—if there's an open space, that's where they'd sit down."

Even with the many opportunities for differentiation among any crew, along with a few groups that stayed closer to themselves, a more general consensus was voiced by Bob Sumner: "We didn't really have any 'groups.' You were friends and socialized with just about everybody onboard. There wasn't really any cliques." Expanding upon Nolan's observation regarding the nukes and their different duty sections, Macaluso acknowledged the existence of social groups, but also saw them as ephemeral in nature: "I think by maybe convenience, some groups held; [they] hung out together because they got off the boat before others got off when they were on liberty. But what I experienced . . . I talked to everybody onboard, you hung out, you joked with everybody, and eventually if everyone caught up with each other, everybody was just one group again."

3
A Unique Culture

"Pride runs deep." This ubiquitous phrase is found anywhere submarine veterans congregate—front and center on their hats, shirts, and bumper stickers. The three simple words epitomize all that has come to symbolize a small, but very defined, segment of American society. But what was so special about this experience? In short, the culture was built around a robust group mentality, and among carefully crafted personalities. There always seemed to be a book of specific rules that a submariner followed, but what belonged in this metaphorical book was open to interpretation. To take one perfect example from the USS *Mariano G. Vallejo* (SSBN-658), Garth Lascink pointed out how "If you came on our boat, and you said something about being a sub-MARE-inner, the COB would come up and say, 'Are you on a sub-MARE-in, or are you on a sub-MARINE? I don't want to hear sub-MARE-in anymore. You're a sub-MARINE-r on a submarine. And that's it!'"

A Brotherhood

When asked what *the* distinguishing feature of the submarine service is, most submarine veterans will point to the remarkable camaraderie among crewmembers. Whether this camaraderie stemmed from the individual character of the sailors or the physical limitations and necessities of being confined in such a small space, the brotherhood that resulted was comparable to what was found in NASA's astronaut corps and special forces units in the Army and Marine Corps: "We're such a small group of people. I'm sure the Navy SEALs are similar, because percentage-wise, you're a very small percentage [of the Navy], and those people are special. At least we think we're special. But you have a camaraderie due to that fact."[1] Another common thread in these elite groups is reflected in the intensity of immersion into their jobs that all members willingly accepted, oftentimes at great or unknown risk to themselves.

In characterizing the foundation of this camaraderie, the integrity and trustworthiness of each man onboard was also repeatedly brought up. As Robert Walters explained, "You could put your white hat on a bunk, and you could put your wallet on the bunk. The white hat would disappear, but the wallet would stay there. I don't think there's any thievery on the boat."[2] Lockers for personal belongings went without locks.

Respect between members of a crew was also a key attribute. Although privacy was hard to come by in such cramped quarters, Mark A. Manzer noted how what little privacy existed, was carefully maintained: "Respect carried over into privacy as well. If somebody's in their bunk, curtain closed, reading a book or something, [it's] just kind of unspoken; you just don't bug them—give them their space. Or if somebody's between the [missile] tubes reading a book, you just kind of leave them alone."[3]

Although a depiction of this brotherhood is easily conveyed through words and examples of hard work, its development onboard any submarine and among any crew was anything but quick and simple. Elbert H. Collins, the hospital corpsman, noted how respect was not automatically handed out: "You have to earn a spot though, too. I was called 'Nurse.' When I first went aboard, I was not qualified, so I was 'Nurse.' And everybody would [say], 'Go see the Nurse' or 'Hey, Nurse.' Until I did something that got their respect, you're [the] Nurse. When I earned my dolphins, I [became] Doc. I had to earn; I had to do something, and I think everybody that goes through the boats earns that respect."

There was also a lot of pride associated with belonging to the crew of a specific boat. Camaraderie generated a team mentality, and it was not uncommon to see sailors take up additional responsibilities in order to help their fellow submariners out. One typical instance occurred before inspections, the most stressful and intense of which was the Operational Reactor Safeguard Examination (ORSE). Conducted onboard nuclear-powered submarines only and lasting for several days, the tests and drills were run by outside examiners to verify that a submarine's crew was thoroughly capable of operating its nuclear reactor safely, and knowledgeable enough to recover from any unforeseen problems. As Charles Fredrick Macaluso remembered, "On the boomer, if we were in a particular run where we had an ORSE inspection coming up, everybody in the front end went to the back end of the boat, in the engineering spaces to help them clean up. ETs, sonarmen, were in the bilges; they were helping machinist's mates back there cleaning up, just to get ready for the ORSE thing. Then it worked the other way. If we had a combat inspection coming on, or a tactical kind [of] inspection, you'd help up forward."

Another example of the volunteer spirit onboard was when repairs were needed. Fred A. Carneau remembered that "On most boats [it] was the same, especially if you had the engine break down, why we had quartermasters, and signalmen . . . and everybody there on the boat [with] spare time was in the engine room working. We got the thing put back together and fixed if it was fixable." Evert Charles Nelson added an anecdote from his time onboard the USS *Blueback* (SS-581): "We broke the crank on the middle engine. It was in the Pacific and we were on our way to Australia, and we had sonar techs and we had quartermasters down there, so when we got to port, it was all ready to be pulled out. We got it out before we even hit port."

What resulted was a workforce that was one cohesive team, with individual sailors playing different roles, and everyone stepping up to help one another out. Such a familial mentality even extended to the uppermost echelons of submarine force administration on shore. David Meade Vrooman recalled how when he first arrived at Pearl Harbor "To pick up the *Plunger*; they were out on a run. The first thing COMSUBPAC did—they assigned me to a boat that was in the yards so I could get sub pay. Then they told me: 'We got you a place down in Waikiki. The *Plunger* will be back in a couple weeks; we'll see you then.'"

Of course, it would be unrealistic to assume that everyone who joined the submarine service was a perfect match. Even some who seemed destined to succeed anywhere sometimes found difficulty adapting to life onboard submarines. As Collins remembered, "We had a corpsman that was the honor man in our independent medical classes. He was the head person in submarine medicine classes. He was the top—number one—in our submarine school classes. He even made chief on his first time up. He got a boat out of San Diego, and he didn't last two months. He did not fit. With all that intelligence and everything, he [still] couldn't fit." Collins pointed to another instance when he had to medically disqualify a new crewmember who couldn't perform assigned duties: "His dad had been on submarines, his uncle had been on submarines, and he wanted on submarines. But every time we closed the hatch, put a little pressure in the boat to dive, he'd hold onto that mess deck, just hold on and watch. He was actually scared to death, [from] the moment we started to dive. So I had to wash him out."

But because maintaining the close chemistry among the crewmembers was so important to their mission, every effort was made to ensure that misfits were taken care of, one way or another. As Christopher Stafford summarized, "If you don't fit in, they get rid of you quickly. If you do something to another shipmate, if it's not in the best interest of the boat, you're gone ASAP. It's a real team. Especially if you're out at sea for thirty or sixty days, if you got a bad apple in the group, you don't want them around, because it'll affect the whole boat."

The limitations of life onboard also created the space for a tight camaraderie to grow among the sailors, and between the officers and their enlisted crews. As Garth Lascink noted, "It's rare to find somebody you don't really get along with." Gary W. Webb pointed out an observation that was echoed by most of these veterans, that "In all the time I was aboard, I don't think I ever heard anybody say, 'It's not my job.'"

Like many brotherhoods, the camaraderie of the submarine force knew no boundaries, and extended beyond the veterans' service in the Navy. As Alan L. Nolan observed, "I've been out of the Navy quite a few years now, and I've never seen that kind of camaraderie anywhere in civilian life, [like what] I experienced [in] those four-and-a-half years I was onboard that submarine. I still communicate with some of those guys to this very day, and I think that's where a lot of it comes from."

As Stafford added, "The big thing is—the camaraderie stays forever . . . When you leave the boat, you have reunions. Ten, twenty, thirty years down the road, you still come together. A couple shipmates and myself—we went up a couple years ago and had lunch with our ex-CO and ex-XO off the boat. That's unheard of in most places, [where] you never [even] talk to officers." Walters recounted a boat reunion where a group of submariners drank with and gave a former Pacific Fleet Submarine Force Commander (COMSUBPAC) a good-natured ribbing, and Collins pointed to an occasion where another admiral stopped a procession to greet old friends. These were classic examples where the rigidity of military ranks was absent, where flag officers were made indistinguishable from reserve sailors.

In a true mark of a robust fraternity, Collins noted how even strangers would come together over the common submarine experience: "If you're going down the street, [or] we've been camping or we've been to parks, and some guy sees your hat, and you're a submariner—you're immediately a friend, [an] old lost buddy: 'What boat were you on?' And they start comparing dates. It's like, my God, where've you been all my life!?" And when Stafford's wife passed away earlier in the summer before our interviews had started, the entire submarine veterans community in Portland came together in support. Collins echoed the sentiment of the moment when he remarked, "I was absolutely proud." Stafford himself noted that these gestures were "Over and above what anybody [else] would do. That's something special."

Blurring of Rank

One defining aspect of life onboard a submarine was in the relationship between officers and enlisted men, where one found a cohesiveness rarely seen in the Navy's surface fleet. Robert W. Sumner encapsulated the predominant feeling among the veterans: "When we threw the lines off, leaving the pier, there really wasn't an officer [or] enlisted rank; you were all members of the crew. You respected the officers; you knew that they were the officers."

Bob Walters finished Sumner's thought: "And they respected you." Sumner continued with a comparison between the surface fleet and the submarine force: "When I first went into the Navy, I spent about eight months on a destroyer escort. And there's definitely a separation between ranks on surface craft. The officers stay in their little corner of the world. But when I went to submarines, it was totally different. And when we were out at sea, there wasn't really any distinguishing between rank. That really is unique to submarine service. You could grab-ass with the officers. I don't think you ever see that even in other parts of [the] military."[4] The unusual bond between officers and enlisted sailors originated in part from the individual personalities of the men, and in part from the realities of the living and working environment onboard a submarine.

Chuck Macaluso expanded upon the type of personal relationship enlisted sailors and officers were able to develop: "You looked at the officer and they were your boss. You called them 'sir' out of respect, but on a submarine, you could talk to each other, you could talk about what you liked, dislikes and likes, talk about family members and stuff. Whereas if you're off the submarine, you have that whole separation. Officers did not get involved in the life of an enlisted person; enlisted wouldn't have that connection with an officer. But on a submarine, it all blended together."

Macaluso also recalled the noteworthy experience and relationships onboard the USS *Parche* (SSN-683). Because of the *Parche*'s reconfigured mission as the Navy's primary special operations submarine, she underwent a refit where a 100-foot compartment dedicated to special operations was added on forward of the sail, complete with all three decks, air systems, and hydraulic systems. And in addition to all the intelligence-gathering electronic equipment, this compartment included separate sleeping quarters for the Special Projects officers, as well as an extra crew's berthing space. These officers were "mustangs," navy parlance for commissioned officers that were formerly enlisted sailors. Some of them would go through boot camp as an enlisted recruit, and then attend the Naval Academy afterward, but in the submarine service, this was rarely seen. For the most part, mustangs in the submarine force served as Projects officers; most mustangs outside of Projects submarines had shore assignments. As Macaluso remembered, "The best officer-enlisted relationship I had was when I was on the *Parche*. We had the mustang [quarters], and we had probably six or seven mustang officers onboard. And you had a great relationship with them because they were all the Projects officers on the *Parche* and we were all the Projects sailors. And it was just like your buddy, cause these guys had just spent several years as enlisted guys, whether they're commanders or they're warrants, and now they're on your boat. It was really, really cool. So they gave you something to look forward to, cause if you wanted to be a warrant or an LDO, those guys were good examples, and they were actually different than the rest of the crew, cause they kind of stayed separate from the regular officers."[5] But even though the *Parche* represented a unique example, close relationships between officers and crew were by no means limited to special operations submarines.

The camaraderie extended beyond the boats, and reached onto shore and into other aspects of navy life as well. Garth Lascink pointed to a crew change on the USS *Mariano G. Vallejo,* when they were loading missiles onto the boat in Bangor, Washington. After the load was completed, a group went up to Whidbey Island, where "We had a weapons officer, [and] he went over to the enlisted man's club, which is almost taboo for those guys to do, and was in there drinking with us and buying us drinks and stuff in the club over there. It is a tight—these guys, the officers were pretty good; it was a pretty close relationship. That's part of the thing about being on a submarine that was a lot different than being on a surface ship." Even off base and away from work, the jovial bonding (and drinking) continued. Alan Nolan recounted a port visit to Victoria, BC, where "In one of the local bars, the captain and the XO sat at the table with me and another guy that was only a third-class at the time; and they bought us four or five beers through the course of the evening. So it was like they were just one of the guys."[6]

In a more proactive approach to alcohol-fueled fun, Collie Collins recalled an instance when "We had a ship's party at the Horse and Cow, and the guys bought a pony keg of beer, and [when] the party was about over with, the old man put it in his vehicle to take it on base. And they took that pony keg into the barracks, put it in the shower—so the guys could continue their party when they got back. Now—this is the old man doing it. If we had tried to bring it [past] the gate, we would've been locked up, key thrown away!"[7]

But in an example of how extreme the familiarity between officers and enlisted crew could get, Chuck Nelson recounted a night of shore leave in Pearl Harbor, right before a WESTPAC deployment: "One of the guys came back; he was drunk [off] his ass. He's being escorted by the shore patrol [and] they went to get the duty officer—'This man's drunk in town.' A couple minutes later, enough time for the guys, the shore patrol to be gone, he's back [on] his way to the beach. I says,

'You going back over?'

'Sure! Duty officer says I could!'"

Not every submarine enjoyed this degree of informality onboard. But for the most part, officers and enlisted alike still treated each other with mutual respect. Although Robert Austin Jackson acknowledged that most of the officers on the USS *Pomfret* (SS-391) stayed to themselves socially, "If you had a concern or if you wanted something, they would see to it. I remember we were overhauling an engine. It was Christmas Eve, and we had it all back together, but we had to fire it off. [The] engineering officer [came] back and said, 'Well, you can't go on liberty until you get it fired off and running properly.' So I asked him, I said,

> 'Well then, everything will be closed by the time I got off. Would you do me a favor? Will you go over to the officer's club and buy me a fifth of Jack Daniels?'
>
> 'I can do that.'

And we fired her off, and we got off of there about eleven o'clock. Of course by the time we got over to Yokosuka, everything was pretty quiet, but at least I had a couple shots." At times, relative age seemed to make a difference in allowing officers to forge a connection with the younger enlisted sailors, for as Jackson added, "We had one ensign—he was the most friendly with the crew, a young kid [like us]."

Even though submariners made an active effort to keep distinctions between ranks to a minimum, in one instance, rank would actually serve as a catalyst for reinforcing the bond between the officers and the enlisted men. This was found in the protective disposition of many officers, who would watch over their crews with paternal vigilance: "If somebody came down on the boat [and] harassed one of the enlisted men, the officers on the boat—you didn't screw with their crew. They'd be all over your case."[8] And if a sailor found himself in trouble away from the submarine, the officers would often be the first to arrive to make sure that their sailor was in good hands. As Sumner recalled, "If you got in trouble on shore, they're really protective. If you got locked up—I can speak from personal experience—they came down and got you out, took you back to the boat. You might have [been] restricted for a week, but it was no big deal. But if that happened on [a] surface craft, you'd be in big trouble."

This kind of camaraderie was also evident in the contrast between the informality of life onboard a submarine and the strict regulations that defined the surface fleet. Submarine officers rarely nitpicked over little details. As Lascink recalled, "There was very little 'Mickey-Mouse' crap you had to put up with. Everybody respected the job that you did, and it was more or less, as long as you perform that, you never got any flak from anybody." Lascink went on to describe one of the common points of dispute that would arise between submarine sailors and surface fleet officers—over the uniforms submariners wore:

> One of the things that our officers would do for us . . . normally [when] you're tied up by a tender, and you go across the tender [to shore], they're writing you up for stuff, cause we wore nonregulation shoes; they called

> the dolphin belt buckles nonregulation buckles. Nobody wore . . . everybody looked like a seaman; even a first-class didn't have a chevron on their arm. So they'd write you up and come over to the boat, but you never heard about them [afterward]. [Our officers] must've just tossed them all in the round file when you got out. From the tender they'd send all that stuff over, and they'd get you up there on that quarterdeck, and says, "OK seaman, what's your name?" I says,
>
> "Well, it's second-class."
>
> "Well, you don't have a chevron! OK, no chevron, nonregulation belt buckle, suede shoes . . ."
>
> Everything, you know? It's kind of funny. It never got anywhere.

The respect also worked in reverse. Because the officers went above and beyond normal expectations for Navy line officers to reach out to the enlisted crew, the sailors felt a reciprocating sense of responsibility to be the best crew for their officers. One of Fred Carneau's anecdotes painted the picture perfectly: "[The] old man, I remember one time he was walking through the control room. There's a piece of paper on the deck that had come off the chart table. He didn't say nothing to nobody. He reached down, picked it up, threw it in the ash can. And everybody's face got red because they didn't see it before."

However, mirroring any organization with a command hierarchy, it was unsurprising that the relationships between the enlisted men and their officers were heavily influenced by individual personalities, not all of which meshed well. As Walters admitted, it "Depended on the officers. Ninety percent of them were squared away." But as Carneau added, "Then there was that ten percent that gave everybody fits." For several of our volunteers, it was the executive officer that gave them the most trouble. As Macaluso recalled, "If I ever had a run-in with an officer, it was with XOs." Jackson recounted his own dispute with the *Pomfret*'s XO: "I was standing watch one morning topside. It was cold [and] foggy down there in San Diego, and I had a cup of coffee in my right hand. And he came across, and he looked at me. And I [said], 'Good morning, Lieutenant.' He went down, and he must've looked in the manual, cause it says in there: 'If your right hand's occupied, you can salute with your left hand.' Well, he put it in the ship's log that there would be no coffee for the topside watch."

Officers new to the submarine service would frequently face difficulties adjusting to the different lifestyle onboard, a result of the often-inaccurate expectations they formulated from their prior experiences. On Sumner's boat, the USS *Sea Poacher* (SS-406), "The entire time I was there, we had nothing but great officers that were really just part of the crew. [But] we had two JGs that came on right out of Annapolis, and I think one of them was there maybe six months—he was going to change the world, and the other one maybe lasted two months. They just didn't understand; they didn't fit in with the crew. They wanted to be more like the surface navy, and it just didn't work."

Midshipmen often bore the brunt of disdain from many sailors. As Mark Manzer recalled from the USS *Sam Houston* (SSBN/SSN-609), "We had a midshipman rider one summer, kind of a cocky kid. And we decided to have a mail buoy run with him. We drew up a qual sheet, had him walk around, get signatures from everybody, got him all dressed up in a harness and rain jacket with the boat hook and everything. CO cleared baffles and went up to periscope depth, [but] sonar came up with a contact, so we had to go back down. And he was pissed off because he couldn't get his mail." "Clearing baffles" is a change of direction maneuver executed by a submarine to scan with sonar, the acoustic blind spot (baffles) directly behind the boat. Normally done to ensure that there wasn't an undetected enemy submarine hiding out behind, unexpected contacts were always a cause for concern. But quite frequently, as demonstrated by this particular rider, midshipmen and new officers alike had trouble adjusting to the unpredictable nature of submarine service. Then again, part of the experience was not of their own doing. As Nolan fondly recalled, "We used to have fun messing with the middies."

However, as far as incompetent officers were concerned, the Academy was not always to blame. Walters noted, "I found that the Academy officers on the *Caiman* were pretty squared away. Two or three of them [had served in] World War II, and a couple others were Class of '47, '48, '49, '50, somewhere in there. But we had some NROTC guys that thought they were God's gift." Lascink also made a similar observation onboard the *Mariano G. Vallejo*: "All of our Academy guys were pretty squared away, but they're older. But some of the new guys . . . in fact, our assistant weapons officer, we called him 'Fluffy.' I mean, this guy was a real piece of work, and so [our] weapons officer—he was a mustang lieutenant; he says, 'Don't let them call you that; c'mon guys, be nice to him.' [But we said], 'Look, get him out of our hair and nothing will happen, but keep him someplace other than back here.'"

Younger officers, caught in a juxtaposition of inexperience and a position of leadership, tended to have more difficulty earning the respect of the enlisted crew. Certain things that were obvious to an experienced sailor may not have been readily apparent to an officer fresh out of the Academy. Collins recounted an instance of flooding in the after battery on the USS *Catfish* (SS-339): "It was only about inch-and-a-half, two inches [of] water. The young ensign came back and saw the water on the deck, and he wanted me to open the battery hatch to see if that water had [leaked] down. And the guys are looking at him like they can't believe what they're hearing! He's getting kind of pissed off that they're not jumping to it and opening that hatch. I said, 'You don't want to open the hatch! You open it up, there's going to be water down there!' But he didn't stop to think. I was qualified at this point, but I may have done it had I not been." Chris Stafford recalled another young officer who had just reported aboard the USS *Barbel* (SS-580) while the boat was in the yards:

> We had high-pressure air lines, high-pressure hydraulic flushing lines, 220-volt power lines, going through the watertight hatches. I had below-decks watch. He came [up to me] and says, "Well, what happens if we start to flood?"
>
> "Well, I'll make sure everybody's off the boat, sound the alarm, and bail out."
>
> And he freaked out.
>
> "You got to close the watertight door!"
>
> "There's no way you can close the watertight door! You got all these steel pipes going through!"
>
> Even with an ax, I couldn't cut it. And he's there jumping up and down and turning red! I could see it [making sense] if we're floating in the water, [but] we were in the shipyard!

It was a very unexpected reaction from the officer, considering that it was rare for hatches, doors, and passageways to be free of obstructing piping and lines while a boat was in the shipyard.

Walters recalled a more innocent misunderstanding by a "JG [who] came aboard from an aircraft carrier, and he made the Tahiti run with us. His name was Jim, and [when] we got down to Tahiti, and he got himself one of these pith hats, got the name of 'Jungle Jim,' 'JJ' for short. Anyhow, one time he was officer of the deck, and we were on the surface, and one of the mess cooks [asked] permission to dump garbage. And JJ says, 'Can't you just take it back aft and burn it?'"

But just as quickly as ridicule was handed out, respect could just as easily be earned back. Walters continued, "One time I was messing around, doing something close to the wardroom, and somebody says,

'Jim, how come you weren't at the party last night for the officers?'

'I didn't feel like going.'

'You'll never get ahead in this life.'

'I'm ahead far enough.'

And all of a sudden, JJ's stock went up about twenty points."

Ultimately though, regardless of how affable or sociable the officers and enlisted men were with one another, what really mattered was that a strong, safe, and efficient working relationship developed to enable everyone onboard to function as one cohesive unit. When it came time to operate the multimillion-dollar submarine, they were all on the same page. What was the most important facet of this working environment? Gary Webb argued that it was because if the officers "Brought something up and you really didn't agree with it, you could question them. And they would accept it."

Cherished Traditions

Because qualifying onboard the boat was undeniably one of the most difficult challenges any submariner faced, some of the most celebrated traditions revolved around the awarding of dolphins. As Richard G. Walker explained, "When you got qualified, you had to 'drink your dolphins.' Get a pitcher [of] every kind of concoction, and you had to drop your dolphins in it and you had to drink it down . . . and try not to puke. But now I think they put a kibosh on that. Then they started 'pinning' [the dolphins] on. They'd hit you in the chest. Then they did away with that [too]."

So what exactly went into the infamous concoction? Garth Lascink elaborated: "They'd take one of those mixers you mix blended drinks in, the metal ones, [and] fill it up with whatever—Tabasco Sauce, booze, put your dolphins in there, and then you drink them. [But] you can't puke. If you puke, they're going to make another one for you."

Because this practice was seen as inherently distasteful and potentially dangerous by some of the higher-ups, it was officially halted by the Navy. As Lascink continued, "When I was out on patrol, we got a [message] that came through, and it says, 'There will be no more drinking of dolphins.' This comes from COMSUBPAC. They had an x-ray of a guy and his dolphins were lodged . . . in the esophagus down there. [So] no more drinking of dolphins. Well, that didn't mean anything; everybody got a big kick out of it really, but everybody still drank their dolphins after that."

Not unexpectedly, these well-established traditions were difficult to abolish overnight, despite official policy changes. As Alan Nolan, one of our younger volunteers, recalled, "When I got my dolphins, I was actually on patrol, and when the captain pinned them on, he made the announcement to everybody on the mess decks that you're not allowed to tack the dolphins on anymore because somebody might break some ribs. And no sooner than he pinned my dolphins on and shook my hand, those babies [got] smacked on good! I did drink them after we got back to port too, and this was long after that was outlawed."

Submariners had another tradition that went beyond the all-important occasion of being awarded dolphins. Any special accomplishment was grounds for ending up off the deck and into the harbor, and it wasn't an uncommon sight to see some twenty-odd members of the crew going overboard for various reasons. In fact, as Walker added, "If you qualified, you made rate, the sun came up . . . anything, they'd throw you over the side."[9]

Collie Collins concurred:

> We would throw people over the side if you got a rank, made rate, or if you had a baby, or for hardly any reason at all. We were tied up at Long Beach, in front of a new [guided-missile frigate (DLG)]. We were having some work done on the boat, so we're all living on the [barracks craft (APL)]. We're on the third level of [the] APL, and they run off the names. Our old man made commander; we threw his butt right over the side, right along with a couple guys that made third-class. And he expected it—cause we were at quarters, and he turned to the exec and he just started taking off his wristwatch and his wallet, cause he knew where his butt was going. And I'm watching, and they get done with quarters . . . [Yes] they do! On the third deck of an APL! They grab the old man like a torpedo and run for the side! And we ended up with eight to twelve people, all swimming around in the bay out there. And this young ensign on the DLG, officer of the deck, comes forward up on their foc'sle, yelling down, "There's no swimming there!" And he wants to know who the hell's in charge. And I can remember to this day, the exec says, "That's our captain . . . swimming over there!" And [the ensign] left.

Evidently, the officers were not only participants in this tradition, they served as enforcers as well. Chuck Nelson added this anecdote: "We're moored in Guam; this guy, a first-class, wanted to [re-enlist]. He was swearing in; the old man gave him the oath standing on top of the rudder. He wanted to do it on the rudder, and I said, 'Why that?' He says, 'It's a turning point in my life!' So they're up there, the old man swears him in, and says 'Congratulations,' then [gives him a shove]—dumps him into the water."

On occasion, this ritual was some cause for confusion as well, especially for one surface fleet officer of the deck (OOD). As Nelson continued, "We were tied up outboard of three tin cans in Japan. The XO had just got word—they had a new child, just had a baby. So that was announced at quarters. And right away, they start grabbing the XO; he's going swimming. Not a big deal. Except . . . the OOD on the outboard tin can [saw that and shouted], 'Put that man down! Put that man down! That's mutiny! Put that man down!' And he calls [for] the Marines! And the XO goes over the side. [But] nothing [more] was ever said about that."

Collins continued with another special occasion down in San Diego: "We had a cook that won the Betty Crocker Bakeoff one year. Came back aboard, a Filipino cook—he was just so proud, and he had all these pictures and everything back there. They grabbed his ass and threw him over the side. About that time, they realized he was a non-swimmer! Three guys go over real quick to save the cook!" Fred Carneau was at least extended the courtesy of being asked if he could swim: "Then over the side I went!"

One of the more unique traditions that only a lucky few were able to participate in was the christening ceremony for boats under construction. Assigned to the new construction crew for the USS *Mariano G. Vallejo,* Lascink vividly recalled the experience of riding the submarine down the ways: "The whole crew stands topside, and then they knock the block, and you just slide into the river, backwards. That was a lot of fun, and that's a proud day. Everybody's standing up there; you got all the ceremonies going on, and then as [the submarine] goes down the ways [into] the water down there, it really picks up speed. It's amazing how fast [it] can get going."[10]

Another special tradition centered on the celebration of Christmas while underway. Although it was difficult being away from home, submariners did everything they could to ensure that their Christmas was memorable. For Christmas 1956 on the USS *Caiman* (SS-323), Bob Walters recalled, "The CO went through the boat, and he must have crawled [through] many, many places, cause he came back with an armful of booze—gin, whiskey, the whole ball of wax. This was not supposed to be there, but he put it in his cabin. So on Christmas Eve, he got the cook to make up a punch with all the booze. He mixed it all together, and passed it onto the guys on watch. We were singing Christmas carols, and here's this first-class electronics technician, crying . . . It really brought Christmas home. That was really the best Christmas I ever had in my life. Then we had the big feed Christmas Day—turkey, ham, and all that stuff; you wonder where that came from too."[11]

Santa Claus was a frequent visitor as well. On the USS *Sam Houston,* Mark Manzer remembered how "One Christmas Eve, Santa came down the snorkel mast and delivered presents to everybody." Santa was also present to help celebrate an unexpected Christmas surprise with Herbert A. Herman and the crewmembers of the USS *Dace* (SSN-607): "We were out for ninety days, and we came back in—in for ten days, and then headed back out—going out to chase the [Soviets]; anyhow they turned back, so we got to come back in [to] New London around Christmastime. [But] they didn't know when we were coming back. We went and took a pillowcase, filled it with everybody's gum and candy, whatever we could find onboard the ship, and we outfitted [a crewmember] with that pillowcase full of presents. He had a full-time beard, some Wellington boots, and we dressed him up like Santa. [So] we [came in] under the bridge there in New London with Santa on the bow."

Rites, Rituals, Hazings, and Toilet Humor

Arguably considered another "cherished tradition," crossing the equator for the first time was celebrated with long-time naval customs, even on a submarine. The amount of hazing associated with "crossing the line" has decreased over time to be in line with contemporary standards of political correctness, but as Garth Lascink pointed out, "In the 'old' days, there was no 'Oh, I don't want to participate,' like they do now. There was no 'voluntary' back in the sixties. When you went across, you went across." Chuck Nelson concurred with an anecdote from the USS *Blueback*: "We crossed the equator. We had a nice ceremony, [and] the last thing you had to do was walk the plank. They had the gangway tied down, so you just walk off the boat. Our quartermaster says, 'I can't go off that. I can't swim!'

'Too bad, we'll tie a line around you if you want.'

'No, no, I don't want to go!'

So they more or less helped him go. Just when he stepped off, the shark watch fired two shots. And this guy, I swore, didn't get his knees wet. He comes up the side of the ship, looks up and says, 'Where's the shark!?' The [shark watch] says, 'I thought you couldn't swim!'"

Lascink went on to describe his initiation onboard the USS *Mariano G. Vallejo*, when he was finally converted from *pollywog* (a sailor who has never crossed the equator) to *shellback* (one who has):

> You go through this—first thing we had was a line where the guys are in between the [missile] tubes with short lengths of fire hose, and you're crawling on your knees, down the length of the missile house, and they're whacking you across the butt. All the pollywogs, the guys who hadn't been across before, [are] in their underwear, and nothing else. And these guys are swacking you across the butt with this fire hose, and you really start moving by the time you get down to the end, from all these smacks on your butt. So then from there, we went into our crew's mess. Since it was so rough up above, we didn't have it topside, so they put a slopshoot in the crew's mess. And so they save the garbage for a week, and put [it] in this big canvas sleeve, like a big condom with garbage in it. So first when you go in, you meet the king and the queen and the baby. You had to kiss the queen's toe—she had her legs crossed there, and she had something in her toes down there that you had to get, mint jelly or some stupid thing between her toes you kissed. Then the baby's sitting there. They find the fattest chief that's a shellback, put him in there, and he's wearing a diaper thing, a white towel or something—looks like a sumo wrestler. You look at his belly,

and it's all yellow; it's mustard yellow, kind of like diarrhea or something. Anyway, what they did, was wipe a bunch of sardine paste and all kinds of crap on there. And so the king says, "Well, you want to kiss my wife's toes, right?" You go, "Oh, yeah, yeah I want to do that . . ." So you kiss that, and [the king] says, "How about kissing my baby's belly? You want to do that, right?" Of course, you say yes. Well, you get up there, you want to get in there and kiss it and get out, right? Well, the baby grabs the back of your head, stands up, and . . . he rubs your nose in all this stuff. You're about ready to barf [with] sardine, mustard, and all this crap on there. So then they look at you: "Oh you're not feeling too well? Doc, give him some medicine." Now they got this jar over here, full of . . . I don't know what's in this thing. They get one of those big metal ladles, and say, "Here, drink your medicine." You drink that and you want to barf. So then after that you go through the slopshoot. You're going through there, trying to get through as fast as you can. Well, these guys are standing on the front, so you're hitting their feet trying to get through this thing. Finally get down to the other end; it was crazy times. You see these guys in there; they're wearing pirate outfits and the queen's got her bra on. You wonder how [all] that got on there, you know? [But] what was funny [afterward], they put on a big spread that night for the people to eat—[and] none of the pollywogs wanted to eat. All you could still smell was that garbage up your nose! And they'd have steak, and all this [good food], and everybody's going "Err . . . I don't feel like eating . . ." The good thing was, you knew if you ever went back, you were going to get retribution![12]

Bob Walters went through an equally elaborate ceremony on the USS *Caiman*: "We started the day at 0800, standing watches. I stood a watch in full foul-weather gear in the forward engine room, with both engines running. Then [after going through the slopshoot], we were topside and we had to walk the plank. We had the gangway strapped down, and you're blindfolded of course, and you're going out . . . all of a sudden, nothing there, and you're in the water!"[13] This quick fix allowed the pollywogs to clean up in the ocean, because the showers onboard were not easily accessible, being prime real estate for the storage of onions and potatoes.

Then there were those initiation rites that one would not be particularly proud of participating in. As Lascink continued,

One of the initiation rites you did not want to join on my boat was called the "Go and Blow Club." That's when you go to the bathroom and blow the toilet back in your face. Every patrol—at least one person would join that club. And you'd have everybody sitting down in the mess hall, eating, [and] all of a sudden, you hear this "WHOOH!" And everybody'd get up and run to the head, [to] see who joined this thing. So we're sitting there one night, and we hear this "WHOOH!" And all of a sudden about two seconds later, "WHOOH!" again. We go, "Oh my God! Two people! Let's go!" Everybody runs down to the head, and we're looking, and there's this guy standing there. He's got toilet paper hanging off his ears, all wet and everything.

"Who's in here with you!? Who's in here!?"

"Nobody . . ."

"Well, how come we heard it twice?"

"I didn't believe it happened the first time!"

The guy spends the next two hours down there cleaning that place up, but oh, that was so funny! The guy did it twice. But you know, you go in there, [and] we used to have a sign you hang on there [that] says: "Caution! Sanitaries being Blown." They're standing there with that in their hand, but you know, you get up out of bed, you're half groggy, you go in there—they know they're not supposed to pull that flapper valve—the sign's in their hand [and] they pull it anyway. Half the time when you're pulling it, you have to bend over that toilet . . .

Pulling the valve while the sanitary tanks were being emptied from the submarine, meant that air pressurized to 225 pounds per square inch, normally used to expel waste from the tanks, now had an extra avenue to travel—through the open valve, and right back into the submarine.

Lascink harkened back to his days as a new submariner, when he recalled his first encounter with a submarine head: "When I went to sub school, they would take us out on fleet boats, out of New London, to go out into the [Long Island] Sound out there, on daily ops. They had a head up in the torpedo room. You're looking at that as a green submariner. You're going, 'I'm not going to the bathroom in that place, cause I know they're setting me up for something.' So you don't drink any coffee, you don't drink any water, you don't drink anything for the day you're out there. You're going 'Okay, what time does this thing get back into New London!?' Cause I'm holding this all this time, till I got back into port to go pee!" As Bob Sumner deftly warned, "You always looked at the pressure gauge first, to see if there's any pressure in that tank!" But in line with Lascink's earlier observation, no amount of precautions or warnings helped. Fred Carneau added, "In the after [battery], we had trouble all the time. It seems like there was always somebody cleaning up something after using the head. They spent [a lot of] time polishing and cleaning back there." And on the USS *Ethan Allen* (SSBN/SSN-608), "It was always in port—somebody coming back from liberty would do it."[14] Eventually though, these relics disappeared from submarines and were replaced by porcelain flush toilets and urinals on the Trident boomers. Although the Tridents retained the ability to blow sanitary tanks, pumps were now the preferred method of expelling waste to the sea.

But just like Lascink described, the heads on older submarines were some of the most complicated pieces of equipment to operate. On the other hand, they provided a convenient apparatus and location for sailors to prank an unsuspecting crewmember. R. G. Walker remembered how on the USS *Capitaine* (AGSS-336), "If you wanted to get somebody, you would go into the head, turn one of the valves on the stool. And then there's a master valve. So he comes and sits down, starts reading his magazine. You turn that valve on, the water slowly starts [rising]—hits him in the ass! Of course, you weren't going to the bathroom; you were getting ready to run! But of course he had his pants down around his ankles, and you'd generally get away!"

The heads were not the only place where someone could get into trouble. Any waste line draining to the sanitary tanks was fair game, even in the mess hall. As Collie Collins recalled, "We had a guy [that] could cause an accident [just] walking through. They were blowing sanitary, and they go around, put the water seal in. This kid came in and saw the bubbling around the drain and around the coffee urn . . . and he opened up [the water seal] that second they blew [the tanks]. And it came up, hit the bottom of that urn, and gave it a big cover effect. It just did a beautiful job to the galley and mess hall. I thought the cook was going to kill him; I really thought the cook wanted to kill him! Because everything had to be cleaned and sanitized before we could eat."

And as Lascink recalled, fun could also be had when it was time to empty the sanitary tanks: "We used to blow our sanitaries at midnight. So when you're in port, you're blowing into the river wherever you're at, alongside that tender there. We had a head [in the] back of the missile house, and we'd crank that sucker up, depending on who we knew was topside. I put as much pressure as I could get in it, [and] still hammer that valve open to let [the contents] go out. Then you got this big 'WHOOSH!' Water and crap is just going up through the air all over the side of the submarine; these guys [topside] are going crazy: 'Missile house, there's something going on down [there]!' And all of a sudden, they start smelling [it]. We're blowing it all over the side of the tender, or the boat next to us, having blowing parties out there at midnight; all this crap is going everywhere."

Sometimes though, the nasty surprise was unintentionally delivered as a result of another sailor's carelessness. Dave Vrooman recalled "One machinist's mate—every time he blew sanitaries back aft, he wouldn't vent it. When you went back there to use it, you quickly learned to check the pressure, cause you knew if he pulled the tanks, he never vented it." Equally problematic were the "Guys that vented too fast. The vent from the sanitary—when you blow it, it goes through a charcoal filter, which 'miraculously' cleans the air. Even at the best of times, it still stinks, but these guys would go in there, and they'll run that thing through there, wide open on that valve; next thing you know, you can be in the engine room [and] you can smell this sanitary smell all the way through the boat. Then the officers start coming down [and complaining], cause their place is right up above."[15]

Sometimes of course, these smell signals were deliberately sent to the officers with a little intent. Other subtle practical jokes were also used to deliver specific messages. Vrooman, the electrician's mate, recalled how on the USS *Plunger* (SSN-595), "Just about everybody back aft carried a little screwdriver to make adjustments with. We got this new division officer, and he decided that he was going to make these adjustments, so he's always grabbing somebody's screwdriver. One morning at quarters, we got a screwdriver for him. We wrapped it all up and presented it to him at quarters. [He] starts unwrapping it and his eyes brighten. Then he gets it all the way open, and [sees that] we cut the tip off!"

Other new officers would receive similar flak from their crews, sometimes for the sole reason of simply being new. Utilizing a feature normally associated with disposing trash from a submarine, Chuck Macaluso described how his fellow crewmembers rigged one officer's bunk. The Trash Disposal Unit (TDU) allows a submarine to remove accumulated garbage while underway, through an apparatus involving metal cans, disk-shaped weights, and a torpedo tube-like ejector. When full of trash, the cans would be weighted down and ejected into the ocean routinely. Weighted cans ensure that the garbage would not accidently make its way to the surface, creating a trail and potentially revealing the submarine's location. But to send a message to this officer, these multipurpose weights were redirected from their original intent and strategically nestled under the mattress pad in his pan-shaped bed frame. This prevented him from opening his personal locker underneath, which was only accessible by lifting the bunk frame. Macaluso recalled the struggle between this officer and his formidable opponent: "We had a brand-new officer onboard who was giving the enlisted guys a hard time. He thought he was a know-it-all. So after each watch, one of the guys would take a TDU weight and put it in his bunk. It would start filling up, and he must have had like thirty dang TDU weights in there before he pretty much caught on, cause he could not lift the damn thing! It took him two weeks to figure it out!"

On the other side of this officer-enlisted battlefield, Lascink was one of the sailors on the more preferable end of the practical jokes:

> We got one of our assistant weapons officers. We're out at Christmastime, just getting ready to leave, and so everybody says, "Well, we need

some Christmas presents!" So we ordered a whole bunch of TL-29s, the old knives they used to have, the jackknives, and then aviator sunglasses. We ordered like sixty of these things apiece through the weapons department. So these things come in . . .

"Here you go, sir . . . uhh Merry Christmas!"

"Where did you guys get this stuff?"

"Oh, you got them for us, sir!"

And he starts looking—he's got all this money paid out for all these sunglasses and all these knives that everybody on the boat got. He was a little bit miffed about that.

But some of the most creative hazing was reserved for the new, fresh submariner: "When you're [a] non-qual, getting on the boat, it's basically trial by fire—the old guys trying to freak out the new guys. And if the new guys can handle it, then they just fit right in."[16] An unlucky Walker found himself assigned to foghorn detail on the *Capitaine* one day:

> We were out in the South Pacific somewhere, and we came upon this huge fog bank. I mean, you couldn't even see the end of the submarine. I'm down cooking and I finished up for the evening, and they sent down word—they wanted the cook up there with his large salad pan and a steel spoon—"And get a life jacket!"
>
> I climb up to the bridge, and they said, "We want you to climb over the side, go out on the bow of the submarine, and we want you to bang that pan. And every five minutes [we'll] blow a whistle and we'll tell you to plug your ears." So I'm sitting out there, banging on this thing, thinking, "I'm going to die first. These son-of-a-bitches put me out here on a suicide mission!" We didn't have any lines up around the submarine, didn't have harnesses. So I'm up there with my pan, banging on it . . .
>
> "Plug your ears!"
>
> [Horn blows.]
>
> "Commence banging!"[17]

Just because Collins had already made first-class did not mean he was exempt from any surprises as the new man on the USS *Catfish*: "We had an animal onboard . . . well, we had one guy we called 'Animal.' I hadn't been on the boat more than a week, our first time out, and of course, they're really pinging for me. About two in the morning, I hear this, 'Doc! Doc! Doc!' You're half-ass awake, look over the side of the bunk, and he's sitting here, and he's got his wazooie in his hand! He's got a flashlight on it, and all the rest of the crew—they're all watching you. And he says,

'Look at that, Doc! Look at that!'

'What's the matter?'

'Nothing. But ain't it a beauty!?'"

Eventually though, Collins got his revenge: "I waited damn near three weeks till I got him. He was sleeping with his wazooie out of his shorts, in his bunk, and I got Gentian Violet, and I painted that . . . purple from one end to the other! But if you didn't have a sense of humor, you'd better not be on the boats!"[18]

Given the boundless limits of sailors' ingenuity, Collins's welcome party to the submarine service was considered relatively mild. Alan Nolan recalled how his initiation pranks on the *Ethan Allen* were a bit less subdued:

> Every time we went to sea, we did a test-depth dive. The upper-level missile house was a pretty cool place to be, to do your leak checks, because the floating decks creak, and you could hear it crunching and crackling the whole way down. We'd always put our greenhorns in there. And we tie the string across for them, so not only could they hear it, they could see the fact we were getting compressed. One time, we took one of our guys, and we hid him up in the upper level with a squirt gun. And we had these kids doing the leak checks around the missile doors. He gave that thing a couple shots of water, and it was kind of dripping a little bit. And this kid started, "Hey! Hey! We're flooding!" I said, "Nah, don't worry about that, unless it streams. That's nothing." So we get down near test-depth, and this kid—he's been watching this [dripping] pretty closely the whole time. And the guy that was hiding out, [as] we get down just about to test-depth, he hits [the kid] right in the face with a big stream from that squirt gun; the kid about crapped in his pants!

But even this baptism was not as ruthless as the prank the whole crew of the *Ethan Allen* concocted as a measure of revenge against a brash, young newcomer in late 1980. As Nolan recalled,

> We were up in Bangor, and the COB on the USS *Long Beach*, a cruiser in the shipyard over in Bremerton—got a hold of our COB and said, "Gee, I got this kid that's never been to sea." So of course our COB says, "Yeah, we'll take him." My boomer was going through the transition to become a slow-attack boat. We're going for two weeks to do some bottom mapping.
>
> This kid reports aboard, and the first thing he says to the topside watch when he came onboard was, "You guys are all queers! Keep your hands off me!"

> And of course, we all know what that meant. The challenge had been laid down.
>
> So for the better part of the next week underway, we as a crew—officers included—did our very best to make this poor kid think he was right. We'd give each other the peck on the cheek, the slap on the rear, [and] we'd do it to him, freak him out. [Later] when I got off watch, that poor kid was sitting in the corner of the mess decks . . . trembling. That night, we had to really calm him down, and finally take him under the wing and say, "You threw down [the challenge] when you came onboard, calling us a bunch of 'queers.' So we've been playing with you for the last week. You want to get the game over with? Start slapping people on the rear when they do it to you!" And he was fine after that. I can't imagine what he must've said to his buddies when he got back to his ship; no doubt they set him up!

And in the end, the world balanced out, and even Lascink was paid his due on his last patrol before leaving the Navy:

> We used to have radiation damage control drills. A lot of times they say, "Okay, you've been radiated, so you guys go down to decon to get decontaminated." So you go down below, and you're supposed to run through the showers and come out through there. Normally it's just "Okay, I've been in the shower," just kind of talk it through. Well, on my last patrol, they says, "Oh no, you got to do this stuff." So [for the] two of us who're getting out at the end of that patrol, they made us go ahead and go in there, take the shower. So here we are standing in the nude. I got a little yellow pair of these booties on—that's the only thing I'm wearing. Yellow booties and you're buck-naked in there. So all the guys stick out of fire control, and they're all taking pictures with their Polaroids, saying, "Oh yeah! Oh yeah!" So [during] the rest of patrol, I'm trying to pay off these guys [for] these Polaroids. I says, "Well, I got to get that!" So anyway, I end up getting it; I had it in all my sea bag stuff. I wasn't married at the time, but years later, I [was] going through all this stuff with my kids around there, and my wife. All of a sudden, this picture comes out . . . and I'm standing there in these little yellow booties—bare naked. And I'm trying to explain how all this relates to the submarine service.

Wearing the Uniform

Aside from the dolphins that distinguished a submariner from any other sailor in the Navy, the uniform they shared was a tremendous source of pride. In fact, greater American society used to regard the uniform as a symbol of entitlement to trust and privilege. Gary Webb noted how "Wearing your uniform was a good thing. If you went on liberty, anywhere, you were treated well because [the public] could recognize exactly what you were and who you were." Bob Jackson remembered how a sailor could "Stick your thumb out in your uniform, and you got a ride, right [there]." Chuck Nelson echoed in agreement: "I'd go out there and thumb. You wear your uniform, you *always* get picked up." Garth Lascink pointed out two more benefits wearing the uniform could bring: "When we went up to Reno, instead of wearing civvies, we wore our uniform. And you didn't have a problem with those waitresses coming over and giving you drinks no matter where you were. All the time. The other thing—in [those] days, you could fly military standby at half fare if you wore your uniform. And invariably, a lot of times if you were back there and they had a seat up forward—'You want to go up to first class?' You get shot up there too."

The level of respect and appreciation the public showed for sailors in uniform was not lost among the veterans. Bob Walters recounted how "One time we're wearing the uniform in LA. We're going to an opera, and we're standing there to buy tickets, and this guy comes up to us and says, 'Are you going to go to the opera, you two gentlemen? Two of our party [are] not showing up. Here are some tickets.' Third row center. Here's [everyone in] tuxes and all this shit, [and] here we are in uniform. It was neat, though." But as Webb harkened back over the years, he acknowledged how "There's a real culture difference between then and [now]."

A popular service that catered to sailors in uniform was the locker club. As Nelson described it, "Anywhere near a Navy base, they have locker clubs, where you could go in to town in your uniform, [but] keep civilian clothes [there] and change clothes. [You'd] go mess around town, then come back in, go to the locker club, get your uniform back on, and [head] back to the base." But these clubs offered much more than just clothing and uniform storage. As Webb added, "One of the big ones was 'Seven Seas,' down in San Diego. [It] was not just a locker club; it was [an] everything club. They had pool tables, they had pinball machines, they sold stripes, they did sewing, and they did dry cleaning." Other services included routine laundry, hot showers, and even impromptu lodging, for as Bob Sumner noted, "You could sleep there if you crawled up on top of the lockers. Did it many of times!"

At the same time, an interesting contradiction existed. For as much pride as the submariners placed on being able to wear their dress uniforms in public, they elicited an equal, if not greater, amount of pride from the informality of their work uniforms within the Navy. By not emphasizing the trinkets of rank, submariners believed that this only served to reinforce the bond of brotherhood among them.

From the beginning of the Cold War era until the late 1950s, chiefs like Fred Carneau would regularly wear dungarees as part of their working uniform, just like the more junior enlisted men, and as Walters noted, "The only [way] you could tell they were a chief [was because] they had the [brown chief's] hat on." Later on though, khakis became standard for chiefs.

The informality of dress lasted somewhat longer for the junior enlisted men. When the USS *Sea Fox* (SS-402) entered San Diego Bay, Webb was one of many submariners who was ordered to have at least "The white hat on, and dungarees, hopefully without holes in them. But that was it." Across the harbor, USS *Caiman* was "Tied up to one side of one of those piers downtown; the *Nautilus* was tied up to the other side. Here we are in our dungarees and white hats, and here are these guys in their dress whites."[19] It was a sign of changing times. Surface ships had always come into port with their sailors primped in dress whites, and now, the submarine force was evolving as well. It would mark the beginning of two decades over which the Navy's uniform regulations were being constantly revised, culminating during Admiral Elmo Zumwalt Jr.'s tenure as Chief of Naval Operations with the sweeping changes he implemented before his retirement in 1974. Widely credited with making major strides toward social equality in the Navy, Zumwalt also focused on improving sailors' quality of life, with various popular directives that relaxed certain regulations he felt were no longer relevant in the present day and age.[20] However, he made one major miscalculation when the order went out to eliminate the sailor's talisman: the traditional dress blue uniform.

For many sailors, the model uniform has always been the service dress blues, with the navy blue jumper and thirteen-button bell-bottom trousers: "That uniform had been around for eons, right? You want to be a Cracker Jack sailor. That was cool; nobody had a uniform like the Navy. The first thing you did when you're out of boot camp was go downtown and get your tie steamrolled—[it] looked like a girl's neckerchief; they were all so wide, so you get them steamrolled so they look good."[21] Many sailors then took it upon themselves to customize the uniform, whether it was a custom-tailored zipper for the bell-bottoms, or dragons imprinted on the inside of the jumper cuffs.[22] And aside from the disciplined appearance the uniforms gave sailors, they also served another practical purpose, as Lascink noted, "Those were really chick magnets! Anyplace where there's not [other] sailors, those are really good uniforms!" The uniforms were also practical in design. As Lascink added, "Plus, you can fold them up; you roll them up. They're made for a ship. Because of the way you'd roll them inside out, they never got wrinkled up." Earlier generations of sailors were issued the blue flat hat or "Donald Duck hat" along with their dress blues. These were eventually phased out in the late 1950s and replaced with the once common, and now ubiquitous, "dixie cup" or white hat.[23]

However, the most turbulent change came between 1973 and 1980, when the jumpers (both blues and whites) were replaced by dress components that resembled the standard chiefs' uniform. The blues were replaced by the "coat and tie," and the summer whites with a white short-sleeved shirt and black trousers, a combination known colloquially as the "salt and peppers," and both sets of uniforms came standard with a chief's hat or "combination cover."[24] These became the dress uniforms for every enlisted man, from E-1 on up. Alan Nolan, who served from 1975 to 1981, remarked, "I feel cheated; I didn't get to wear those [jumpers]." Chuck Macaluso added incredulously, "When I joined in '79, in boot camp, they were not issuing sailors jumpers. I joined the Navy and I didn't have a jumper!" But one year later, the jumpers made an emphatic return to the fleet after many sailors voiced their displeasure with the abandonment of tradition.[25] Michael A. Stephens, who joined in 1974, noted, "I never had a jumper until I was an E-6, and I had to find me a seaman to show me how to tie that tie!"

But the biggest shock to the older veterans was how sailors no longer regularly wore uniforms on liberty. Since the 1970s, civilian clothes had slowly become the standard dress for sailors off base and off duty. As Lascink recalled, "We used to have to wear them; if you're under E-5, you had to wear a uniform off base." In fact, as Webb noted from his experience, "The only person that had civilian clothes onboard was the captain. None of the [other] officers, none of the chiefs . . . You did not go on liberty—you did not leave, unless you had your dress uniform on. Period."

All in Perception

One of the most significant positives to come out of the submarine experience was pride, and submariners elicited a certain sense of pride by juxtaposing their own service against the rest of the Navy and other branches of the military. They perceived themselves as the US military's oddball "A Team." This opinion was especially apparent among the more senior enlisted ranks, who saw themselves as guardians of the submariners' paradigm. Garth Lascink recalled this exchange from the noncommissioned officers' (NCO) club in Guam: "We were over at Anderson Air Force Base. We're getting ready to fly out. We used to have charter flights back to Hawaii, [after a] crew change. So we're in the NCO club there, and we're all drinking. And there's all these tail gunners—in those days they still had tail gunners [on] B-52s—and these guys [were wearing] wings. So we're all drinking, [and] next thing you know, we're switching wings for dolphins. Then we show up the next day at muster, [and] we got these wings on. So we're all saying, 'Well, we're going to join the Air Force!' Well, that went over like a lead balloon with the COB! 'What *the* hell is this!?' He really got a kick out of that alright . . ."[26]

A distinct privilege submariners were always proud of having was that they were trusted with keeping their own liberty cards. As Gary Webb explained, "[For] the bulk of the Navy, [they] would take your liberty card. And when you were okay to go on liberty, they'd hand them out [again]. In the submarine service, you carried your liberty card all the time. And that was a *big*, big privilege." Lascink added, "[In] some of the schools, E-5 and above could carry [their own cards], but below that, you had to turn them in."

As Collie Collins reflected upon his career, he noted how "Of all the duty I ever had in the Navy, and in twenty years I had aircraft carriers and destroyers, the best group of guys I was ever with was [on a] submarine." Herb Herman joked about the dichotomy between the submarine force and the rest of the Navy with an anecdote that was symbolic of the bond between the entire crew of the USS *Baya* (AGSS-318): "We pulled into port at Hunters Point; the boat tied up [to the pier]. There was an aircraft carrier [on the left] and there was an aircraft carrier [on the right], and the last thing the skipper said was, 'Don't start any fights. I think they've got us outnumbered!'"

At other times, submariners weren't as discreet about their feelings toward what they called the "skimmer fleet." While stationed out of Pearl Harbor, Chris Stafford observed the prank of a lifetime:

> The sub base there looks out over several other piers where cruisers and destroyers hang out. And a submarine came in, the *Archerfish*, and it [had] an all single-men's crew. You had to be single to be on the boat. If you were married, they kicked you off. It was basically an R&R boat. They did some oceanographic exploration, but they hit all the little fun places to go, and they were a rowdy crew. They pulled into Pearl, were there for a couple of days, getting refueled and new stores. They took off really early one morning, and [when] everybody came down to the boats [later], you could see across the bay, on the bow [of] one of the big cruisers, it says, "You have been sunk by the USS *Archerfish*." Right on the bow. Big letters. Everybody on the sub base could see it. And they were laughing their butts off! And about two hours later, there was a couple of seamen over there on a float, trying to paint out [the words].[27]

Ultimately, what distinguished the submarine service from the rest of the Navy and the military in general was not found in dolphin pins or ingenious pranks; instead, it was inherent in the physical and mental self-containment these sailors faced. As Bob Sumner explained, "The way I would describe it—'We all go down together. We all come up together.' You depend on everybody on that boat. [If] one person screws up, none of you might come up." Fred Carneau added, "Everybody's life depends on [any] one person, all the time."

The theme of risk and danger with regard to serving on a submarine was central to this discussion and was brought up repeatedly. Although the specific nature of these dangers was addressed in chapter 2, the veterans noted how an awareness of the risks helped to reinforce the community bond. Alan Nolan placed an emphasis on this observation when he noted, "Part of the camaraderie also goes with some of the inherent danger that's involved in being on a submarine. Our very lives depend on each other, so we took care of each other. We played hard together; we worked hard together." Lascink added some historical perspective: "When you think about it, the period [I was] in [the service], you're talking maybe twenty years after World War II. You know, the submarine service lost the most people per capita unit, than anybody in the [Navy]. I mean, it was a dangerous job. I was in for six years, and during that [time], two submarines went down—*Thresher* and the *Scorpion*. And it was still a dangerous job. Still a dangerous job today, but you haven't seen one go down. But in that period, God, submarines are going down left and right all the time. So that is part of that mystique of being a submarine sailor. Everybody's in there together; you really got to rely upon everybody in there." A submariner essentially had to trust his life to all the other sailors onboard every time the boat went out to sea. Sumner expounded upon this fact when he noted, "My wife asked me one time: 'How could you go to sleep, knowing that you're submerged and that there's other guys that are up doing their job?' And I said, 'Because they're *doing* their job.' That's how you could go to sleep and feel comfortable because you trusted the guys that were there with you."

Figure 1. Fred Carneau, standing next to an antiaircraft gun mount on the USS *Entemedor* (SS-340) in San Diego, California, 1947. Note the larger 5-inch deck gun on the main deck in the background. Courtesy of Fred Carneau.

Figure 2. Collie Collins, official Navy portrait, 1962. This photograph was used for his admiral's staff billet at Naval Hospital Oakland in California. Courtesy of Collie Collins.

Figure 3. Bob Jackson (*far right, shaking hands*) is congratulated by CO Charles K. Schmidt after receiving his dolphins in a topside ceremony on the USS *Pomfret* (SS-391), 1955. The *Pomfret* is tied up next to the submarine tender USS *Sperry* (AS-12) in San Diego Bay. Courtesy of Bob Jackson.

Figure 4. Bill Bryan, official Navy portrait, 1958. Courtesy of Bill Bryan.

Figure 5. While on deployment in the Mediterranean, Bill Bryan visits the Parthenon in Athens, Greece, 1957. These port calls provided young sailors with the opportunity to see what they had previously only read about in history books. Courtesy of Bill Bryan.

Figure 6. USS *Thornback* (SS-418), a typical GUPPY fleet boat of the *Tench* class, seen underway, 1963. Note the step-sail and several crewmembers standing watch on the bridge. A source of consternation for the lookouts, this step-sail design exposed them to roiling waves during foul weather. NHHC Photograph Collection (USN 1086056).

Figure 7. While topside on the USS *Caiman* (SS-323), an amused Bob Walters (*center*) cracks a smile as he listens to two shipmates behind him discussing everything they should know about the opposite sex, 1957. The USS *Diodon* (SS-349) is tied up alongside. Courtesy of Bob Walters.

Figure 8. Bob Sumner, standing in front of the barracks that housed the crew of the USS *Sea Poacher* (SS-406), while the submarine was being overhauled in Charleston, South Carolina, 1961. Courtesy of Bob Sumner.

Figure 9. Gary Webb, official Navy portrait, 1960. Courtesy of Gary Webb.

Figure 10. Herb Herman, standing on the after deck of the USS *Baya* (AGSS-318), 1961. Courtesy of Herb Herman.

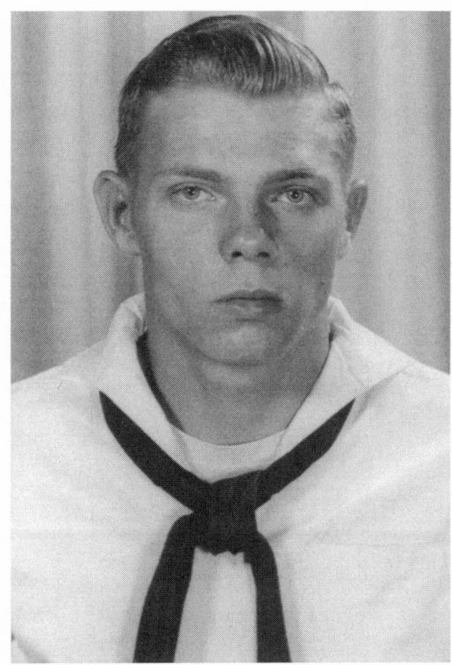

Figure 11. Dave Vrooman, official Navy portrait, 1962. Courtesy of Dave Vrooman.

Figure 12. USS *Plunger* (SSN-595), a *Permit* class fast attack submarine, seen underway off Oahu, 1963. Bestowed with a Navy Unit Commendation (NUC) for special operations conducted in the winter of 1966, most crewmembers are still not sure what the prestigious award was for. NHHC Photograph Collection (USN 1067833).

Figure 13. Chuck Nelson, standing topside on the USS *Blueback* (SS-581), the last diesel-electric attack submarine built for the US Navy, 1963. He is flanked by the starboard side of the sail and a submarine tender in the background. Courtesy of Chuck Nelson.

Figure 14. USS *Patrick Henry* (SSBN-599), once home to Chuck Nelson and Chuck Macaluso, loads a Polaris nuclear ballistic missile from the submarine tender USS *Proteus* (AS-19) in Holy Loch, Scotland, 1961. In late 1981, the second-oldest boomer in the US Navy suffered a flooding casualty that was exacerbated because the Navy neglected to maintain working pumps onboard. NHHC Photograph Collection (USN 1053952).

Figure 15. R. G. Walker (*far right, wearing shades*) poses with shipmates from the USS *Capitaine* (AGSS-336) following a successful souvenir run in Saigon, South Vietnam, 1963. In addition to the wrapped package, Walker is holding an *erhu*—a traditional Chinese stringed instrument. Courtesy of R. G. Walker.

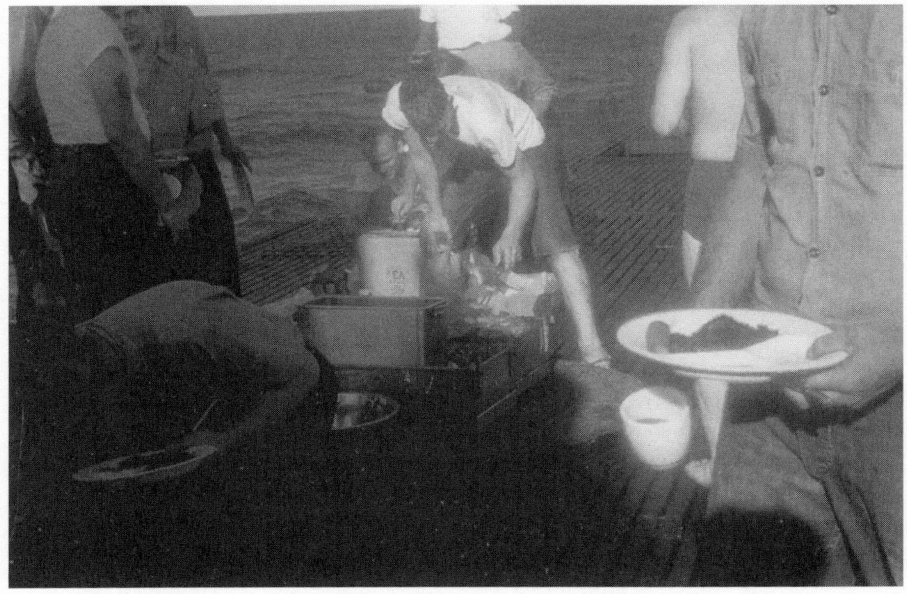

Figure 16. While on patrol in the South China Sea, commissaryman R. G. Walker (*center*) fires up the grill on the USS *Capitaine*'s steel beach, 1963. Courtesy of R. G. Walker.

Figure 17. Garth Lascink, official Navy portrait, 1968. Courtesy of Garth Lascink.

Figure 18. Garth Lascink strikes a pose in the torpedo room of the USS *Mariano G. Vallejo* (SSBN-658), 1967. Primarily for defensive purposes, torpedo tubes were nonetheless installed as secondary armament onboard all American ballistic missile submarines. Courtesy of Garth Lascink.

Figure 19. USS *Mariano G. Vallejo,* the penultimate ballistic missile submarine of the *Benjamin Franklin* class, seen during her launching ceremony at Mare Island Naval Shipyard, 1965. Note the sombrero adorning the port side of the sail. Garth Lascink is among those topside. NHHC Photograph Collection (L45–175.04.01).

Figure 20. During a port visit to Hong Kong, Chris Stafford stands watch topside on the USS *Barbel* (SS-580), 1967. Note the open engine room hatch. Courtesy of Chris Stafford.

Figure 21. Easily recognized as a symbol of economic stimulus throughout port cities worldwide, Chris Stafford sports the summer white uniform with the ubiquitous "dixie cup" hat during liberty in Hong Kong, 1967. Courtesy of Chris Stafford.

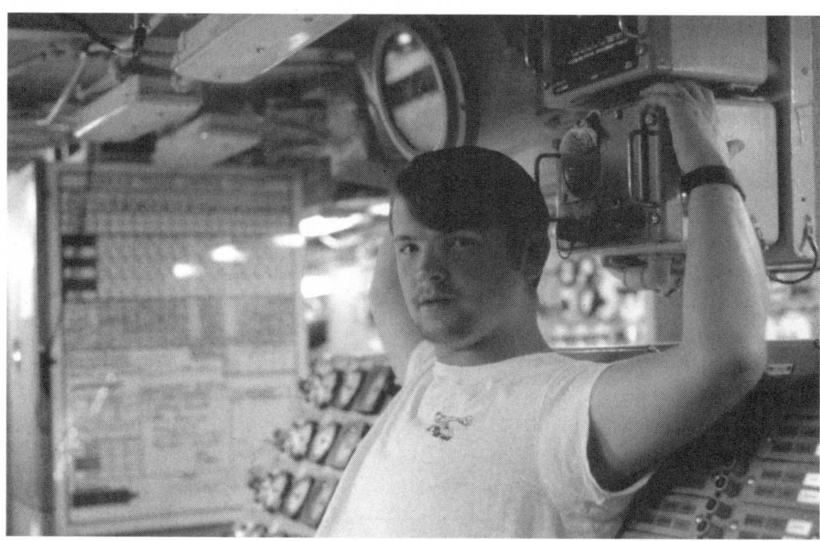

Figure 22. Leaning against the supervisor's console in the Missile Control Center (MCC) of the USS *Thomas Jefferson* (SSBN-618), Mike Stephens patiently waits to go on liberty in Guam, 1979. Courtesy of Mike Stephens.

Figure 23. During a refit in Guam, missile technician Mike Stephens (*far left*) and his shipmates on the USS *Thomas Jefferson* enjoy a brief respite from greasing missile muzzle hatches, 1978. Note the open muzzle hatch behind them. Courtesy of Mike Stephens.

Figure 24. Alan Nolan, standing next to the #3 missile tube in the missile compartment of the USS *Ethan Allen* (SSBN-608), 1978. Note the yellow dosimeter attached to his belt. These film badges measured radiation exposure and were checked to ensure that crewmembers did not exceed acceptable limits. The long passageway behind Nolan, a luxury available only on boomers, offered ample space for recreational pursuits. Courtesy of Alan Nolan.

Figure 25. Just offshore of Waikiki Beach, Hawaii, Mark Manzer relaxes topside as the USS *Sam Houston* (SSBN-609) waits for clearance to enter Pearl Harbor, 1980. Courtesy of Mark Manzer.

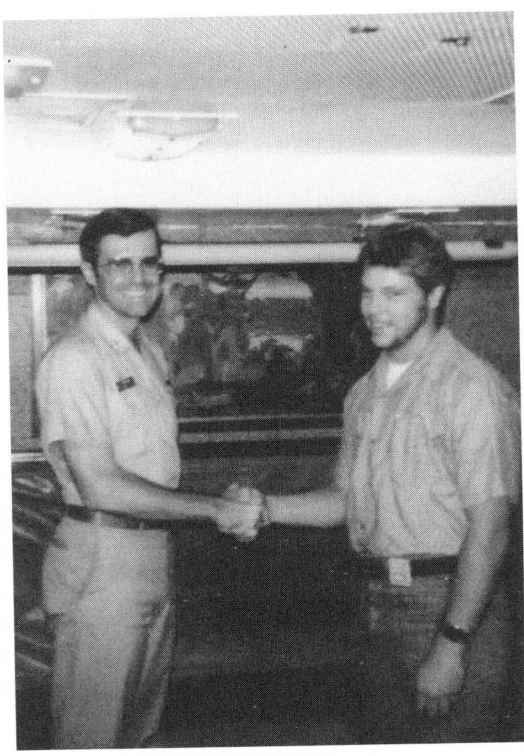

Figure 26. After completing his qualifications and receiving his dolphins, Mark Manzer (*right*) is congratulated by CO William Owens onboard the USS *Sam Houston*, 1979. Courtesy of Mark Manzer.

Figure 27. Chuck Macaluso, official Navy portrait, 1988. Note the qualified diver insignia pin on his uniform (below the ribbons). This photograph was used for Macaluso's Sailor of the Year nomination and subsequent selection. Courtesy of Chuck Macaluso.

Figure 28. Six months prior to his retirement, Chuck Macaluso attends a Change of Command ceremony at the submarine base in Kings Bay, Georgia, 2000. Having risen up the enlisted ranks, he is now sporting the uniform of a warrant officer (W-2). Courtesy of Chuck Macaluso.

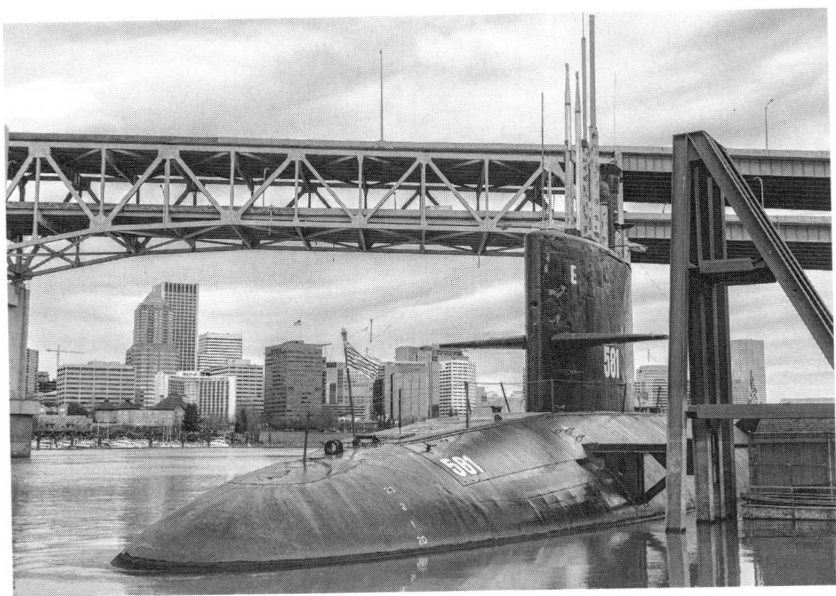

Figure 29. The USS *Blueback* is now a floating educational resource and tribute to submariners at the Oregon Museum of Science and Industry in Portland. The submarine veterans featured in this book all volunteer onboard the *Blueback* by leading public tours, working on boat maintenance, or contributing to other special projects that help preserve the history of the Silent Service. Courtesy of Corey Walden.

Figure 30. Known as "Officers' Country," the wardroom of the USS *Blueback* was home for her eight officers. The central dining table also doubled as a medical emergency operating table. Staterooms are located off to either side of the passageway. Courtesy of Corey Walden.

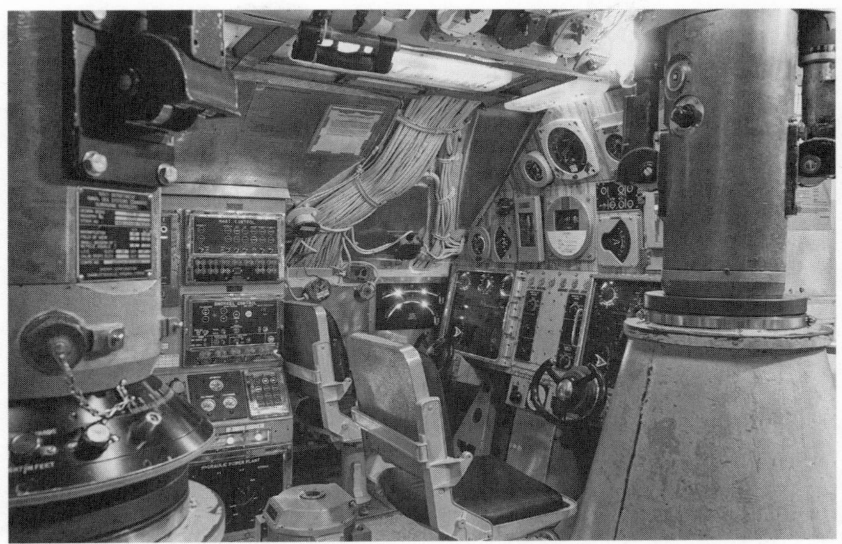

Figure 31. Facing port, the two periscopes in the control room of the USS *Blueback* frame the helm and dive stand in the background. Courtesy of Corey Walden.

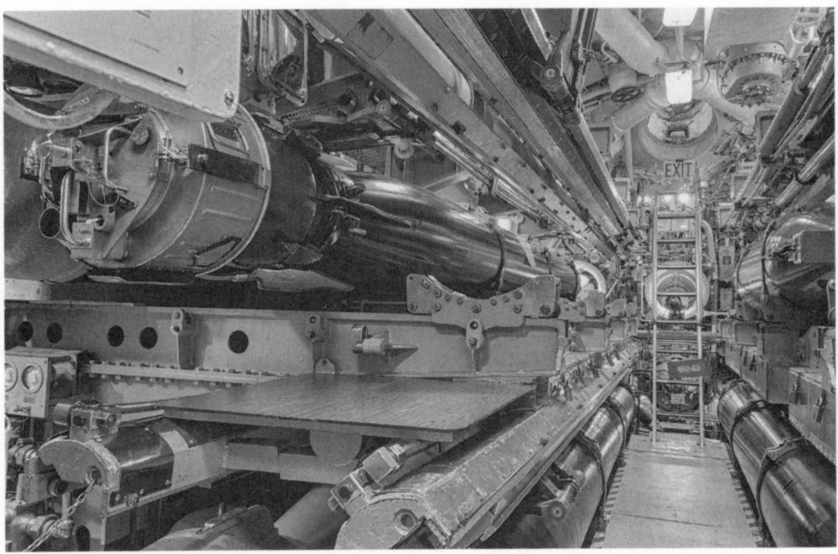

Figure 32. In an unusual configuration for a US Navy submarine, the only torpedo room of the USS *Blueback* has six torpedo tubes, arranged in two rows of three. The torpedoes were loaded into the boat, tail-first, through the angular hatch above the ladder. Courtesy of Corey Walden.

Figure 33. The crew's mess of the USS *Blueback* served as the dining room, living room, and everything room for the enlisted men. Shown here facing the galley, which was the one and only kitchen onboard, where four meals a day were prepared for eighty-five sailors and officers. Courtesy of Corey Walden.

4
Fighting the War

Arguably the longest war in American history, the Cold War pitted the United States against one primary adversary, a superpower that held keys to an arsenal capable of obliterating entire countries. Because this was the first time in history the United States, or any other state, faced a rival with such destructive firepower, all the rules and practices developed through centuries and centuries of warfare naturally went out the window, and were replaced by the mutual understanding that any full-scale conflict would probably be the last war human civilization ever fought.

Because war really was the *last* resort, the competition between the United States and the Soviet Union inevitably spilled into other arenas, be it economic practice, political rhetoric, or national defense strategy. And because the potential consequences of starting a hot war were unacceptable, the overarching goal of defense policy on both sides favored gaining the biggest advantage over the adversary while minimizing antagonization. To no one's surprise, secrecy became the calling card throughout the American defense community. But while the CIA independently managed its covert operations, the Department of the Navy called on its own double agents, members of a force predicated on stealth since its very inception. Worlds apart from how Hollywood glorified the CIA's cadre of secret agents though, the Navy's submarine sailors were often more detached from the enemy, and pursued missions that made the war seem abstract and impersonal. Depending on their captains' command philosophies, it was not uncommon for the sailors to know little, if anything at all, about their big picture objectives and whereabouts. But they were all aware that their special missions and patrols operated at combat levels of readiness, and that their submarines packed a much greater punch than the world had ever seen.

Who Is the Enemy?

In war, as in any scenario in which two parties come into conflict, a common sociological question regarding the nature of an opponent inevitably arises. That is, from each respective party to the conflict, how is the concept of an adversary or enemy perceived? In the submarine service especially, this proved to be a difficult question to answer.

Christopher Stafford provided the common perspective from the sailors when he noted the absence of a big picture: "I don't think I was taught anything about the Soviets. It wasn't something that they focused on. If you were spying on them, you knew you were spying on them, but you didn't know what you were doing or why you were doing it."

Charles Fredrick Macaluso pointed out that the Soviets were not given a human face in any way: "I don't remember ever really looking at the Soviet military and humanizing it. All you had to do was just understand their technology, whether it was a torpedo sound [or] a screw sound. [We were] never taught Soviet uniforms and different rates and ranks, nothing like that, never humanized . . . My overall perception was: it's them or it's us. It wasn't them as an individual, just them as an entire country that we had to be out there ready to shoot our missiles [at], in case they attacked us. It was really this 'big umbrella' kind of concept, which is kind of vague and remote when you're out there in the ocean."

Part of the impersonal disconnect between American sailors and their purported "enemies" also stemmed from the absence of an active, shooting war. As Robert Walters added, "There wasn't any animosity to them like there was to the Axis during World War II. [This was] a completely different thing." The Soviets certainly weren't demonized like the Germans and the Japanese were in the preceding world war, but taking evil out of the equation seemed to make the Soviets less humanlike, as opposed to less than human.

Stafford continued by noting how the American government "Didn't try to indoctrinate us on that the Russians were bad guys." The juxtaposition was instead made in terms of a "chess match" or a "football game." This was a contest being played by bishops and pawns, by quarterbacks and receivers, and not by human beings with personalities and emotions. For these veterans, their game pieces just so happened to be submarines. And as for the nature of submarine patrols, "You were just doing what was normal to do in those days."[1]

Meet the Soviets

Due to the very nature of the submarine service, even in times of full-fledged war, contact with the enemy was usually only represented by the machines he built. Thus for these veterans, most of what they knew about the Soviets was what they gleaned from encounters with Soviet submarines. And the one resonating feature of these submarines was that they were remarkably noisy and could be heard from miles away. As Garth Lascink noted, "They were so loud in those days—sounded like a train going by out there." Audible contacts aside, working on a submarine ultimately did not lend itself to many opportunities for interactions with the Soviets. Onboard the USS *Mariano G. Vallejo* (SSBN-658), Lascink added, "The one time we saw Russians, was [when] we were going through the [Panama] Canal, and there's a Russian freighter going that way; we're going this way. We're taking pictures of a Russian freighter for whatever reason—'Hey! Look at those Russians!' And they're taking pictures of us."[2]

Opportunities for contact were also a function of the type of boat a submariner served on, and were closely correlated with the particular submarine's mission. The operating principle behind Lascink's boomer, along with all ballistic missile submarines, was entirely wrapped around the ability to remain undetected, far away from snooping Soviet submarines. As Chuck Macaluso remarked about the sailors' notion of the enemy, "It was very ambiguous—[especially] on a boomer."

With the exception of picking up sonar contacts of the noisy Russian submarines, the only regular occurrence during which boomers were in detectable proximity to the Soviets was with their trawlers: "When you go on sea trials off San Francisco, they're out there taping you for 'future reference,' and then of course when you leave Guam, there's a trawler sitting out there. You try to lose him once you get out; it's not that difficult—all they're trying to find out is when you're leaving anyway. [But] the one in San Francisco would follow you . . . You'd come up and you wouldn't see him, and then an hour later you'd see him sitting back off about 2000 yards or so."[3] On one occasion in August 1979, the trawler stationed off Guam boldly retrieved a practice Mark 37 torpedo shot by the USS *Sam Houston* (SSBN/SSN-609).[4] This incident sparked a twenty-four-hour standoff between State Department officials and their Soviet counterparts. The Navy also dispatched two aircraft carrier battle groups, which intercepted the trawler off Okinawa.[5] A combination of these efforts finally coerced the trawler to jettison the torpedo back into the ocean, from where it was finally recovered.

But out near the Soviet Union's Pacific coast, there was much more activity: from diesel fleet boats prior to the mid-1960s, and afterward, from the fast attacks that replaced these relics of World War II. Robert Austin Jackson recalled how starting in the mid-1950s, "One boat would come back, and another boat would go in. And it was constant surveillance. At that time, we were just keeping tabs; they weren't a real threat [yet]." One of the most common surveillance activities conducted by submarines was to make sound recordings of propellers (screws) from Soviet ships and submarines. The different screw revolution frequencies provided a unique sound signature, much like a fingerprint, and could be used to identify distinct types of enemy vessels. William M. Bryan Jr. described a typical surveillance mission in the Gulf Stream of the western Atlantic, where on the USS *Thornback* (SS-418), "The only thing that we did was take sonar counts of screws. We'd sit down there [with] everything shut down for four, five, six hours at a time and then we'd come up, run the snorkel up, take on a little air and then go back down if everything was clear, and we'd sit another four, five, six hours, just counting whatever passed over, taking the sound of it. All that got put in this big black box and we never heard anything [more] about it; didn't really know what was going on; didn't care. Then you came up at night, recharge the batteries, [get fresh air]—gorgeous out there. But in the day, we'd go back down, stay all day, from sunrise to dusk."

Toward the end of the 1950s, sonar surveillance efforts were stepped up, and the fleet boats played a more active role. Onboard the USS *Sea Fox* (SS-402) during one such mission in the northern Pacific, sonarman Gary W. Webb told of how "We would present ourselves as a target to [the Soviets]. Then we'd run like hell, go silent, back off a little ways, and then turn on the tape recorder. Basically, we were building a database for the computerized sonar systems that they were designing for the later nuclear boats. So we were purposely picking different Russian craft and trying to get them to do different things that would allow us to make recordings. And then when we got back to San Diego, I took this box of recordings up to the Eleventh Naval District [headquarters] and turned them in."

Onboard boomers, the operation of passive sonar was mostly for defensive purposes, to help them detect if there was an unfriendly target nearby. But Lascink noted how secretive sonar surveillance was, even on a submarine that was not ostensibly engaged in any active special operations: "You had those paranoid sonarmen, when they [deployed] that towed array [sonar] . . . They're doing something; they're working back in there. Nobody could know they were putting that towed array back in there. When we went in to do that, boy that was hush-hush."

Bob Walters's USS *Caiman* (SS-323) participated in close-up photography reconnaissance: "We took pictures of a cruiser, and had to take two shots—one forward and one aft. We were *that* close."[6] This was a manageable feat because, as Walters added, Soviet sonar technology "Wasn't all that great, because we were in the middle of a fleet and they didn't hear us." Jackson's USS *Pomfret* (SS-391) was also involved in visual intelligence gathering: "We were going through the straits [near] Hokkaido; once we got inside, we took pictures out of the periscope. We had a first-class that was pretty talented in drawing, and they had schematics—they would relay information to him and he would draw things in. We went in pretty close, and we got a lot of intel."

But these close-proximity maneuvers also multiplied the risk of exposure, and eventually the *Pomfret* found herself desperately needing to escape. As luck would have it, her captain discovered a thermocline, a layer of water with a radically different temperature characteristic as compared to surrounding layers. A godsend for a submarine facing pursuit, the difference in temperature is enough to distort sound waves emanating from either the enemy's active sonar or the submarine itself, helping to hide it from detection. As Jackson continued, "They knew we were around. They got on us one time . . . They were pinging us pretty good. We went down—I was on the trim manifold—I think it was about 410 feet; it was test depth. And we hit a [thermocline], and we slipped out. Our sonarman said they dropped five [grenade-like] depth charges." And even though neither country was ostensibly out for blood, this was a reminder that such a game was still a high-stakes, high-risk affair.

As nuclear-powered fast attacks gradually replaced the fleet boats, surveillance equipment was upgraded, but the mission did not change. Learning anything and everything about the Soviets was still priority number one. And this process of intelligence-gathering led these sailors through a journey that was significantly different from the path their boomer counterparts took. Macaluso provided this contrast: "On a fast attack, it was a little more defined and narrowed in because you're actually following another submarine, or doing an underhull on a submarine, taking pictures of it from underneath. That's a little more personal."

Over the decades, as technological advances were exponentially integrated into both the US and Soviet navies, and submarines became increasingly quieter, their underwater encounters closed in proximity and the risk of collision multiplied. Although the inevitability of such a collision is debatable, its high probability was not; and eventually, it did happen. But unlike the earlier collisions depicted in chapter 2, which were best described as freak (though sometimes avoidable) accidents, these collisions with Soviet submarines were also a product of risk-taking by both captains, where a gamble failed in embarrassing fashion.

Mark A. Manzer was certainly not the only sailor who knew of this dangerous game being played, but he also saw some shreds of evidence: "One time at Pearl Harbor, one morning, all of a sudden, a fast attack was tied up to the pier with a big old tarp draped over its sail. They wouldn't tell us what happened, but the imagination went wild." This imagination was fueled by stories and rumors of submerged maneuvers gone wrong, leading to collisions so violent, that they were probably capable of inducing paralysis and instigating heart attacks. The most terrifying of these underwater impacts occurred in June 1970, when a Soviet Echo II submarine crashed belly-first into the sail of the USS *Tautog* (SSN-639), grinding her propellers into the steel of the American fast attack. At the time, both crews assumed that the other submarine had been sunk. However, this grim hypothesis turned out a miraculous conclusion when it was publicly revealed two decades later that both the Echo and the *Tautog* had been able to limp back to port. But in the immediate aftermath of the crash, the US Navy lowered the iron hammer of secrecy on the crew of the *Tautog*, ordering the fast attack to slink into Pearl Harbor under cover of darkness, with her sail covered in a shroud. The sailors were all required to sign an oath of secrecy, and the higher-level briefings were verbally communicated all the way up to President Richard Nixon, as to leave no paper trail. Every particle of evidence was hidden or removed, and the official posture was denial.[7]

Although the byproduct of these special operations was quite sobering, it didn't deter either government from its insatiable appetite for intelligence. In a world where any information about the enemy was potentially useful and the market price for any advantage was astronomically high, the submarine service remained a good business to be in. But from top to bottom, it was a business of secrecy: secrets were the main export, silence was the mission statement, and most of the workers would never see the final product.

Uncommon Knowledge

Not billeted as the "Silent Service" without reason, the availability of job-related information to submarine sailors was asymmetrical in many facets. Knowledge of the overall mission and the whereabouts of their submarines was often kept to a need-to-know basis, and for most sailors, there was simply very little need to know. David Meade Vrooman noted how "Nobody really talked about it . . . In fact, we didn't know what we were doing." Vrooman's fast attack boat, the USS *Plunger* (SSN-595), received a Navy Unit Commendation (NUC) for special operations in the winter of 1966.[8] But to this day, he still has no concrete idea about what the award was for.[9] In fact, his official NUC citation reads, "In successfully accomplishing a mission of great value to the Government of the United States . . . resulted in the attainment of a significant milestone in submarine warfare."[10] These were the juiciest details the Navy would divulge.

The availability of information varied by the type of boat on which these sailors served, with such information being even more restricted onboard boomers, due to sensitivity surrounding the payload of nuclear weapons. Michael A. Stephens recalled how "We weren't even allowed to know where we were; own ship's position, the date and time was top secret." The quartermaster's chart in the control room was covered up, and as Stephens added, "We weren't even allowed to go over there. Most of the crew, they [only] knew we were in the Pacific somewhere."

But these secrets didn't necessarily spur curiosity. As Chuck Macaluso observed, "My perception was [that] most people didn't care where they were. When you're out in the middle of nowhere, you're just punching holes; that's the boomer world—you don't care." The one exception for Stephens, the missile technician, was when the USS *Thomas Jefferson* (SSBN-618) received a nonroutine radio message: "[I] only wanted to look one time. That's when we got an urgent targeting change and half our load went to one place—'We should find out where this is, where we are, and where it's going . . . '"

Strings were left a little looser for crewmembers of submarines not involved in deterrent patrols. As Macaluso continued, "Now when you're on a fast attack, we used to put our position up on the wall; we kept everybody informed. And we'd just track it, a map of where we were in the ocean, how close we're getting to where we're [going]. When we got on station then, the map was taken down and the quartermaster's chart would be covered up. [But] it really depended on the kind of ship you were on."

Even with all the secrecy shrouding the whereabouts of individual submarines, there was still one major indicator of latitude available to the men onboard: water temperature. Robert W. Sumner's boat, the USS *Sea Poacher* (SS-406), was based out of Key West, in "Tropical waters, somewhat warmer than a lot of places. [But] then we went to England; we were in England for awhile and then we picked up a couple of spooks, and you could tell pretty much where you are by the water temperature outside, because the hull starts getting pretty cool when you start getting up far north. And so you might not know exactly where you are, but you have a pretty good idea in general." The change in temperature was very apparent, even inside the submarine. As Garth Lascink added, "The water starts getting really cool; your bed's cool, even though you have that heater thing. So you're putting on your watch cap and a sweater when you're in your bed, because it does get cold. We start off in Guam, and the water's pretty warm when you open up the tap. But you go north—starts getting colder and colder."[11]

If a submarine was operating close enough to land to receive radio signals, Russian or Japanese music might be occasionally piped into the mess halls. Sometimes, sailors were even rewarded with "periscope liberty," and afforded the opportunity to sneak a peek at the outside world. As Bob Walters remembered, "[To] see the sun after forty days was kind of cool." But Walters also noted one instance when periscope liberty revealed the location of his submarine, the USS *Caiman*: "When we were up charging batteries, we got to look, and you could see the glow of Vladivostok."[12]

Then there was the occasional surprise giveaway. Chris Stafford remembered an instance on the USS *Barbel* (SS-580) when "We were cruising up north, and I knew not where. All of a sudden, the bottom drops out—and we're heading toward the bottom. We're sinking like a rock. 'What the hell happened?' We ran into a freshwater river. And when the water density changes, you sink, cause you lose all your buoyancy. And you go, 'Well, how close do we have to be to hit a freshwater river!?'"

Although a protected secret for most submarines on patrol, the location of any particular boat wasn't truly consequential information in the day-to-day lives of these submariners. But for a very select group of boomer sailors known as the "Targeting Team," their security clearances combined with a "need to know" brought home the reality of their mission. Comprised of the CO, XO, weapons officer, assistant weapons officer, and specific enlisted crewmembers such as the radiomen and watch standers in the Missile Control Center (MCC), this team was permitted various levels of access to the top-secret targeting publications that were stored in the MCC safe. If anyone else (other officers included) wanted to view the publications, the MCC watch was under orders to deny them access.

However, the need for secrecy sometimes bordered on absurd, as Stafford recalled, "I was on the *Barbel*. There's only three submarines like it in the world. They're, all three, built with the same plans, even though they were built in three different shipyards, but yet you could not tell a guy on the *Bonefish*, how fast or how deep you were, even though you were on the same class of boat. I mean, they were just paranoid about everything, so the *Parche* was just ten times more paranoid than the normal submarine service." The USS *Parche* (SSN-683) of course, was the Navy's premier special operations ("spy") submarine at the end of the Cold War. Like her famous predecessors, she had been specially refitted for intelligence-gathering missions, and both the submarine and her crew carried some of the most closely guarded national defense secrets.[13]

Macaluso's experience onboard the Parche redefined the "Silent Service" for him:

> When I was on the *Parche*, I had to go to training . . . I mean the Silent Service is already—you don't talk much about where you go, but [while] I was on the *Parche*, it was even more locked down. So I'd go to all these schools; none of it's in my service record, and I couldn't tell my wife where I was going. I could tell her what state I was traveling to, to get training. [But] I couldn't tell her who I was training with, and all our training was done with civilian companies and physicists and scientists. We'd log in at the building:
>
> "Who's your employer?"

"Self-employed . . ."

You didn't travel with your uniform; you couldn't talk about the military; I couldn't take anything with me; I couldn't show my ID card when I was on travel. I was on the boat for three years and my wife didn't know what department I was in, what division I was in, what equipment I worked on, and I can tell you, it was kind of stressful because I remember after I got off the boat, after three years, I didn't realize how stressed I was after actually being on that boat, cause of all the things you couldn't say. You always had to be careful who you talked to. I had friends out in [the] civilian community. You couldn't tell them what you did, so conversations didn't go very far that way. It was a tight group [onboard the boat], but it was just so locked down.

The need to have complete control over all aspects of classified and top-secret information at all times often resulted in great inconveniences, even under circumstances in which it was not likely that the information would leak. As Macaluso remembered from the USS *Guitarro* (SSN-665), "We were six hours from pulling into port when one of the spooks realized he lost some kind of confidential disk . . . and we had to find that disk before we pulled into port. We suspected it was in one of the one hundred and forty-four TDU cans. Because we kept all the trash onboard, it was all in the freezer. Every can was pulled out. We started opening cans of trash, can by can, in the mess decks. Something like the twenty-fifth can, they found it lying right on the top. [But] we had to search the whole ship, every compartment, every locker, under every rack. Everybody's searching the boat for this disk, a floppy disk." Stephens recalled a similar incident onboard the *Thomas Jefferson*: "We lost a top-secret overlay off a plot . . . and oh yeah, 'All hands, get up. We're going to find it.'"[14]

There was also a heightened emphasis placed on the reliability of the sailors. Although most of the crew would not have enough information to be able to complete the security puzzle, the individual pieces they did hold were still extremely sensitive. Sailors were subjected to background investigations, and sometimes even extended monitoring. Sumner noted how "You knew that everybody was being checked out. I only found out about it because my mother, when I was talking to her on the phone, she mentioned that a couple of FBI guys had come around. And just before you get ready to leave Key West, three of the guys all of a sudden leave the boat. Nobody knew why, but maybe they didn't check out . . . [It] was the only thing we could surmise."

This wariness was especially evident on May 11, 1962, when the USS *Sea Fox* participated in Test Swordfish, a nuclear antisubmarine rocket (ASROC) detonation that was part of Operation Dominic, a series of thirty-six nuclear weapons tests in the eastern Pacific. The *Sea Fox* was present, not as a weapons platform or an observer, but rather as a participant in the experiment. Her primary mission was to take hydroacoustic measurements from attached hydrophones suspended below the submarine at a depth of 1000 feet.[15] As Gary Webb recalled,

> We were in San Diego and the captain came aboard Saturday morning, about seven o'clock, and told the chief of the boat to round up as many guys as he could. At eight o'clock muster that morning, he said, "Okay, everyone that's nineteen or under, [or] not a natural-born citizen, has two weeks of leave, compliments of the Navy. We're getting underway in about five minutes." Part of the formula for figuring out how much radiation you can tolerate—your age is a factor. The older you are, the more you can take. [And] because it was at the time considered a top-secret operation, that's why the [non-natural-born] citizens were not allowed to go. We had seven or eight guys that qualified to stay and take their two-week liberty: a couple of Filipinos, one Canadian, and about four or five guys that were under nineteen.
>
> We went downrange of the Pacific Missile Range, dove to 100 feet, and . . . come to find out that we were [23.5 miles from] ground zero for a five-megaton air explosion at 5000 feet above sea level. After the shot, we were about a mile [displaced]. You heard a big boom, but we really didn't feel anything [weird]. We did feel the motion, but at the time, it was just a motion. You didn't know what it was, but it was definitely a sideways motion. If you've been up in the Aleutian area, in rough seas, at 100 feet or so, you can feel the groundswells, and it felt about like that; the whole [boat] just moved along. To me, that was real impressive. The outer hull had a little [radiation], but we didn't detect any inside. And we all had the little badges; if you got too much radiation, they'd change color.[16]

Known as dosimeters, and regularly worn by many crewmembers onboard nuclear-powered submarines, these film badges were developed weekly by the corpsmen to check and confirm that no one onboard had been exposed to an excessive level of radiation. For the *Sea Fox* sailors, the only thing they were able to glean from this experience was an unusual measure of physical motion. And although this particular mission had nothing to do with the Soviets, the Navy made it clear that certain requirements needed to be met to even come along for the ride.

Ultimately, even with the Navy's paranoid efforts at maintaining a strict environment of secrecy, it was inconceivable that these restrictions on the spread of information could, and would, remain watertight. As Evert Charles

Nelson recalled, "I was going through new construction on one of the boomers, and this was in Newport News, and I said, 'Well, I'll take the bus home today.' And I'm surprised if you listen to how people talk, if you knew anything about what they were talking about, you can pick up all kinds of interesting information. I see how now they say during World War II: 'Loose lips sink ships.' Hey, that's really an easy thing, you know."

In a startling instance from the *Parche*, Macaluso noted how effortlessly sensitive information was compromised: "We're getting underway; we're going to go down to San Diego. Had a senior chief, he was by-the-book and he didn't give you the light of day—you couldn't make any mistakes. All of a sudden that morning, we were stationed in maneuvering watch, and . . . he's not around. Apparently, he'd been telling his whole family about everything he did on the *Parche*. He felt guilty, and he went over and talked to Navy investigation people, and they pulled him off the boat. We got underway; never saw him again. It was a shocking kind of thing, cause apparently he'd been telling everybody what the *Parche* was doing."

To take another specific example, Walters told of a conversation he overheard on a water taxi in San Diego: "Had this surface craft sonarman talking about the *Nautilus*; they were out playing games with the *Nautilus*. And he said, 'That damn thing does 40 knots underwater!' And . . . nobody else knew that."

The Cuban Missile Crisis

Photographs taken by American U-2 surveillance overflights on October 14, 1962, revealed that the Soviet Union was installing offensive nuclear missiles on the island of Cuba.[17] As President John F. Kennedy and his staff of advisers debated back and forth as to what the most appropriate American response would be, the military was placed on high alert. About a week later, on October 22, Kennedy announced an executive order that established a quarantine on arms shipments into Cuba, and called the Navy into action to enforce the quarantine.[18] But as early as three weeks before the actual crisis was publicly revealed, the action had already begun heating up. As Bob Sumner recalled from the USS *Sea Poacher*, "We were in Gitmo, where a lot of boats [from] Key West would go for ops and everything. And we were on the way back to Key West, and we were in the southern part of Cuba, going around. In those days, the territorial waters were twelve miles [from shore]. And we were outside the twelve miles. It was at night, and the officer of the deck called down for the captain because he kept seeing what he thought was a signal light of a boat in trouble. But it was inside the twelve-mile limit. So the captain went up, and they watched it for awhile . . . and come to find out what it was: tracer bullets that a Cuban gunboat was firing. They watched it for a short period of time, and then we dove."[19]

Although the naval quarantine was primarily handled by the surface fleet, submarines still formed a crucial part of the armada. As Sumner continued,

> We had just come back to Key West a day or two before the actual blockade started. So we all thought we were going to be in port for awhile. And all of a sudden, everybody was called back to their boats, every one of the boats. And we all left port the next day. Nobody really knew where you're going, [but] everybody loaded live torpedoes before we left. So you knew something was going on . . . All the boats went out of Key West, and we were part of the blockade for a short period of time, until the nuclear-powered boats came down. They relieved most of the diesel boats, and we went up to different ports all along Florida [and] the Carolinas. Key West at that time put up Constantina wire all along the beaches, and they had gun batteries, antiaircraft batteries—it was pretty well fortified at that time.

The heightened alert and lockdown extended up and down the East Coast. Stationed at the submarine base in New London, Connecticut, Chuck Nelson recalled: "I was in sub school at that time. There's normally six or seven boats in port. You go down the next morning, and there was one boat along the pier. Everything else got sent downriver. And the reason is because they were afraid if somebody blew the highway bridge, you couldn't get your submarines out. [So] one by one, they'd be coming back upriver to get loaded out. As a student up there, the day before, you could get down on the river, down [near] the shop area. [Now] you couldn't go underneath the railroad trestle unless you were assigned to a shop or a ship, one of the boats. It just really surprised you." And in sub school, many sailors were pulled out from training and pressed into active duty. Nelson continued, "They'd say 'Johnson, come with me.' Johnson's a radioman. 'Smith, come with us . . . ' You'd never see them again, because they needed them for the boats."

Implications of a Cold War

Although the Cuban Missile Crisis became its epic climax, it was still barely imaginable that the Cold War could and would ever turn hot. But if a shooting war ever started, the submariners with the most to ponder were the ones who served on boomers. Altogether, it was not easy to grasp the idea that the enclosed steel hull within which the men worked and slept, carried enough firepower to instantly obliterate several cities, not to mention any effects from the calamitous war that would surely follow. But interestingly enough, what could be seen as a burden of knowledge was not treated as such. Fred A. Carneau summarized the predominant viewpoint among the sailors when he noted, "I don't think many people even thought much about it."

But for those who had direct responsibilities in the weapons release process, such as our missile technicians (Garth Lascink and Mike Stephens) and fire control technician (Bob Walters), the consequences of their decisions and actions were more pertinent; yet the line of thinking was still fairly straightforward. Walters described his duties on the USS *Caiman* as simply being prepared to follow orders, and trusting that those orders had been well thought-out: "When we were in the middle of this Russian fleet, we were at battle stations, silent running, all the hatches were closed . . . and my battle station was 'push the button,' and we're sitting there, waiting for it, and if something happened, I would've pushed it. But we also had faith in the CO that he knew when to blink and when not to blink."

Not surprisingly, the process of launching nuclear missiles was slightly more intricate than that of shooting torpedoes from the *Caiman*. Onboard ballistic missile submarines, multistep procedures were developed to ensure the security of the launch process and the validity of the launch order. Many fail-safe measures made it logistically impossible for any madman to launch the missiles by himself. For the launch process specifically, there were several separate control points, two of which were a key switch for the captain in the control room, and a key switch and trigger located farther aft in the Missile Control Center. Each switch was activated independently by an individual turning his respective launch key, and both switches had to be concurrently engaged in order for a missile to fire.

On Lascink's USS *Mariano G. Vallejo* and in the majority of the American boomer fleet, the weapons officer stood behind the trigger in the Missile Control Center. But on the USS *Thomas Jefferson*, as was initially the case with all *George Washington*-class and *Ethan Allen*-class boats, the final responsibility for missile launch rested in the fingertips of an enlisted submariner like Stephens.[20] The CO would turn the launch key in the control room, and as soon as the weapons officer uttered "Fire One," the fate of humanity suddenly shifted onto the shoulders of a young man who would likely have enjoyed carousing on a college campus in an alternate universe. But Stephens described how the Navy removed conscious thought and emotion from the equation: "That's when your training just basically takes over. That's why you had to go through one week, maybe two weeks of team training in off-crew, and at least two or three training countdowns a week underway, so if it happened, you would just kind of shift over to whatever your training was."

However, when asked if he would actually shoot the nuclear missiles,

Stephens responded, "The only real answer to that is 'I don't know.'" Lascink approached the circumstances similarly: "One of the times that I started thinking about that . . . We were interviewed one time about what we thought if we had to shoot our missiles. Two or three people in this room asking you, 'What would you do? Would you shoot the missiles? What do you think about that?' In that discussion, then you start thinking about . . . the Cold War [and] of course you give the old pat answer, 'Well, if they shot at us, we're going to shoot back—that's what we're here for.' [So] you learn to give these pat answers." However, Lascink's thinking also had a line of logic: "What I said to them—I says, 'Well, I figure my family is probably dead if we're shooting . . . somebody shot at us is why we're shooting . . .'"

But aside from this mysterious interview he went through, Lascink noted one other occasion when the thought of nuclear war would rear its ugly head. Volatile world events, such as the *Pueblo* incident of January 1968, often magnified a boomer's mission, and these heightened stakes manifested in nonroutine messages. The USS *Pueblo* (AGER-2) was an electronic signals intelligence ship that was fired upon, boarded, and captured by North Korea, sparking a major international fracas in the Sea of Japan, and as Lascink explained, "The other time it just kind of creeps in your brain is . . . You get in a routine with these WSRTs, Weapons Systems Readiness Tests, that come along. They [usually] come in a routine order. [But] all of a sudden, they'll have one come back on you pretty quick after that—and then if things are going on, like when the *Pueblo* got captured, and things like that . . . it does stick in your mind, just a little bit: 'Well, what's this one for?' You start thinking about it if there's something going on in the world, and this test comes in right after another one, cause generally, they're spread out. But of course you get so far in the countdown you know it's a readiness test, not a full countup." Just the sheer amount of activity associated with the WSRT was enough to send shivers down spines, because if the preparation for a missile launch was in fact the real deal, and not just a test, there was a high probability that each man onboard only had minutes to live. The submarine's key advantage, stealth, would be compromised, and its location inevitably revealed: "We'd have all these tubes breathing in air—air is going in and out of these tubes, and everything's spun up. You know, it can get a little [nerve-racking] . . . You figure you're not going to get many of [the missiles] off. If there's a Russian attack boat there, you know—'Here I am!' Soon as that missile goes, they know where you are. And there's all kinds of noise. DCT tanks are pumping."[21]

Mark Manzer harkened back to his childhood to make a similar connection with the strategic implications of his job: "I grew up in Omaha, Nebraska, right off the final approach to Offutt Air Force Base, and I can remember lots of times B-52s scrambling over my head, an endless stream of these things. Then on the boomer, when you had the WSRT, all I could [do was] think back."

Kindly Old Gentleman

Widely regarded as either the most infamous politician or the most effective leader in the naval community during the Cold War, Admiral Hyman G. Rickover left an undisputed legacy of controversy. As Director of Naval Reactors, Rickover was often praised for his leadership and initiative in advocating a tremendously successful nuclear power program, and in making the Navy a key component of the American strategic deterrence infrastructure. Created in 1949 and headed by Admiral Rickover until his forced retirement in 1982, Naval Reactors is the Navy's citadel of nuclear power. Stressing safety above all else, Rickover guided a nascent technology to engineering maturity with an unblemished record. On the other hand, the admiral was widely criticized for his unorthodox, often ruthless, methods of administration, which he employed at his leisure, a result of his ever-growing power and influence. As Fred Carneau noted, "[Any] person that gets that kind of power, has a habit of being a little overbearing; they can get away with it."

The legend of Admiral Rickover is most popularly enshrined in stories about the outrageous interviews he conducted. As diesel submarines were gradually phased out, any officer with aspirations to begin or continue a career in the submarine service would eventually encounter this particular challenge. On the way up the career ladder, all roads ran through Naval Reactors, and specifically through the personal office of Rickover, who sat on the throne. The admiral was the gatekeeper, and he would personally interview every officer candidate for the nuclear power program, as well as make the final decision to accept or reject each individual. The stories about these interviews are wild and rampant.

In Rear Admiral Dave Oliver's *Against the Tide*, a book about Rickover's leadership principles, he detailed his own interview experience fresh out of the Naval Academy:

> The admiral spoke, "You are about to graduate as the first literature major in the history of the Naval Academy—so write down the titles of the last ten books you have read." I quickly wrote down nine and handed him the list. [. . .] His high-pitched voice began, and for the next half hour, this admiral, this man who was the Father of Nuclear Power, responsible for managing a brand new engineering science, leisurely summarized the concepts each of my authors had avowed. [. . .]

> So far, my interview had not yet required me to say a single word, much less recall an engineering principle. [. . .] "You will find that anyone can study literature and history by themselves, but," and he looked down as his right hand closed on and crumpled my list, "you need a professor to help you when you are studying mathematics and engineering, or you will make mistakes." He looked up at me. "Do you understand?"
>
> "Yes, Sir."
>
> "Get out of here."[22]

Captain Alfred Scott McLaren detailed a more adversarial interview in the first of his memoirs, *Unknown Waters*:

> His eyes literally riveted me to the chair that I was ordered to take, and his first words set the tone. Fortunately for me, they ignited my fighting spirit. "What are you, a wrestler?" the admiral snarled. My puzzled "Sir?" was followed by his declarative and mocking, "Well, you have cauliflower ears!" [. . .]
>
> Suffice it to say, my adrenaline was up. "No, I do not!" I shot back. Rickover's next remark was, in retrospect, my moment of truth. "Well," he growled, "we have determined that you are stupid and lazy and will be of little use to the nuclear power program!" I rose from my chair. He started to dismiss me from his office with a wave, but I stood my ground and protested vehemently that I was neither stupid nor lazy. [. . .] A senior member of his staff immediately entered the office and attempted to usher me out. I shrugged off her light touch on my sleeve and, refusing to go, spoke my mind for a few moments more.[23]

Both Oliver and McLaren were accepted into the nuclear power program.

Officers who remained in the submarine service and advanced sufficiently enough to be considered as prospective commanding officers (PCOs) would have to make a return trip to Crystal City in Alexandria, Virginia, for a tour of duty and undergo a grueling training course. Most of the three-and-a-half months spent in the offices of Naval Reactors were devoted to studying, but one of the side duties PCOs were tasked with included that of the "inside man," which entailed accompanying candidates for the nuclear power program (just like they were years ago) for initial interviews with Rickover and taking notes of the proceedings. In April 1969, McLaren began his course as the PCO of the USS *Queenfish* (SSN-651), and shortly thereafter, found himself as the inside man for one riotous interview, the story of which quickly made its way out to the fleet:

> Certainly, one of the shortest interviews on record had to be the day I escorted a confident young Naval Academy graduating midshipman of excellent bearing into the admiral's office. Without a greeting or even a preliminary question, Admiral Rickover asked the midshipman, "Do you think you can make me angry?" The young man blinked, thought for just a second or two, and replied, "Yes, sir!" The admiral then said, "Go ahead!" The midshipman immediately approached the admiral's desk chaotically loaded with books, stacks of articles and papers, pencils, pens, and several partially filled cups of coffee of unknown age and, with his right hand and arm, swept everything off to hit the floor with great thuds and crashes.
>
> Admiral Rickover made no attempt to stop him, but his face grew beet red, and he jumped up and down shouting. Now, I cannot say whether he was really angry, but I quickly grabbed the young man and pulled him as far away from the desk as possible. Rickover's senior secretary or executive assistant and two, possibly three, other female staff members rushed in and had their hands full trying to calm the admiral down. The most senior of the group shoved us out of the office and told us to stay out of sight.[24]

This particular young man was also accepted into the nuclear power program.

Having developed a folklore reputation within the submarine service from the stories of these interviews, Admiral Rickover garnered attention wherever he went. Almost everyone who has ever come into contact with Rickover has a story to tell. Our volunteers were no exception. Chuck Nelson underscored a typical interaction with Rickover as one which "You can't win." Elbert H. Collins "Ran across him three times, and made a point of staying the hell out of his way." Collins added, "You get almost paranoid, you know . . . You see him come this way, you go that way." Garth Lascink compared it to boot camp, where, "You wanted to be invisible; you wanted to blend in [with] the bulkhead behind you." However, it was a popular belief among the sailors that Rickover had more respect for the enlisted ranks than he had for the officers, as he would frequently spar with officers over frivolous details. But even the enlisted men were by no means spared, especially those standing watch, for "When he'd come onboard late at night . . . If you didn't challenge him, actually challenge him, then your ass was grass."[25]

Herbert A. Herman was spared a personal encounter with Rickover, but did however face an interview panel of Rickover's so-called henchmen while stationed at the Naval Reactors Facility (NRF), a training complex located northwest of Idaho Falls, Idaho. The interviews were designed to test the trainers at NRF, "Just to see if you knew as much as you're supposed to know."[26] Herman recalled his interview experience, "Answering questions, and one of them I wasn't sure about . . . I answered the question and they tried to convince me to change my mind, and I wouldn't do it cause as soon as you changed on one thing, they're backing you down on fifteen other things . . . And you could spin the guy completely around!"

During new construction, Rickover insisted on riding each and every one of the nuclear-powered submarines on sea trials, to make certain that these submarines met the high standards and specifications he set. Although it was not necessarily true, popular rumor among sailors noted that he rarely went on the first dive. But from the moment it was announced that the admiral was on his way, until the moment he finally stepped off the boat, officers and crew alike were always continuously on edge. Not only did they have to worry about the submarine's technical performance but they also had to pay particular attention to the admiral's every quirky personal need, such as his demand to always have a provision of fresh seedless green grapes on hand.

In November 1965, during the new construction sea trials of the USS *Lewis and Clark* (SSBN-644), Nelson experienced his own personal moment with Admiral Rickover, after consciously trying everything he could to avoid one. As an electronics technician, Nelson was standing watch as the reactor operator when the order went out to scram the power plant. During the process of restarting the nuclear reactor, Nelson kept his hand on a selector switch that would allow him to monitor the statuses of several different meters: "I usually would pick the highest-reading meter and go by that, but [now] I got the admiral behind me, I'd better periodically take a look at the other panels." And without warning, Rickover suddenly appeared and asked, "Reactor operator, what are you trying to do? Break that switch?" Nelson did not touch the switch again.

One year later, Lascink found himself as the sea trials planesman when Rickover descended upon the USS *Mariano G. Vallejo* in November of 1966: "One of the things that came out, was when he was sleeping up there, you couldn't use the sail planes. So you're driving the boat with the stern planes only, trying to maintain a level depth because it's just hard to keep on depth with those unless you're really staying on them all the time; but the reason given was [that] they didn't want the hydraulics for the sail planes, which were right next to the cabin he was sleeping in, waking him up." Unsure as to whether this order originated from Rickover himself, or just from paranoid officers of the *Mariano G. Vallejo*, Lascink jokingly speculated that they actually came from officers in the engineering spaces, "Because they knew anytime he started walking aft . . . you could hear the phones ringing back there, and you just knew a [reactor] scram was coming . . . Everything would be going gangbusters by then. Everybody knew: 'OK, get ready, here we go!' That was a whole different submarine when he was on there."

Personal encounters aside, Rickover left a legacy that was mixed. Even though enlisted personnel had very limited, if any, interaction with the admiral, most sailors who served in the nuclear navy were cognizant of Rickover's relentless emphasis on safety. As Nelson acknowledged, "I had a lot of respect; I think the guy did good. I think he was kind of overbearing in the way he handled things, but he went out and had a goal and he accomplished it." Mike Stephens added, "It was kind of hard to argue with his results." And although Collins attributed part of Rickover's personality to the fact that the admiral had to work with, and was responsible to, Congress, the same personality did not win many rave reviews from a good portion of the older submarine establishment. For them, Rickover had radically altered the aura and culture of a service that had been defined in the dark depths of the Second World War. But for better or worse, the Navy was moving on. Diesel boats would not last forever.

In the Public Eye

Given Rickover's tightly controlled bureaucratic operation and the general secrecy shrouding the submarine force, it is easy to forget that military service isn't a profession that is kept in isolation from the public. To be sure, the daily lives of many people don't intersect with those of service personnel, especially after the draft ended along with the Vietnam War. But just as we are able to easily pass a day without concern for military matters, the existence of a war allows such thoughts to enter our consciousness more frequently. During Vietnam, as during the immediate aftermath of the terrorist attacks on September 11, there were very pronounced public responses, albeit very different ones. Our volunteers have been subject to the whole spectrum of public reception, from open derision to a hero's welcome.

In the early 1960s, Bob Sumner was based out of Key West, Florida: "It was a real small town in those days, and it was really a navy town, but they really treated the Navy great. They really appreciated the Navy." The Florida Keys were home to an underwater demolition school, an oiler station, and a sonar school, among other facilities, and the Navy presence was cherished by the local community. Mike Stephens placed Bremerton, Washington, in the same vein. Other popular ports among the veterans included Portland, San Francisco, and Fort Lauderdale (especially during spring break). And as Garth Lascink noted, "Some of those towns really liked it because there was a lot of money coming in."

However, navy towns did not always get along with the Navy, even if the local economies were boosted by the fleet. Lascink summarized this dichotomy: "If you could get out of a major navy city, go somewhere else—good times. If you were in a major navy city, sailors and dogs, keep off the grass." There was a general consensus that the communities around two of the largest Navy bases on the East Coast, Norfolk, Virginia, and Groton, Connecticut, along with those surrounding the big Pacific bases of Pearl Harbor and Guam, were not very hospitable to sailors. Addressing Norfolk, Stephens commented, "I felt like a third-class citizen [there]." But the zones of animosity were limited to the immediate areas around the bases. Lascink added, "You get out away from there, people treat you pretty [well]. You could go up to Hartford, from Groton, and it was altogether a different [world]."

It's not difficult to imagine numerous reasons why locals in navy cities disliked the permanent omnipresence of thousands of sailors, but few of these reasons were enough to ignite active protests. The one exception was visibly demonstrated by a subset of unhappy citizens that was primarily concerned with the culture of war in a broader sense, but more specifically with the existence of nuclear weapons. Their protests would naturally tend to spawn at homeports of ballistic missile submarines. As Stephens recalled, "The anti-nuke protestors would show up at Bangor about once a week. They didn't bother anybody [though]."[27] But the perceived possibility of a threat to the core of the Navy's nuclear arsenal meant extra precautions were necessary, in the event that someone attempted to breach the security of the weapons. Lascink was present when these changes were being implemented, and recalled, "That is one thing that started changing—depending on where you went into port, you could have drills for repelling boarders. We had two topside watches—generally somebody after the missile deck and a guy forward. But if you're in a non-military port, even like in Cape Kennedy when we shot missiles down there, we would sweep the hull, make sure there's nothing on the bottom of the boat—divers go down. Generally when you're in a naval port [though], then there wasn't any of that stuff going on."

However, the greatest challenge to the American military ethos began to gather momentum in the mid-1960s, as the Vietnam War heated up. Although Chris Stafford served in the Navy as President Lyndon B. Johnson heavily escalated American involvement throughout 1967 and 1968, he was spared the most acrimonious attacks: "I was in college before I went on active duty, and then [back in] college when I came off active duty, and I hung around college people when I was on active duty, and . . . nobody said a peep. If you were in the Army, that was something different, but in the Navy, it was really a non-issue. I think it was the circle of people you went around with [also]. If you were hanging around anti-war people, then you were probably ostracized. But I was with a group that really could care less either way. And I never had any problems. I lived on campus while I was going to college, and I would wear my uniform to reserve center; nobody said a peep." Sumner added, "I don't think most of the American public would associate the Navy with Vietnam. You think of the Army, and the Marines, National Guard, and all that, but I don't think you think about the Navy." Even so, Stafford seemingly enjoyed an isolated experience. As the war dragged on, public reaction became increasingly vociferous. As Lascink noted, "It all changed with Vietnam. Near the end of Vietnam, you couldn't even wear your uniform [in public places]." But Lascink, who left the Navy in 1969, also observed that the antimilitary sentiment was not ubiquitous: "When I got out, I went back to college, and half the guys you're hanging around were ex-military there, so in that case, there was no problem."

Chuck Macaluso joined the Navy in 1979, just a few years after the conclusion of the Vietnam War. From his initial entry into the military and until the first Gulf War, "People were very indifferent. They didn't have anything against me, but they didn't really care that I was in [the military]. And I had a lot of people that I knew out in the civilian world, that if I talked about submarines, before you knew it, we're off to talk about something else—not really interested."

But as the US defense establishment redefined itself and learned its lessons from Vietnam, the enormous success it experienced in the first Gulf War greatly changed public opinion. As Macaluso continued, "There was a huge change. Everybody came back as heroes, so it got much better in the '90s, and then after 9/11, it's on a whole new level. The respect that the military has out there right now, in a way I'm kind of jealous because I never had that when I was in, in the '70s and '80s. I only started seeing some of it in the later '90s, about the time I got out, after twenty-two years."

Retirement continued to be a boon for Macaluso: "Now it's great. The other day I had a beer over at 'Green Dragon,' and I walked in and I had a submarine shirt [on]. The guy looked at me and he says, 'Thank you for your service.' He bought me a beer and said his grandfather was in World War II, on submarines. I mean it's really different now. I got people from the last three or four years all the time thanking me for my service. In the '80s, it didn't happen."

This story quickly got everyone's attention—for various reasons, free beer notwithstanding. Lascink seemed much more disconcerted:

> You know, that "thank you for your service" thing, for me, I don't quite understand that. I mean, there wasn't any "thank you for your service." You did it. You went in there; a lot of people I knew went into the service.

> That's almost a calling, right, when you got out of school? There was a draft, but I wasn't drafted. I went in; a lot of guys went in. But when they say "thank you for your service," it's like you did something really great. Well, I don't feel like I did anything great; I just did what a lot of people do—you go serve your country, and I don't feel like they need to tell me [and] thank me for my service. To me today, it kind of bothers me, cause I don't see it the way they see it today, in that respect. You're expected to do something for your country, I think. Or you should . . . The way I think about it, why don't you do something instead of thanking me; everybody's got the ability to do that.

This was clear evidence of a generational gap, a difference in societal expectations and a change in how the American public viewed its active servicemen and its veterans. As Sumner observed, "In those days, you just did it. Today, you see, they don't feel that way."

5
Foreigner

"Join the Navy, see the world." This recruiting pitch echoed from one American coast, across a continent, and down the other coast, taking a path that drew in the interests of many a young man. But the world these sailors eventually saw was often viewed through a different lens, a perspective that was not shared by the local population or even by other American visitors. After all, they were there on business, for work, at the pleasure of their country. And although the sailors' foreign world took on a distinctly military hue at times, such experiences were also often devoid of the artificial coloring of commercialization and the tourism industry.

It should also be acknowledged that not every sailor had the privilege of experiencing a foreign culture. Due to the nature of their sensitive payloads, nuclear ballistic missile submarines rarely surfaced while out on deployment, let alone enter a foreign port. So it was quite possible that a sailor could serve out his entire enlistment period and not step foot on foreign soil. This was especially the case for many missile technicians, who by default held a rating limiting them only to service on boomers. Over the course of a twenty-year career that included eighteen deterrent patrols, Michael A. Stephens enjoyed a grand total of three liberty port calls. Even some fleet boat and fast attack sailors missed out on the world tour. As Herbert A. Herman recalled, "I was in the Navy for six years, and I didn't think they had any foreign ports! We went down the East Coast, did some sonar calibrations, went to the Virgin Islands for a week, and that's a US possession! Then back home, and that was it."

An Out-of-Element Experience

In the modern world where technology and globalization have drastically decreased the figurative distance between countries, it is increasingly more difficult to picture a time when the thought of visiting foreign soil frequently conjured up wild imaginations of unfamiliar peoples and lands. But a mere thirty years ago, this now-outdated perception was once commonplace and cherished. As Christopher Stafford noted, "When you're young and you're seeing the world, from fresh eyes, it's a wonderful thing. You see all these different places that are exotic."

Stafford described what such an unfiltered experience felt like:

> Most bases stateside have got everything you've ever seen in your hometown. [But] you go over to Japan, Hong Kong, I mean, it's a whole new world. For an eighteen-year-old kid, holy smokes! It's stuff you'll never see again . . . in your lifetime. We were on our way back from Hong Kong, and we stopped in a place called Beppu, Japan. We were the first American ship that had been there in fifteen years. And you had to anchor out and take the little boat in. Everybody was broke, because they'd spent all their money in Hong Kong.
>
> Beppu was a resort town for the Japanese people. They had a small planetarium, an amusement park, and a little bitty zoo, and some hot baths and stuff. And they'd bus these school kids in every day, and they'd go up to the amusement park and play. My buddy and I are out walking around, and there [were] no Americans in this town, except for [those from] our submarine. Everybody [else] was Japanese, and you could actually see how they lived. They had a huge Buddha there, and you could walk around the town, and [not] have to worry about all kinds of shops and people trying to sell you junk. We were walking past this grade school, and all the kids came out, and they're waving at us, and we're waving back. And it was really a neat place to go, because you could actually see how the people lived without having to go through all the bars and the cheesy hotels. You know, that's a once-in-a-lifetime thing for a lot of us.

Hong Kong was a tremendously popular destination for the submarine sailors. Stafford continued with highlights from the city:

> [From] watching people on the walla wallas, floating around the harbor, [to] Victoria Peak, where you can take a tram up to the top, and see almost 360 degrees around the island, and over in Kowloon, where in '67, all the new businesses were [beginning] to start up. And then the New Territories was basically all rice paddies. Rice paddies for miles and miles and miles. They used to have guard towers up there, because there was a lot of influx of refugees from China. You'd ask the guard,
>
> "Well, where's the border?"

"It's out between the fourth and the fifth rice paddy!"
You wouldn't have known the border from anyplace else because there was no separation like a wall or a fence.

Richard G. Walker remembered in amazement how even by the mid-1960s, "The thing that struck me about Hong Kong most was the tall buildings there. Most of the other places you go to, they're maybe one or two or four stories, but [in Hong Kong], they had skyscrapers. And the scaffolding—they used all bamboo. [You're like] 'Whoa, how can they build stuff like that!?' Looked kind of scary to me, but it was interesting to see the building techniques compared to what we have over here."

Having captains like William M. Bryan Jr.'s was also a catalyst for adventure: "The first trip we went out, we had twenty-two ports. The next trip we went out, we did forty ports. We had a new captain; I guess he was trying to prove that he was better than the first one! It [even] got tiring after awhile, going into ports! But I got to see the whole [Mediterranean] in two trips over, twice." And for Bryan, the opportunity to see (and sometimes touch) what he had previously only read about in history books, was awe-inspiring: "I thought I knew a little bit about history, but you get over there and you see the real thing—and you know zip. You found out what [it] was [really] like. I think that's probably the most educational [experience] I got. I got to see things that I had read about in ancient history, but now, it's modern history because you're standing there looking at it, and it is the real thing."

Robert Austin Jackson was also able to relive some of the sobering drama from history books: "My skipper went on a joy trip, a sightseeing cruise, when we went to WESTPAC; he visited quite a few islands—Okinawa, Saipan, Tinian, Guam, through the Marianas, [where] there were still grass huts. There was one called Chichi Jima, a small island north of Iwo Jima. We pulled into this lagoon, and we had several hours to get out and explore the island. There was a ship there that had been either bombed or torpedoed. And then on the beach, there was propellers from the airplane engines, [and] all kinds of casings laying there. Then there was a dirt path [that] went up to the mountains. We went up there, and there's a cave there that'd been carved out by hand. It was real rough, and the gun emplacements were still there. It really left an impression on me."

But on the flip side of these enlightening experiences were other slightly less impressive aspects of community life that required a little adjustment and adaptation. As Gary W. Webb noted from Japan, "In Yokosuka, all the septic was in ditches, open ditches. You did not want to get drunk enough to where you'd fall in one or step in it! [And] the other thing that just really turned my head was communal bathrooms. You go in and sit down to do your business, and this gal would come in and sit right alongside of you and do her business. [And] there was no partition in between. That was a little hard to get used to."

Fitting into the local social dynamic also presented a challenge for many sailors. Charles Fredrick Macaluso recounted his experience learning the transportation system in the Philippines:

> Had to get in these things called jeepneys, that were pretty damn scary. They don't have streetlights out there in town, and these guys don't drive with their headlights on; there's no centerline to stay to the left or to the right. I don't know how they don't hit each other . . . it was frightening! The head-ons were close . . . I don't know how these guys . . . and they were yelling and screaming; it was chaotic. The jeepneys are all decorated with all kinds of weird fluffy, dangly things, and dice, and little Jesuses everywhere; it's bizarre.
>
> [And] I didn't know how the money worked over there. I didn't know the difference between a centavo and a peso. So four or five of us on there—they all jumped out of the back and left me to pay the guy. I guess instead of giving him three dollars, I tried to give him three cents . . . and they're screaming and yelling at me; I didn't know what was going on! Then everyone in the back of the car started yelling at me, and my friends are all running off, laughing! I just put my hands out with the money, and said, "Take what you need!" I thought I was going to get killed! They were all waving sticks at me! [So] learning the money is important!

The Military Economy

As much as these sailors were able to immerse themselves in a local day-to-day experience, it is not accurate to say that they did not partake in local tourism. In fact, it was quite the contrary; American sailors were renowned for their contributions to the local economies of port cities around the world: "You're young—eighteen, got a few bucks, you go do things!"[1] Sometimes the source of income came from more creative ventures. As Mike Stephens recalled from South Korea, "For some reason, they couldn't get Japanese goods. There was still some trade issue going on. So you got your little Nikon camera. About every third person I walked past wanted to buy it for about eighteen times what I paid for it. [When] I went back the second time, [the] Korean gate guards wouldn't let you off [the base]. They discovered that you were playing the black market game. 'No, can't take that off the base. Can't take that off the base . . . How much you want for it?' So I sold it to the guards instead!"

But in the same manner that benefited local communities stateside, US

Navy sailors were equally well-received as economic stimulus overseas. Local shops and businesses "Could smell us coming a mile away . . . and what they smelled was money."[2] However, until the mid-1970s, this money was not in American dollars; instead, the sailors were issued Military Payment Certificates (MPC): "You couldn't have American money in Japan or Hong Kong. You had to have MPC—trade your American dollars on the boat for the MPC or the yen, because they thought at the time, the Communists would get the greenbacks and infiltrate [our economy]."[3]

But the use of MPCs created other unintended problems in local economies. Because local businesses accepted the MPC banknotes in lieu of US dollars or their own currency, a black market in currency trading sprung up every time the current MPCs expired and a new edition or print was circulated: "They switch it every now and then. All these [locals] that have all these MPCs off-base—they can't come [onto the bases] and change their money. So now they're looking for Americans to give that money to. The wheelers and dealers on base know this is happening; they're going out there and they're buying [old MPCs] for nothing, because now they can come back and turn it in and get the full value [in] new MPC. The guys that are money-changers: 'Well, I'll give you twenty-five cents for this dollar . . .' And they're making a killing out there on this."[4]

Figuring out how to protect American currency overseas was not the only headache the US government had to deal with. There was also the issue of black market goods coming back stateside. Chris Stafford provided this example: "If you bought stuff in Hong Kong, you had to have a certificate of authenticity that said it wasn't made in Red China, or the customs guy would grab it when you're coming in to the United States. But on submarines, you could stash a lot of stuff in the torpedo tubes and never have to worry about it. There was still a lot of formality going on, but you didn't worry about it that much; you tried to follow the rules, but you could [also] push things and not get caught. [On] submarines, you can get away with a lot of stuff."

Usually, the goods that were smuggled back were more for personal use and had little monetary value. However, Bill Bryan recalled taking part in the haul of a lifetime down in Cuba:

> A fifth of the best rum in the world cost you a dollar. And we were negotiating for enough rum to sink that submarine! We had two lockers under the deck that were both [for] paint, and we had to find a place to stow that stuff so we could get the rum in. The old man says, "I got a good idea of how much rum we've got; I need to know where it is, so when we make that first dive, we're not [at an angle]!" So I said, "Well, I think we need to add about four torpedo weights forward!" So we get

in [to Key West], and people come aboard to inspect you. This [customs agent], he had us haul out a torpedo [to] look down the torpedo tube. Couldn't see a thing. The torpedo gang had gotten smart by then, [and] pushed in one of the short ones. So this [inspector] figured [he'd] pull the short one out [to] see what's forward of it. When he didn't find anything, he says, "Alright, lift the decks." [The] old man came up there and [asked], "What are you looking for?"

"I'm looking for the hooch that they've got stored that I can't find!"

"Have you ever been on a submarine before?"

"No . . ."

"They're qualified. You know what that means?"

"Uh, well . . . they know about the submarine."

"You know anything about submarines?"

"No . . ."

"Well, you're not going to learn this way either!"

And that was the end of it. [But] they [also] had Marines at the gate; they had a fellow that was pretty sharp. [When] he got to checking, he'd move tires, look under the seats, make you move [the] back seat, pull out your back seat . . . After we tied up, the old man says, "How're you getting it [off the base]?"

"My father is in the tire business." He looked at me and it went over his head for a second.

"Which tire?"

"The spare tire!"

"How do you do that?"

Well, in vulcanizing, you can make a tire solid enough that it feels like it's got air in it. But you can put three bottles or four bottles of hooch in that sucker, close that thing up, and drive right on out. We came by that Marine twenty or thirty times [and] we got it all off the base, got it over to the officers' house, and they started dividing it up. This lieutenant JG says [to me], "Are you going to stay in the Navy?"

"I don't think so. Why?"

"Boy, I've never seen so much stuff come off the base in my life! How did you get all this stuff off?" The old man says,

"What are you asking dumb questions for? It's here!"

We'd take [the car] up, put [the tire] in the trunk, go over to the barracks, and that's when we'd put it inside the wheel, when nobody's looking; [The Marine] tore my car up. He literally took my car apart three different times. He finally laid down [to] look up under the [car], but he never did catch how we were getting that stuff off the boat. For some

> reason, he was always on us. Once he got off the base, really a nice guy, [but] he knew somebody was hauling something off the base.[5]

Scarcity and Dependence

One recurring observation by many sailors centered on the surprising extent to which local civilians relied on the US Navy, not just in terms of employment, but for other resources as well. Chuck Macaluso provided this example from the Philippines: "We pulled into [Subic Bay]. They put us up in the barracks there, cause we're going to be there for six weeks. In the morning, you'd see everybody out in town riding their bicycles on base with empty plastic jugs tied up under their bikes; they're walking in with six or seven jugs, cause if they worked on the base, they got to take the free water—clean water. It wasn't contaminated like it was out in town. I thought that was really, really odd; I'd never seen that before, where the civilians that worked on base brought all the water home, cause they didn't trust their local water in the Olongapo area."

Local children however, seemed to be less concerned with the terrible water quality, especially if it meant making some pocket change. As R. G. Walker remembered, "We're pulling into port [in] Subic Bay, and these little kids on these rafts would paddle out to you. They want you to throw money so they could dive into the water after it. But of course in that harbor there, you thought, 'God, this kid's not going to live to get back and spend that money . . .' It was so filthy there; everybody's pumping their sewer in there, garbage . . . It's just disgusting, but everybody's [still] throwing money to this kid."

Eventually though, the Navy started paying more attention to the welfare of local children, and banned the sailors' money-throwing practices. About twenty years had passed since Walker had been in the Philippines, when Macaluso finally noted:

> They kind of shut that down. From that base, to get over to the town, you had to cross the little bridge over the river, [which] smelled like shit. But it got to the point that they had Marines on each end at the gate, and there were signs saying, "Just walk across—no one's allowed to stop on the bridge," because too many people were stopping on the bridge and throwing money out and just having fun with the kids down there, money diving in that river, and it was a pretty nasty river; it was really, really bad. Lots of kids [had] to make some money. [And they're] jumping in and coming up with it in their teeth. So they shut all that down. But as soon as you got on the other side of the bridge, there'd be about twenty kids swarming you in a circle, and you had to be ready for

that. I don't know what they were saying, but they're spinning in circles around you, and all touching you. [So] I had it zipped up, locked up, hands in my pocket, just kept moving, and they eventually left me alone.

Food shortage was another recurrent theme. In Japan, Chris Stafford noted,

It seemed like the Japanese in Yokosuka were starved for meat. You could get anything for a couple of steaks or some chicken. When we were onboard, cooking fried chicken, and you had extra chicken left over, and you wanted something done, you'd ask the yardbirds. And then they'd take their hard hat, fill it up with napkins, and take a whole handful of chicken, and take it home. We had a bunch of sea vans, that we're filling up full of personal stuff like stereo equipment and furniture. And it started to rain, and some of the sea vans weren't very watertight. So we ask them for a tarp, and we got a tarp that must've been fifty yards long! I mean, it was huge! And it covered up all the sea vans. We were having a barbeque at the time, and we're barbequing steaks, and all the yardbirds lined up. They took a stack of six steaks . . . each. And they took it home; they just didn't get much meat there.

Meat wasn't the only commodity in high demand in Japan. As Robert Walters recalled, "In Yokosuka, I wanted to build a shelf on the bunk above me. I made the measurements, drew a picture, and bought two cartons of cigarettes—gave it to a yardbird. [I] took off, came back, [and] that thing was installed, worked perfect. They would work for you. They'd do anything for you. And we threw some clothing away in Sasebo . . . I remember seeing people just coming out of the woodwork, going through that clothing. About five minutes later, there wasn't a stitch left."

In 1957, already twelve years removed from wartime occupation, segments of the local community in Hong Kong still struggled to acquire day-to-day sustenance. Robert W. Sumner was stationed on a destroyer escort at the time, but remembered that "All these junks would try to come up next to the ship, and [we] would select one of them. That junk—the guy, his wife, and his kids lived on it. They would come up every meal, and you'd hand them your tray of whatever was left over. And they'd scrape that food into different barrels. And they'd take that [back], what we threw away. And they chipped and painted that whole superstructure of that destroyer escort, just for the leftover food that we didn't want."

Farther south, in Thailand, Walker, by now the only remaining cook on the USS *Capitaine* (AGSS-336), was taking inventory in Bangkok and recalled how the boat's galley "Kept missing stuff, missing all this food; we couldn't figure out where it was going. Finally one night, I went up topside, and [saw] these boats pulling up beside us. I saw these guys jump in these boats, carrying some of our food! So I finally cornered a guy, and found out their little boats were coming up servicing [the sub]. The guys, they wanted food; they wanted these big cans of Spam that we had, hams, whatever it was these guys could steal out of the boat—[in a] trade for services."

Oddly enough though, Mike Stephens recalled how in South Korea, one of the locals' most in-demand commodities was something that most boat sailors were more than happy to give away: "They loved the Taster's Choice coffee. We didn't have a regular coffee pot on *Thomas Jefferson*. We had this awful mud-spitter. You pour Taster's Choice in the top, push a button, and you get your instant coffee. But [the locals] would kill for a jar. You could get anything! When we left, there wasn't a jar of coffee left on that damn submarine! We had the great coffee investigation, [and] they actually restricted some people to the boat."

But for Mark A. Manzer, one of his most eye-opening experiences came from serving the community in Korea:

> In the middle of a boomer patrol, we had a port call in Jinhae, Korea, over Christmas 1979. We had three days off [during our] four days there, so we had to stand duty one day. Being over Christmas, I decided I'd take advantage of the cultural opportunities available. The USO arranged a bus tour [on] the first day to an ancient kingdom capital [of] Gyeongju, [which had] these thousand-year-old buildings. [But on] the second day, we went into town and went to the town market. Everybody, for five dollars each, could buy just more toys than you could hold, just overflowing. Then we went to this children's orphanage. And this is right at Christmastime, in the middle of winter, and this orphanage had dirt floors. [The] kids barely had clothes on, no shoes . . . So we're giving out toys and singing Christmas carols to them in English; they're singing Christmas carols back to us in Korean . . . lots of hugs; that was a good time. Then the next day, we did pretty much the same thing, [at] this children's hospital. That was probably my most memorable Christmas ever.

The same theme of scarcity was equally present halfway around the world in the Mediterranean. As Bill Bryan remembered,

> We went into Malta, and we stayed [for] two weeks there, [because] we messed up a screw and had to have one shipped in. Those people were the same way all through the Med. They were starved to death to see the Americans. Those people there, they still lived down in the caves from

> World War II. They had not moved back up into the houses up on the top. When you go into the city, the city was underground. Nothing on top. And the English had not left [yet]. They still had a base and warships there, a couple tin cans and a squadron of subs, and when we went in [the] floating drydock, the yardbirds on that worked for the English. Anything that was left over, you don't throw it away. You give it away. And you could get just about anything [in return]. And . . . the ladies . . . They had them lined up for you, if that's what you wanted.

Throughout the Mediterranean, it was commonplace to see local communities that were extremely grateful for the American visits. As Bryan continued,

> We went into Syracuse, Sicily, and we were the first Navy [vessel] to dock [since] '45. We went there January of '57. We had to do a Mediterranean dock—you drop the anchor and tie up and back in. You can't walk the lines, so to get across, this guy had one of these rowboats, and he could probably do a half a knot [for] 400 yards to get you in. He would take us in and bring us back; he could take six people at a time, whenever we wanted to go in, and he'd start at eight o'clock, and we were due back at ten o'clock at night. [And] during that time, he stayed there just for the food that he could acquire. He was a fisherman by trade, and he would give us, each day, probably enough fish to feed the crew maybe three or four times over. They were cleaned and ready for cooking, and we just took them to the freezer and froze them, so we had fresh fish later on.

In general, especially during the first two postwar decades, Stafford noted how the locals were "Very grateful for what they could cumshaw [or] borrow off of us, or work a deal where they'd trade their workmanship for food, for whatever [they] needed—[even] the yardbirds, [who] got paid pretty well, compared to everybody else."

A Spectrum of Hospitality

An appreciation of American generosity by local peoples stayed relatively independent of the geopolitical situations playing out in their respective countries. But while overseas, American submariners nonetheless prepared themselves for more dangerous encounters. As military representatives in novel lands, these sailors became accustomed to expect everything, ranging from security lockdowns to incomparable hospitality.

Bill Bryan went back to Cuba in 1958, "Just as Castro was getting ready to take over. Oh my, you talk about a wild area. Now you had Castro on one side, and you got the mafia on the other side; that war was strictly [between the] mafia and Castro. But the people themselves, they loved to see you come. You could hold up a dollar, and they'd break your arm to get it. A dollar would get you almost anything."[6]

And throughout the USS *Thornback*'s (SS-418) tour of the Mediterranean with the Sixth Fleet, Americans were usually well received by the locals, whose ports were equally enjoyed by the sailors. But there were always exceptions. Istanbul, Turkey, fell under this category. As Bryan recalled, American sailors were warned to stay in line and cautioned about getting into trouble in a country with relatively draconian laws. Most locals cast a wary eye toward the Americans, and the local officials never seemed to trust the visitors. But during this 1958 deployment, there was another port of call that stood out in a different sort of eye-opening way: "We were tied up at Lebanon. We actually stood top watch there with a Thompson. That was the only time in the three years I was in the Navy that we actually loaded our side arms. [Normally] we couldn't even carry live ammunition topside. And we actually had two top deck watches, one fore and one aft, and we had lights, turned out into the water, so that we could see down in the water. And we had a diver on call, twenty-four hours a day, while we were there. We stayed two days—that's when that Lebanon crisis was going on. And I don't know what we were taking on, but whatever it was, it was covered coming on, [and loaded] in the forward torpedo room. It was sealed, we left, we went to Malta, [and] whatever came off was [still] covered."[7]

For Chuck Macaluso and Mike Stephens, their respective journeys to the United Kingdom elicited a similar level of shock and surprise. As Macaluso recalled, "I went to Scotland—I was on shore duty doing inspections at Faslane, the submarine base there. So we stayed in a hotel outside the base, about six miles away. What stunned me was . . . people don't wear their uniforms out in town there, at all, period. You're told not to. Local sailors do not wear uniforms out in town. They keep them at the base. When they go home, they take them off, and they go home in civvies, because there's people out there that'll shoot at [them]. They're just not liked by everyone. The IRA's out there. It was . . . different. I thought I could wear my uniform, but I had to wear my Eisenhower jacket, could have nothing on the epaulettes, no hat, no trinkets or anything, and you went from point A to point B [and] didn't stop anywhere in between."

Stephens observed a similar atmosphere of cautious vigilance: "When I was at TTF, the American training centers, they'd have the big posters about no drinking and driving, stuff like that. [In Scotland], we'd go from the hotel to the training center. What I noticed at the training centers [over there]: 'This is the latest IRA bomb,' and what it looks like, and yeah it's really bizarre. You come out of the base headed back towards Helensburgh, and they had a permanent encampment for the protestors. Permanent."[8] Because of all these perceived threats, the security presence was intense, and the base perimeter was locked down by Ministry of Defence (MoD) guards: "Their gates are manned to the hilt. It's like you're going into a commando camp. It's just a submarine base; [but] there's no rent-a-cops at the gate."[9]

During the early 1960s, certain problem areas in the Philippines and Hong Kong prompted the Navy to warn its sailors about venturing into dangerous spots. In the Philippines, especially around the Subic Bay and Olongapo areas, sailors were discouraged from leaving the base, and were told to travel in groups and only in the daytime if they did. Specifically, R. G. Walker recounted being cautioned about the presence of Communist guerillas.

In Hong Kong, sailors were initially prohibited from going to Kowloon, but by 1967, the restrictions had been lifted. Chris Stafford remembered taking a tour through Kowloon and the New Territories, "All the way up to the Red Chinese border. But the night before we left, they were having Communist riots in Hong Kong. The British soldiers came in with submachine guns, cleaned out all the bars, and told [all of us] to go back to the boats." Similarly, Jinhae, Korea was kept under tight control during the mid-1970s. Stephens noted how "They rolled the streets up about ten o'clock at night. Martial law was still in [effect]. But the people loved us. I never saw any animosity."

Regardless of location and problem areas specific to certain localities, American submariners consistently marveled at the hospitality of foreigners in general. When Walker was in South Vietnam at the beginning of the war, he noted how American sailors were well-received and could travel around safely: "We were in Saigon and I bought this violin. So we went around; I was playing this thing, and going all over, [through] the back streets and back alleys. [I] must have had fifty kids following me! And they were happy and laughing." And even though Walker admitted that things would probably have been very different four years later, "Fortunately, everybody was pretty friendly then."

Although Japan was generally considered to be very safe for American servicemen, there was one special consideration that impacted the submarine force stationed at Yokosuka. The issue at hand was Japanese aversion to the use of nuclear energy for military purposes, which was of course systemically rooted in the calamitous experience of Hiroshima and Nagasaki. As a result, the Japanese government had an overt agreement with the United States, stipulating that nuclear weapons and nuclear-powered warships were prohibited on Japanese soil and in Japanese ports.[10] But even with these restrictions in place, it was clear that the Japanese did not fully trust American military intentions.

In one such instance, Walker and his friend were stopped and questioned by Japanese law enforcement regarding American compliance with this agreement: "We went to Tokyo, so we got on the bullet train and rode that in. Everybody's looking at you, cause we're in our uniforms, and they don't see that many sailors getting further inland. We got to Tokyo; we're in this nice bar, drinking, and all of a sudden this guy walked up to us, showed us a badge, and told us he wanted us to sit down. He was apparently the equivalent of our FBI. He wanted to know who we were, what we were doing, what submarine we were off of, and if it was a nuclear submarine. He interrogated us for about an hour. Of course, he kept buying us beer, so we didn't care! Loose lips sink ships! 'Well, give us some more!' After about three or four beers, he says, 'Okay, see you later,' [and] turned us loose."

Another manifestation of this suspicion was seen during the arrivals of *Barbel*-class submarines, which were greeted by protestors off base. This was because the streamlined *Albacore*-hull design of these boats created a close resemblance to their nuclear-powered cousins. Stafford, a machinist's mate on the USS *Barbel* (SS-580), noted how each time they entered port, "We had to make as much smoke as possible, out of the diesels, so we wouldn't look like a nuke [and] so they wouldn't protest everything." In Yokosuka, a surprised Evert Charles Nelson recalled how the "*Blueback* had just come out of the yards. She got fairwater planes [installed]; therefore, [the protestors thought] this is a nuke; this is not the *Blueback*. [Then] on Saturday, they're going to have a demonstration. They're going to demonstrate from nine to one, so nobody could come on or off the base between nine and one. [But] after that, everybody's still friendly."

All things considered, Navy sailors were well treated by the local populace of most countries. In comparison to the communities back at home, Walker noted how, "[In] the United States, you had more problems than you did in foreign countries." Our veterans rattled off names of port after port, in which their foreign hosts treated them like royalty. Whether it was Bob Sumner in Ocho Rios, Jamaica, and Portsmouth, England, or Bob Walters in Papeete, Tahiti, and Brisbane, Australia, or Alan L. Nolan in Victoria, Canada, Sumner echoed the prevailing sentiment when he remarked, "The locals really liked us. I can't say anybody ever had a bad time."[11] In Victoria, Nolan observed, "You just had to wear anything with the boat's name on it—hat, coat, uniform, and those folks took care [of you]. Your money was no good there."

Multinational Affairs

The foreign experience of many sailors extended into another arena, one more closely associated with their day-to-day work. On many occasions, American submarines participated in naval exercises with allied navies. Several of our veterans had opportunities to work with the Canadian Navy. And they came away impressed. The general consensus of the Canadians' tactical ability? "They were good."[12] Their skills were especially evident in antisubmarine warfare (ASW) games, during which some older US fleet boats would play the role of target. As the sonarman Gary Webb recalled from the USS *Sea Fox* (SS-402), "We would make runs, and then they would [try to locate us and] drop these little phony depth charges, which were [concussion] grenades; they would get frustrated occasionally and take their grenades and wrap four of them together, so they could get a little bigger bang when it came down. But the Canadians were really fun to work with. They were really a nice group."

In a slightly different version of the ASW exercise, Bob Walters, our fire control technician, explained how the USS *Caiman*'s (SS-323) mission was to imitate a Regulus guided-missile submarine: "You had to surface to fire [the missiles]. And you had to be on the surface for five minutes. The Canadians were protecting the Los Angeles basin, and we were supposed to steam in there, surface, stay [up] for five minutes, and then dive. Well, we tried to do that for roughly twenty hours. And people [onboard the submarine] were falling like flies [from the] lack of oxygen . . . [even though] they bled oxygen in the boat, and they had CO_2 absorber. [But the Canadians] were good. You stand an ECM watch and you come up, it's quiet . . . [Then all of a sudden, you get buzzed]. They pick you right off! I gained respect for them."[13] This was a stark contrast to the US Navy, which always seemed to encounter difficulties in locating its own submarines during fleet exercises. Such a commonplace experience was echoed by many of our submariners and, as a disgusted Chuck Macaluso mockingly added, "They couldn't find you if you told them we were in this patrol box, operating at this depth, running at this speed . . . and they still can't find you! It's . . . kind of embarrassing!"

American forces also regularly participated in exercises with many of their East Asian allies, to maintain good military relationships and to ostensibly help stem the expanding influence of Communism in the theater. Before the United States normalized diplomatic relations with the People's Republic of China (PRC) in 1979, both Walters and R. G. Walker recalled working with Republic of China (ROC, commonly referred to as Formosa or Taiwan) forces—the *Caiman* in an ASW fleet exercise as a mock target for Taiwanese destroyers, and the USS *Capitaine* in a covert operation, transporting Taiwanese commandos. Chris Stafford's USS *Barbel* also provided local services to the Japanese Maritime Self-Defense Force (JMSDF).

And as Vietnam began to heat up, American forces became more involved in training their South Vietnamese counterparts. Walker's *Capitaine* was involved in an intense battery of ASW exercises during April 1963. Operating with a flotilla of Republic of Vietnam Navy (RVN) patrol craft, the *Capitaine* embarked sixteen RVN liaisons and played target for eight straight days. Even in rough sea conditions, steady improvement by the patrol craft was observed, as they held contact well during the first six days. However, their success rate tapered off dramatically during the last two days, when fatigue started to wear on the South Vietnamese crews. Operationally, the RVN units showed an incomplete mastery of ASW maneuvers, leading to struggles in re-attack positioning and misplaced depth charge patterns. Altogether, observers from the *Capitaine* noted the enthusiastic and aggressive prosecution of the mission by the patrol craft, and considered the results excellent.[14] And although the Vietnam War ultimately did not heavily involve the US Navy outside of air sorties from Yankee Station, many submarines, including Stafford's *Barbel* in May 1967, operated patrols in the Vietnam combat zone, responsible for everything from intelligence gathering to minelaying.

The Italian Navy though, was not quite as sharp as the Canadians, nor as dedicated as the South Vietnamese. Operating in the Mediterranean with the US Sixth Fleet, the British Royal Navy, and an Italian fleet, Bill Bryan's USS *Thornback* embarked on its mission:

> [Our skipper] told [the] captain on this radar picket submarine to string lights on it [and] make it look like a fishing boat. [We] would run down and to the side of it. This Italian group had a carrier, and the old man says, "I'm going to get that carrier." We eased up close enough to fire, and when the old man fired that signal out to let the [Italians] know we had fired on them, that Italian [captain spoke] the most plain English you've ever gotten. He called [our captain] a dirty SOB and a few other things, [and] said, "You can't sink my carrier!" And the old man told him, "I think that flare just told you I did!" And all of a sudden [the Italians] realized that the radar picket wasn't a fishing boat; it was a radar picket! That was really embarrassing; boy, the captain was really upset with [our old man]. But [our skipper] was a sharp dude. He knew exactly what he was going to do to get that aircraft carrier.[15]

During these Mediterranean operations, Bryan was also afforded the opportunity to experience life as an engineman of a different submarine service when the *Thornback* engaged in exercises with the Royal Navy's First Submarine Squadron:

> [I] went aboard the [HMS] *Tally-Ho*; we were in Malta, and that probably was the smallest submarine I've ever been on—three compartments and it had fifty-eight people. They were still sleeping in hammocks!

> If you were in the engine room, you slept in a hammock in the engine room. And you didn't hear [any] complaining. They thought that was the greatest thing. And if that engine was running, if that engine changed tone or anything, whoever was in that hammock, he was on his feet. He was [ready] to help whoever had a problem. I happened to be on [for] just a day-run, but whatever was going on, they included us [Americans] into what they were doing, and when they came aboard and went out with us, we did the same [for] them. But when they saw [our] bunks, they said, "Oh my!"

In engagements with different foreign submarine services, our veterans noted how the camaraderie and culture of their own service extended across borders. Mike Stephens recounted giving a tour of the USS *Blueback* to an elderly gentleman who was accompanied by his granddaughter. As the young lady translated, Stephens learned that the man was once a sonarman onboard a Soviet submarine. Despite the language barrier between former adversaries, an instant kinship was created for two submariners. Following the tour and some shared moments of reflection, Stephens handed his silver dolphins to the Russian submariner as a keepsake. As Walters explained, "You meet a submariner from a different country; there's the bonding there [too]. When I was in Japan [recently], I finagled my way to go topside aboard a Japanese submarine. And [the] camaraderie was there. The CO pointed to his dolphins and said in broken English, 'Do you have these?' He took them off his [uniform] and handed them to me. I don't think one of our officers would do that. Not [for] some third-class fire control technician that's seventy years old!" These were shimmering moments of humanity that bridged language, culture, and history, and revealed a resolute connection forged by common experience.

6
Looking Back

Regardless of whether the career spanned a full count of twenty-two years or lasted for less than two years, all of our volunteers reflected back on their time in the submarine service as an indisputable and defining highlight of their respective lives. Without a doubt, there were a seemingly unlimited plethora of obstacles to overcome, as well as facets of submarine life that simply weren't all that attractive, but these lowlights were what made the experience and the accomplishments that much more rewarding. There was no other way to go about it. After all, they were all in the same boat, literally.

Challenges and Accomplishments

Weather was often a formidable opponent. This was especially true if one had to stand watch, exposed to the elements. As Robert Austin Jackson duly noted, "Riding a typhoon out is no fun, up there hanging on for dear life." Mark A. Manzer was among a sizable group of sailors who experienced these storms first-hand, and recalled how the USS *Sam Houston* (SSBN/SSN-609) was "On the fringes of a typhoon in Guam. I was topside watch; I had my harness on, strapped into that I-beam on the deck, standing in the lead of the sail, [with] the winds blowing by me about 50 miles an hour."

But the most daunting challenge was probably standing lookout watch on a GUPPY boat with a modified step-sail. These lookouts were placed a mere twenty-two feet above the waterline, lower than those on any other US Cold War-era submarine, and even lower than the old World War II fleet boat designs these GUPPYs were originally converted from. Lookouts on World War II boats stood watch up in the shears (on which the radar and radio antennas were installed). But on their converted replacements, the same lookouts were literally "Right down where the action is. And you get water coming down on the top of you, and it comes up to your legs and up over your head. So you're spending two-thirds of your time underwater."[1] The waves would also often slam the lookouts against the side of the sail. William M. Bryan Jr. remembered one such storm, front-row center on the USS *Thornback* (SS-418): "That forward [sail door] came off, came back past us, and cut a hole in the sail. You talk about panic-stricken, but it's too late, cause that sapsucker just went that way! I was the starboard lookout and got two cracked ribs. I'm tied down, got the safety lines on, up against that rail. And you're hanging on for dear life, cause the water's going over you, and it's green . . . and you're hoping that you can hold your breath long enough . . . [And then] the old man says, 'Uh, can you stand a four-hour watch!?'"

Further compounding the unpleasantness were the modifications that some of the older diesel boats had undergone, making them more sensitive to the pitching sea. Bryan's submarine, the *Thornback*, served as a target boat, and was therefore fitted with extra steel around the hull, along with a steel deck: "You could be in calm water in Key West, and it would still [roll]." Another boat, the USS *Baya* (AGSS-318), once home to Herbert A. Herman and Gary W. Webb, was also notorious for being unstable, primarily due to its redesigned bow, which was flat on top and rounded in the front: "When you got it in water that was less than calm, that sucker would really roll. It would wallow in the surf."[2]

But sometimes, the challenge with weather was entirely mental. This was especially evident when the boats started rolling in rough seas. Robert W. Sumner recalled one such storm in the North Atlantic during which the USS *Sea Poacher* (SS-406) "Rolled over to port, and I'm in the forward engine room; I'm standing on the coffin covers on the number two engine, and the number one engine is up here [above me]. You're waiting . . . is it going to come back? And it just hangs there for a few minutes, then finally comes back." Fred A. Carneau could also relate: "The boat would roll over on its side, lay down there, and just sit there . . . You just knew the damn thing was going to go over! And then it'd come back and [roll] down on the other [side]!" Webb remembered another similar experience onboard the USS *Sea Fox* (SS-402): "We were giving services up in the Aleutians to the Canadians, and we sent all the destroyers home. The [aircraft carrier] *Kitty Hawk* and us stayed [behind]. When you could see the *Kitty Hawk*, they were taking green water across the flight deck. As a matter of fact, it looked like it was going about halfway up the island! I got a chance to see what ninety-foot groundswells looked like. We took a sixty-seven-degree roll to port and hung there for a minute-and-a-half . . . just scared the living crap out of you." Alan L. Nolan was especially thankful that the USS *Ethan Allen* (SSBN/SSN-608) didn't roll when it was stuck in drydock as a typhoon hit Guam: "Everybody got underway except us. The *tender* got underway. We're sitting in that floating drydock, [on] those blocks. That was challenging . . . cause I knew what we were sitting on."

As taxing as it was to make it through foul weather, the sailors simply buckled down and survived. The hardest hit were those topside standing watch, but in such circumstances, job performance level was of little concern. But in other stressful situations, productivity mattered. For several of our submarine veterans, their job duties would occasionally force them to work overtime. And this was no ordinary overtime; it was well beyond what anyone would reasonably expect to encounter in the civilian workplace.

All the abnormal work demands placed on these sailors were unsurprisingly draining, and many submariners would have to be kept awake by artificial means. And "artificial" wasn't limited to just coffee. As Webb recalled, "For some reason, we were at sea, and the active sonar, which at the time was BQS-4, malfunctioned. I was second-class at the time, so I was the highest rated sonarman onboard, other than the chief, and I started working on this particular problem. And with the help of the hospital corpsman and his Benzedrine that he administered to me, I was up for about thirty-six hours straight, working on figuring out why this thing wasn't working. It was challenging—I really had no one I could ask [for help]. I just had to dig it out of the books."

However, the use of artificial stimulants sometimes became routine, leading some sailors to question this practice. Garth Lascink, a missile technician, remembered how "We were up in Bangor loading out missiles, going well beyond a day. [The] corpsman came along and gave us all Benzedrine to keep us awake while we're loading these things. Years later, I got to thinking about that . . . Here we are, loading these nuclear-tipped missiles down into that submarine [and] everybody's pumped up on 'bennies' to stay awake. You go now, 'Wait a minute. Was that really what should have been done?'"

Although the missile load was certainly fatiguing, Lascink's most difficult challenge actually came from the preparation in advance of attending diving school: "I just got back [from] patrol and went right to scuba school, so all [throughout the] patrol, I'm sitting there doing pushups and sit-ups and stuff, to try to be ready for when I get back in. We had a stationary bike, but that's pretty boring, sitting down there in lower level of the missile house, cranking away on a bike. Cause [in] scuba school, everyday, you start off in the morning doing a run, and then you come back and do calisthenics. And then in the afternoon, you go into the pool. And they're messing with you in the pool, ripping your mask off and pulling your regulator out of your mouth. That's pretty tough; it's a lot of exercise you're not really used to, and you don't get a whole lot of exercise out [on patrol], unless you put yourself to do it."

Coming from a medical background, Elbert H. Collins had a huge adjustment to make in learning the different technical systems onboard a submarine. Hospital corpsmen could be qualified to stand anything from sonar watches to chief of the watch: "To make it through all that mechanical [knowledge], [and] on the electrical systems, for us [corpsmen], it was hard. I had a bitch of a time! But I had a good time. Sounds crazy, [but] I enjoyed damage control, with water going all over; it was cold and I remember that, but I enjoyed that, cause for me, it was a learning experience. Right from the first day, I got my hands into the grease, the guys got me dungarees, and I learned something. [Normally] at sea, there's not a lot for a corpsman to do. [But] if I had somebody sick, be it a sonarman or a radarman, I would relieve him—and there'd always be somebody there that would work with me—and I would learn something [or] get back and refresh stuff."

And specifically as a hospital corpsman, Collins faced some of the most demanding training and on-the-job pressures relative to his peers: "In the medical end, they really stuff it to you. The majority of your instructors are doctors. [But] they don't want to give up any [responsibilities]. Eventually, they want you to be on independent duty, but they don't want you to be independent of them. They train the hell out of you; it's very extensive, and I didn't think I'd ever make it. I really didn't. We started out with fifty-two guys and graduated twelve. All the time, they're dropping out. But [it becomes] a goal; you want to [finish]. And I also wondered if it was well worth it when I got to the boats. I really did." And on top of all these challenges, Collins was part of the first class of submarine corpsmen required to attend dental school: "Some admiral had been on one of the boats with a toothache, and he came back, was upset, and made every corpsman in our class and after, go down to the dental clinic and put in a three-week course. And it paid off. I had to do a root canal on a guy. That was a lot of fun . . . didn't bother me a bit!"

For Collins though, all the challenges he battled in submarine medicine were eventually worth it. The countless hours of hard work he had put in all paid off one day: "I [got] to do a little surgery on one guy. It was an emergency. He burned his hand on high-frequency [radiation], on each one of his fingers. I worked on him for probably two-and-a-half, three hours. Everybody thought I was nuts; I had guys come in, and [they] couldn't eat [afterward]; the blood kind of got to them. But in the end, when I got him back to the tender, the doc that saw it—he said what a good job [I did] . . . I felt ten feet tall!"

But ultimately, many of the submariners mentioned something associated with their training when asked to address the toughest challenges they faced during their careers. Detailed in chapter 1, the qualification process was undoubtedly one of the most difficult and rewarding hurdles submariners had to tackle. And therefore it came as no surprise that in looking back on careers rife with adversity, the greatest accomplishment overall was more often than not, qualifying on the boat.

Nostalgia and Riddance

Unanimously, our volunteers agreed that out of every possible aspect of the submarine service, they missed the camaraderie and the relationships formed with their fellow shipmates the most. Among the veterans, it was very common to hear the remark, "[It's] never been the same since."[3]

For sailors who served on the diesel fleet boats or the newer fast attacks, the opportunity to travel, visit exotic ports, and see the world was part of a job they fondly looked back upon. For whatever reason that each veteran put forth for leaving the Navy, a good number of our shorter-tenured volunteers ended up with tinges of regret after the transition to civilian life had become complete. Some of the submariners later wished that they had stayed in the Navy longer; others looked back on their time in the service and mused about missed opportunities, especially pertaining to career development and related experiences. The Key West-based Bill Bryan concurred with San Diego-based Gary Webb, who ruminated how "The one thing if I had to do [it] all over again—I would've loved to put a tour of duty on the West Coast, and then put a tour of duty on the East Coast. I think that would've really been worthwhile."

And while daily life onboard could hardly be termed as exciting, the exceptional quality of food the sailors enjoyed roused many memories (and stomachs). Covered in chapter 2, Robert Walters went as far as to claim that submarine service food was "The best damn food there ever was."

Of course, most submariners and their submarines were still not exactly a match made in heaven. As much as they cherished their experiences in the service, there undeniably were aspects of their jobs that they were all too thrilled to leave behind. For starters, there was a less glitzy side to having all that gourmet food aboard, because on the flip side of the same coin, few sailors enjoyed mess cooking.

Another theme every sailor repeated was the dreadfully long time spent away from home, at sea, and on deployment. The toll on marriages, relationships, and family life was also addressed in chapter 2. As Bryan, who himself went through a divorce, admitted, "I paid dearly for that with part of my life." Though strong commitment and experience helped families adapt to life in the Navy, it certainly did not make it any easier: "You're gone so much . . . Even for single guys, [if] you're not married, then all those relationships go by real fast, because those girls aren't going to hang around . . . You. Are. Gone. So you'd have a girlfriend there, and next thing you know, she's with someone else by the time you get back. It just seems like if you're not out at sea, you're getting ready to go back again . . . always gone."[4]

Some of the least popular aspects of working in the submarine service were specific to a limited group of sailors. To say that reactor operators and other nuclear-trained sailors detested the Operational Reactor Safeguard Examination (ORSE) boards is a substantial understatement. Yes, it is true that ORSE was deemed a necessary comprehensive evaluation of a nuclear-powered vessel's safety preparations with regard to the nuclear reactor. But for the sailors involved, the pressure, stress, and both physical and mental fatigue they were subjected to were parts of the job they were all too happy to leave behind.

Other unpopular features of shipboard life included the accidental venting of sanitary tanks inboard, and additionally on diesel-electric submarines, a similar but more dangerous problem of poor air quality. After a diesel boat submerged, it would not be able to replenish its air supply from the environment until, at a minimum, it went back up to snorkel depth. Diesel-electric submarines, with the limited amount of battery power available to the boat while submerged, didn't have the capability to generate oxygen through the electrolysis of ocean water like their newer nuclear-powered counterparts. Instead, they carried auxiliary oxygen bottles or tanks that could be bled in, but this did nothing to reduce the amount of carbon dioxide in the air. Carbon dioxide scrubbers or filters, using lithium hydroxide, could be employed to absorb some of the excess CO_2, yet this provided only temporary relief. In earlier days, when methods were cruder, this simply equated to spreading the white chemical powder throughout the submarine to act as an absorbent. As technology became more refined, a purification filter system was developed and installed onboard. And even some of the older nuclear submarines, sailing with inoperative oxygen generators, were forced to improvise. Herb Herman's USS *Dace* (SSN-607) "Went on a long patrol, out for ninety days, [and] we had every single crevice and crack on the boat filled with chlorate candles that give off oxygen . . . and that was spooky."

How bad could it get? As Webb recalled from one particular instance, "You're sitting there with the Zippo lighter and you cannot get it to fire. You shouldn't even be thinking about smoking if you've been down that long. A stick match would just fizzle. Wouldn't burn. We were down [for] about seventy-four hours. [The air] gets real bad. When you go from control [room] to conning tower, you rest a few minutes." And although the oxygen deficiency was of major concern, it was actually carbon dioxide that caused the most health problems. An excessive concentration of this poisonous gas quickly limited sailors' capacities to function normally. As Bob Sumner recalled, "Sometimes it gets so bad, that your head would just start splitting from all the headaches."

To a significant extent, poor air quality was a problem that was influenced and induced by man. But additionally, there was one uncomfortable rite of passage that was reserved by, and administered at, the pleasure of the sea. But "passage" was often a misnomer, because for many sailors, there was nothing ephemeral about seasickness. Fred Carneau pointed to "One young fellow that came aboard . . . they'd set the maneuvering watch, and the minute they'd start the engines, he'd run to the head and start heaving. Everyday, every time, and all the time we were underway—he was sick, couldn't keep nothing down and had a horrible time. We had him there for about a week-and-a-half, before they offloaded him." David Meade Vrooman noticed another sailor facing similar problems: "We had one kid that was so bad, that even in port . . . we'd be sitting around the mess decks, and we'd start [rocking] back and forth, [and] he'd start getting sick."

Sometimes, sailors would be affected only if they were in certain areas of the boat. As Walters recalled, "I thought I had my sea legs for the longest time. But every once in a while [when] I had to go back aft [to] the after torpedo [room], I was getting woozy [from] the heat, plus sort of a circular motion [of the boat]; you go up and down and sideways." And being topside certainly didn't help. While standing watch on the USS *Baya*, Herman remembered how he "Was a vengeful guy. Up in the crow's nest, standing the lookout watch, the [sail] is [pitching] back and forth, and I got sick. The officers were out there with their sextants, practicing on figuring out their position . . . and I got all five of them scrambling down below decks! I wasn't appreciated that day!"

But for easily impressed submariners teetering on the edge, many were done in by "The one that takes care of everybody—the mess cook [who] throws up just before chowtime."[5] Garth Lascink vividly recalled one such mess cook: "He's sitting up in there, [barfing]. Then he'd be cleaning the dishes. You're going 'Oh my God, I hope he doesn't get confused with all this stuff!'" On the flip side though, the mess hall was empty in choppy seas, and food was plentiful for those who managed to beat their stomach demons. Webb noted how "Rough water was the best time for meals. You were lucky if there were twenty guys that [felt like eating]." At the same time, it wasn't uncommon for the overall selection of food to decrease. Carneau remembered how "We used to have soup around ten, [but] underway in a storm, none of that. The only thing the cooks put together was sandwiches. And if it was three, four days in a storm, you didn't eat very good."

Although Carneau and his crew took pity on their young nauseated sailor, some submariners on other boats were merciless. Many a seasick sailor could be seen onboard with a number-ten can hanging around his neck, just for convenience. Sumner noted how he "Used to enjoy sitting in the mess hall, eating sardines. And [for] the guys I knew were getting seasick, I'd leave a couple tails sticking [out] . . . They'd come in and just turn around and go back!" But as Christopher Stafford replied, "I used to get revenge. On the *Barbel* class, you had to walk through the mess hall to get to the head. So you could carry your full number-ten can . . . through the mess hall, [and] the odor permeated everywhere." Collie Collins was one of the easily swayed: "I'm a sympathy puker. I had no problem until a whiff came by. If a whiff came over this way, man, I'll join you!"

But Collins had his own theory about the mystery of seasickness: "It's psychological. Coming out of San Francisco Bay, you got about ten miles of those long rolls. My first time [out] was on a carrier, and I was sick as a dog. And the odd part was, for the next twenty years, every time, whether I was on a tin can or on the *Catfish*, or any other boats, I would get sick. So I went and got me a number-ten can; I knew I was going to be barfing!" Evert Charles Nelson provided some supporting evidence for Collins's hypothesis when he noted, "We had a machinist's mate aboard. And he was fine [while we're] tied up to the pier. [But] as soon as they just threw off the last line, hadn't moved at all, this guy would start getting sick. And he was sick until we submerged. And after that, he was fine. [But] you know, underway [and] submerged, you've still got some [movement and] action [on the boat]." Stafford suffered through the same experience: "Well, we'd be up at quarters, [and they'd say] 'We're going to sea, you guys!' They'd throw off the first line, and man, I was a hurting dog! It's tough, when you're seasick and in the engine room when it's 130 degrees and you're barfing your brains out . . . You wonder if you're going to survive to the next day. You just hope for the diving alarm to come." Herman tried to convince himself of the psychological origins to no avail: "When I first went out on [the *Baya*] from San Diego, I got seasick, and I thought, 'Well, it's psychological; I'll just stay up until I get over it.' About two days later, I'm still [up]! That was a bad plan!"

Nonetheless, seasickness was an affliction for which there were no obvious or straightforward medical recommendations for treatment. Bryan was even sent to the Bethesda Naval Hospital for examination, where the doctors ordered him to be "'Put to bed [for] the first watch.' The old man told me, 'I don't care whether you go to sleep, but you're going to be in that bunk.' And that first watch, I was in my bunk. But I could stand any watch after that, never got seasick again." But even with all the trials and travails throughout his submarine career, Bryan was not alone in steadfastly declaring his fondness for the Silent Service: "I miss it . . . even today. It's a love affair that has never gone away."

A Learning Experience

As rigid as the structure of military life was, the time these submarine veterans spent in service of the national defense also allowed an opportunity for personal growth. On the lighter side, Bob Walters noted he "Learned how to have a sense of humor. Cause if these guys that you are with, know that they can find where your weak spot [is], they'll push and push and push. Pretty soon, you got to learn to laugh, and laugh at yourself." Although initially described in chapter 3 under the broad categories of hazing, toilet humor, and practical jokes, submariners had their own term for it: "We call it 'pinging.' So we find your weak spot; we're going to ping that spot until you give up and go with the bunch, because otherwise, you're going to get it every time you walk in."[6] As much enjoyment and entertainment submariners received from giving their shipmates a relentlessly hard time, the reverse was also true: "You'd better be able to take every bit that's dished out. Because the second that you complained or backed away from it, you were dead meat!"[7]

In a piece of sage advice, Gary Webb added, "You don't want to be tough. We had a second-class cook come aboard, and he had put [in] sixteen years on surface craft. So he was non-qualified, and when a qualified seaman would give him a ration of shit, he would just almost bite nails. He just could not handle it. And of course, the chiefs are right there egging him on. [But eventually], he made it."

One gift that kept on giving was education, including both the instruction these veterans received in the Navy, as well as the opportunity to go to college afterward. Our volunteers held steadfast in their belief that during the Cold War, the Navy had the best schools in the military. And as Garth Lascink acknowledged, "The military allowed for a lot of us to go to college. [We] would've never been able to go had it not been for the military. The GI Bill . . . probably ninety-five percent of the people I know that were on the boats with me—[when] they got out, all went back to college and got a degree, and moved on with their lives. I would've never been able to go to college without the GI Bill [and have] the means to be able to go to college."[8] But ironically enough for Lascink, his Navy education was initially misinterpreted by the civilian world: "When I got out, I went down to the unemployment office. You took your DD-214 in there. They says, 'Okay, you were a missile tech.' So they go to their book, and flop open this big book. 'You can be an ordnance carrier . . . ' They talk about all this bomb stuff, that I can go handle ordnance. I'm going, 'I was a missile tech, not an ordnanceman! I spent two years in electronics school!' But that book didn't equate to that. It was kind of funny the way that translated across; electronics had nothing to do with that rating, according to this book."[9]

But in most cases, having a Navy education paid off, literally, in the civilian workforce. From the observations of our volunteers, Navy veterans were hired at a greater rate than other service members. And when it came to submarine veterans and employers, Bob Sumner noted how, "A lot of companies recognize that guys coming out of the submarine service had a pretty broad background, because they get qualified in the boat. You understood mechanical and electrical [systems], and you got along with people. They appreciated [that]." Each citing his background in sonar, Webb and Alan Nolan noted how IBM and Intel, respectively, immediately recognized their qualifications. As Webb depicted the hiring process, he explained how "It went from 'we'll talk to you' to 'we want you' in the minute they found out [about my experience]." Walters, who was also hired by IBM, noted that seventeen of the twenty new hires in his basic training class were veterans.

Although many of the veterans were, to mixed degrees, disappointed with certain facets of civilian life after leaving the service, they also noted how their experiences and association with the military continued to support them, even after their commitments were long over. As Lascink elaborated, "You got the structure and the discipline. You knew what you wanted to do, you stuck to that, and you got through. You know you're going to have to be somewhere at a certain time, you don't show up late. That is one thing the military does give you, [that] translates into civilian life." Another important attribute was found in their development of a lasting team-first mentality. As Herb Herman acknowledged, "That's something you had in the submarine [service]. But when you got out of the military, [you hear], 'That's not my job.' You hear that all the time. You go to work out in private industry, [it's always] 'Not my job, not my responsibility . . . ' You really get upset about [an] attitude like that."

The Navy gave our volunteers a solid foundation to build upon for the rest of their lives. Bob Jackson expounded on how the submarine experience impacted him: "It was structure, compassion, humor, discipline, and goal setting. Every one of those fit. I've always been a person with those characteristics, and [as] I look back, had it not been for the naval experience, I probably wouldn't be [where I am] today. I was in education for thirty years—set a lot of goals, did a lot of things, and got a lot of compliments . . . and I give it all back to the time I spent on the boats. Every bit of it."

In this sense, the submarine service perhaps allowed more room for personal growth than other branches of the military might have provided. Webb noted how "It's the only place that I worked, [where] I was given the ability to do everything that I could do, [if] I wanted to do it. I didn't have to check with other people; I could actually grow to my potential."

Epilogue

Parting Legacies

Just two of our seventeen volunteers served in the post–Cold War Navy. With the winding down of hostilities and the reconfiguration of the submarine service away from a blue-water threat, the nature of the submarine's mission had to be redefined in a rapidly changing world that had no interest in seeing another half-century-long game of nuclear brinksmanship anytime soon.[1]

One crucial aspect of the nuclear drawdown was reflected in the plethora of arms limitation and reduction treaties signed by both countries. For the US Navy's submarine service, this specifically meant a reduction in the number of strategic platforms available—in other words, a decrease in its fleet of ballistic missile submarines, the boomers. Both Michael A. Stephens and Charles Fredrick Macaluso were present during START (Strategic Arms Reduction Treaty) verification visits by the Russians. Initially signed in 1991 by the United States and the Soviet Union, START continued the arms limitation efforts of previous treaties by further decreasing the number of nuclear warheads permitted for each country: "The Soviets came over to verify we didn't have any missiles hidden in any particular buildings. They were measuring door accesses to verify that a missile couldn't be stored in this room. They had an entire inspection team on the base—Soviets running all over the place. And we did the same thing at their end [that] they did at our end, to verify that our assets was what we said we had."[2] Although Russian inspection teams were allowed unprecedented proximity to the American nuclear arsenal, their access was by no means unlimited. As Stephens, one of our missile technicians, explained, "We had to put the missile condoms on. They weren't allowed to look in at the actual warheads, but we had to take the nose fairing off, and put a device on there that proved that it didn't have more than x-number of heads. It seemed like every week they came to TTF and looked inside our fake missile launcher to make sure there wasn't a real one in there."[3]

As relations between former adversaries thawed, the variety of friendly encounters between Russian and American sailors increased, on occasion to a degree unfathomable several years earlier. Macaluso pointed to an instance on the USS *Kentucky* (SSBN-737) when "We had Soviet admirals come onboard. The Soviet admiral in charge of [their] submarine force came over to visit, and came on our boat. It was really odd to, first of all, see Soviets walking around on your boat. And then to have them speaking on the 1MC through your boat with an interpreter right behind them . . . kind of gave you goosebumps. It did not feel right—it was really odd."

As Submarine Veterans and Volunteers

Two months into the first year of the new millennium, Chuck Macaluso retired from the Navy, the last of our volunteers to do so. While he became a newly minted veteran, some of the other USS *Blueback* volunteers had been out of the Navy for almost half a century, since the late 1950s. But regardless of when they reentered civilian life, these veterans would carry with them a special legacy for the rest of their lives, as they reintegrated into mainstream American society.

But how did they choose to define their legacy? What does it mean to be a submarine veteran?

Unanimously first and foremost comes a solemn duty. As Elbert H. Collins rhetorically asked his peers, "Don't you think we have the responsibility to keep the memory alive . . . of the guys that paid the ultimate [price]?" Our veterans place the burden on themselves to faithfully and accurately preserve the memories of those passed, because as fellow submariners, they are the only ones who had shared the same experiences and wrestled the same challenges. Collins focused particularly on the World War II submarine veterans, many of whom "Haven't told their *families* what the hell they went through in the war. They don't talk about it. But . . . they will talk to you as another submarine veteran. He'll open up and tell you all the things about making holes in the water. And it's fun to listen to them. I watched a couple of old farts argue [about] how many depth charges [they took], whether it was twenty-eight or thirty." The reluctance of older submariners to share their traumatic experiences, save to their peers, places these younger veterans in a position to safeguard a history that would otherwise vanish. As Collins reiterated, "That's our responsibility . . . to spread the word [about] what they did."

Pride is another common theme that bonds the veterans. As Robert W. Sumner explained, "Having been in that branch of the service, with guys that understand what you were doing, to me . . . I really feel proud to be associated with guys like [those] sitting here at this table." And as Alan L. Nolan added, "Because it was such a major part of my young life, I mean, I was nineteen to twenty-four years old when I served onboard my boat; it's also a huge sense of pride, because it was something that meant so much, and something I'm so proud of doing . . . Pride, and the camaraderie, and the friendships that developed—I've never seen that anywhere since, in my life." Even long after these sailors left their submarines, the sense of family didn't depart as easily. These sailors volunteered the prime of their lives in service of a navy and country, and it came as no surprise that these experiences would be able to elicit such poignant sentiments.

Educating the public in a more general sense is also an important facet of the collective responsibility shared by submarine veterans. Christopher Stafford noted how "A lot of people are interested [in] submarines, and you like to give them as much information as you can—just because they're interested, and you've got the knowledge." Nolan agreed: "[We need] to get the word out. Because there are people that do want to know something, because it has been such a hush-hush society. Now you start to see more of it on TV, and so people will ask." For many of the volunteers, teaching inquiring minds about the science and history behind submarines is also a way to give back to the communities they came from.

Having an actual submarine as a focal point and a tangible educational resource also resonates well with the veterans. Not only does the *Blueback* serve as a gathering place for this community, it also allows our volunteers a product to show for their efforts in preserving American history. But even though the *Blueback* has been open to the public since 1994, these submarine veterans have not always felt able to speak freely.

Opening Up

The paradigm of the "Silent Service" and the practical necessities of the Cold War precluded the creation of a space for submariners to share their stories. From day one, it had been engrained in each individual that all the experiences and memories from their service were to remain buried in their collective consciousness: "For years, we were all told, 'You don't talk about nothing.' And we didn't. And that's one of the reasons that [if] you ask people about it, they still don't say nothing."[4]

William M. Bryan Jr. added some perspective to the dilemma submariners faced with this anecdote from his temporary duty aboard the USS *Nautilus* (SSN-571):

> They sent me over for two weeks. [*Nautilus*] had come in to Key West and they were doing ops in that area. When you go from a diesel boat to a nuke, the difference, when you watch that depth gauge—you're used

to coming out at about 200 feet, and that sap-sucker just keeps on [spinning] at 400! [For the] three or four of us that [were] on it, I know our eyes had to be that big [and] round. You're used to doing three, four, five knots, and this sucker's like an airplane! As we leave, the chief of the boat says, 'You know everything that you've seen, heard, and talked about [these] last two weeks? You can't talk about it anymore!' So my father, must've been eighty, a couple years before he died, says, 'You never talked about the *Nautilus*. Why?"

"I was told not to."

"You mean that you can't even tell your father?"

"I haven't even told my children or my wife!"

"You mean nobody knows what happened when you were on there?"

"Not from me . . . "

And that was the first time I talked about it and I had been out of the Navy [for] thirty-five years.

But as the years passed following the fall of the Soviet Union, the wall of silence began to show cracks. With the former adversary vanquished, secrecy under the pretense of national defense became arguably obsolete. And thus, bits and pieces of once unthinkable stories began to leak their way out to the public.

Many people in both the naval history and submarine veterans communities agree that the watershed event in which the dam finally burst occurred with the 1998 publication of *Blind Man's Bluff* by Sherry Sontag and Christopher Drew. Not only was this work groundbreaking in terms of the unprecedented history that was revealed to the public, it also sent a signal to a heretofore anonymous community of submarine veterans. This was the first time their contributions to American security and world peace were being publicly acknowledged, and perhaps even more importantly, as Bob Sumner noted, "[*Blind Man's Bluff*] was a eye-opener for everybody . . . [and now] maybe you *can* talk about some of that stuff."

The new outpouring of stories also helped heal a surprising rift within the submarine veterans community. As Robert Walters explained, "For the longest time, World War II guys wouldn't have anything to do with you: 'You weren't depth-charged, you weren't this, you weren't that . . . All you did was go out there and drive around.' Then the book *Blind Man's Bluff* came out, and all of a sudden, these [World War II] guys come up [to you]: 'You guys do that!?' All of a sudden, they opened up. All of a sudden, we were accepted by them, so to speak."

Simultaneously, the book generated tremendous interest from the public. With the burden of silence on the veterans now ostensibly lifted, coupled with a grateful and inquisitive public eager for stories, the close-knit submarine veterans community set off on a mission that was part enlightenment, part catharsis. Several former high-ranking officers wrote their memoirs. Many other officers, enlisted crewmembers, and associated civilians opened up to curious authors and journalists. And even more submariners chose to carry their legacy through the plethora of museum boats across the country, and through their local and national submarine veterans' organizations.

But for our volunteers, this is just the next chapter in an adventure that began all those years ago. And throughout it all, it continues to be an adventure written in camaraderie and told through brotherhood.

Appendix A

Biographical Information

Name	Rate/Rank	Hometown	Service Years	Submarine Assignments
William M. "Bill" Bryan Jr.	EN3 (SS)	Largo, FL	1953–1960	*Thornback* SS-418 *Trutta* SS-421
Fred A. Carneau	ENCS (SS)	Portland, OR	1942–1978	*Entemedor* SS-340 *Stickleback* SS-415
Elbert H. "Collie" Collins	HMC (SS)	Portland, OR	1947–1968	*Catfish* SS-339 *Thomas Jefferson* SSBN-618 (Gold)
Herbert A. "Herb" Herman	ETR2 (SS)	Portland, OR	1960–1966	*Baya* AGSS-318 *Dace* SSN-607
Robert Austin "Bob" Jackson	EN3 (SS)	Camas, WA	1952–1956	*Pomfret* SS-391
Garth Lascink	MT2 (SS)	Los Angeles, CA	1963–1969	*Mariano G. Vallejo* SSBN-658 (Blue)
Charles Fredrick "Chuck" Macaluso	CWO2	Buffalo, NY	1979–2001	*Patrick Henry* SSBN/SSN-599 (Blue) *Robert E. Lee* SSBN/SSN-601 *Parche* SSN-683 *Guitarro* SSN-665 *Kentucky* SSBN-737 (Gold)
Mark A. Manzer	STS3 (SS)	Omaha, NE	1978–1982	*Sam Houston* SSBN/SSN-609 (Gold)
Evert Charles "Chuck" Nelson	ETCS (SS)	Seattle, WA	1962–1984	*Blueback* SS-581 *Lewis and Clark* SSBN-644 (Blue) *Patrick Henry* SSBN-599 (Gold) *Snook* SSN-592 *George Washington* SSBN-598 (Gold) *Sam Houston* SSBN/SSN-609 (Gold)
Alan L. Nolan	STS2 (SS)	Kalispell, MT	1975–1981	*Ethan Allen* SSBN/SSN-608 (Blue)
Christopher "Chris" Stafford	MM2 (SS)	San Diego, CA	1964–1968	*Barbel* SS-580

Continued on the next page

Name	Rate/Rank	Hometown	Service Years	Submarine Assignments
Michael A. "Mike" Stephens	MTC (SS)	Scotia, CA	1974–1994	*Thomas Jefferson* SSBN-618 (Gold) *Florida* SSBN-728 (Gold) *Tennessee* SSBN-734 (Blue)
Robert W. "Bob" Sumner	BT3 (SS)	Alamogordo, NM	1957–1963	*Sea Poacher* SS-406
David Meade "Dave" Vrooman	EM1 (SS)	Portland, OR	1960–1968	*Plunger* SSN-595
Richard G. "R. G." Walker	CS2 (SS)	Portland, OR	1962–1968	*Capitaine* AGSS-336
Robert "Bob" Walters	FTU3 (SS)	Portland, OR	1955–1957	*Caiman* SS-323
Gary W. Webb	SOS2 (SS)	Grants Pass, OR	1959–1962	*Sea Fox* SS-402

NOTE: The far-right column of "Submarine Assignments" does not include all TAD (Temporary Assigned Duty) or Naval Reserve assignments. Therefore, some of the preceding anecdotes in this book reference submarines not listed in this appendix.

Appendix B

US Submarine Losses (Cold War)

Cochino (SS-345) – August 26, 1949, 1 on eternal patrol
6 from the *Tusk* (SS-426) lost during rescue operations

Stickleback (SS-415) – May 29, 1958, no casualties

Thresher (SSN-593) – April 10, 1963, 129 on eternal patrol

Scorpion (SSN-589) – May 22, 1968, 99 on eternal patrol

Appendix C

Common US Navy Rates and Ranks

Pay Grade	Title	Colloquial Terms
E-1 through E-3	Seaman Recruit, Seaman Apprentice, Seaman	"Seaman"
E-4	Petty Officer Third Class	"Third Class"
E-5	Petty Officer Second Class	"Second Class"
E-6	Petty Officer First Class	"First Class"
E-7	Chief Petty Officer	"Chief"
E-8	Senior Chief Petty Officer	"Chief"
E-9	Master Chief Petty Officer	"Chief"
W-2 through W-5	Chief Warrant Officer	
O-1	Ensign	
O-2	Lieutenant (junior grade)	"JG"
O-3	Lieutenant	
O-4	Lieutenant Commander	
O-5	Commander	
O-6	Captain	Commanding officers (CO), or "skippers" of Navy ships, are often referred to as "captains," although they do not necessarily hold that rank
O-7 through O-10	Commodore (*obsolete*), Rear Admiral, Vice Admiral, Admiral	"Admiral"

Notes

Introduction

1. Three of the men held ratings that no longer exist today. Although Sumner was rated as a boiler tender (BT) from his surface-ship days, he worked as an engineman onboard the USS *Sea Poacher* (SS-406). Webb's sonarman (SO) rating was soon renamed to that of sonar technician, the specialty of both Manzer and Nolan. Walker's commissaryman or "cook" (CS) rating was later changed into mess management specialist, which was recently revised back to culinary specialist.

2. Norman Polmar and K. J. Moore, *Cold War Submarines: The Design and Construction of U.S. and Soviet Submarines* (Dulles, VA: Potomac Books, 2004), 6–8.

3. GUPPY: Greater Underwater Propulsion Power (plus the "Y" added for pronunciation).

4. William R. Anderson and Don Keith, *The Ice Diaries: The Untold Story of the USS* Nautilus *and the Cold War's Most Daring Mission* (Nashville, TN: Thomas Nelson, 2008), 13.

5. Polmar and Moore, *Cold War Submarines*, 121.

Chapter 1

1. V-12: Navy College Training Program. Similar to ROTC and employed primarily during World War II as another venue of training for prospective officers.

2. "A" school and "B" school: Training courses for specialty ratings. Covered in Chapter 1: Specialty Training.

3. On the beach: Shore duty assignment, as opposed to sea duty.

4. Sumner.

5. Because some submarines did not have ensigns onboard, the lowest-ranking officer would be a lieutenant junior-grade.

6. EAB: Emergency Air Breathing mask. Resembles a firefighter's mask with a hose attached to the submarine's internal air supply tanks.

7. In reference to Bryan's surprising assignment to yeoman school, Webb noted that naval bureaucracy has "A way of getting what they want."

8. A-ganger: Slang for an Auxiliary Division submariner.

9. Hogan's Alley: Slang for one particular dimly lit berthing section on a diesel boat. Usually not occupied by the most refined sailors onboard.

10. Lascink.

11. As Walker added, "Oh my God, what a fatal error that would've been!"

12. Submariners responsible for operating the diving planes are referred to as planesmen or helmsmen.

13. Carneau.

14. 1MC: 1 Main Circuit.

15. This meant standing a six-hour watch every twelve hours, instead of the standard six-hour watch every eighteen hours.

16. When asked how he managed, Walker remarked, "I had my mother send a Betty Crocker cookbook!"

17. Walters.

Chapter 2

1. 35MC: 35 Main Circuit. Communications circuit local to the missile compartment.

2. AEF: auxiliary electrician, forward. IC-man: Sailor with an interior communications electrician rating.

3. Stafford.

4. ECM: electronic countermeasures.

5. Once the air banks are depleted during the emergency blow, they need to be "recharged" or refilled so that a submarine can return to the surface following its next dive.

6. Macaluso.

7. A hilarious moment ensued when Nelson's comment triggered a well-practiced chorus of "A bitching sailor's a happy sailor!" from the other veterans.

8. Walters.

9. Macaluso. Also the self-proclaimed "[IBM] Selectric Typewriter Repair Instructor."

10. Stafford.

11. Manzer.

12. The soupdown is also known as mid-rats or midnight rations.

13. In reply to Jackson's pleasant mess cooking experience, Walters responded, "I was on the wrong boat!"

14. Macaluso.

15. As a disgusted Walters added, "And it stunk too!"

16. Although Walters admitted to the officer of the deck that he didn't have a good solution for cleaning up the mess, Lascink offered a brilliant fix: "Dive the boat, sir!"

17. Nelson.

18. When Collins brought up his experience of using trays in an aircraft carrier mess hall, the unanimous response from the other subvets was, "What's a tray!?"

19. Bryan.

20. Walters.

21. Lascink.

22. Lascink.

23. This popular hangout in Guam was serviced by "Andy's Hut," a bar of sorts that many sailors affectionately referred to as "Andy's Chateau by the Sea."

24. Sumner.

25. Lascink.

26. Stephens, a missile technician for twenty years, noted that he never heard the moniker "Sherwood Forest" while on the boats. His fellow sailors called their missile compartment the "mouse house."

27. Collins.

28. Nolan.

29. Sumner.

30. Although spooks weren't required to qualify in submarines, some of them did indeed take the time and effort to do so.

31. Yardbirds: Shipyard workers.

32. Walters.

33. Walters.

34. One interesting byproduct of inebriation was a so-called invincibility effect. As Collins (the corpsman) explained, "I have had broken bones in the hands from clearing the bridge, broken noses from the binoculars, I've had twisted and broken legs on deck, and that's sober, dead sober. But . . . they come in off the beach, drunk as a skunk, fall down the after battery hatch . . . all the way down! [And] they [just] pick themselves up!"

35. NCIS: Naval Criminal Investigative Service.

36. The assassination attempt on President Reagan took place on March 30, 1981.

37. For Carneau, back at the end of World War II, his starting salary as a submariner was $21 per month.

38. Peter Maas, *The Terrible Hours: The Man Behind the Greatest Submarine Rescue in History* (New York: HarperCollins, 1999), 18–51, 76–77, 82, 177–216, 281–83. The genius and catalyst behind the *Squalus* rescue, Lieutenant Commander Charles Bowers "Swede" Momsen, had actually designed the rescue chamber prior to the *S-4* sinking. But in typical bureaucratic fashion, it took the lives of forty more men before Momsen's creation was finally brought to fruition.

39. The depth at the deepest point of the Mariana Trench is just less than 36,000 feet.

40. Due to extenuating circumstances, I was asked to omit the names of both the volunteer and the boat.

41. Gregg K. Kakesako, "Sub Accident Eerily Similar to 1981 Incident," *Honolulu Star-Bulletin*, February 27, 2001, http://archives.starbulletin.com/2001/02/27/news

/index.html. In a sickening déjà vu moment, an almost identical accident occurred twenty years later when, in February 2001, the USS *Greeneville* (SSN-772) surfaced under a Japanese fishing boat off the coast of Oahu.

42. Stephens's former division officer on the *Thomas Jefferson* was the diving officer on the *George Washington* when the collision occurred.

43. Lascink.

44. In a moment of truth, Stephens added rhetorically, "Where's the rescue buoys? The only right answer was 'motorcycle parking.'"

45. Sumner.

46. Because the lifeboat was obviously too big to fit through the hatch, Bryan surmised as to how it was installed in the torpedo room in the first place: "You know how it got in there? It got put in there before the plates were put on at the yard!"

47. Although Sumner emphasized that this type of danger was limited only to diesel boats, Macaluso quipped, "Dangerous things happen too on boomer boats!" To which Vrooman quickly added, "Fast attacks too!"

48. To place this experience in a quantitative context, Stafford cited an incident that happened on the USS *Barbel* (SS-580) before he was onboard, when a sea piping valve failed and the boat took on one ton of water per second, nearly sinking the submarine.

49. Collins, in a moment of empathy and mock disgust, remarked, "Have you ever noticed it's always cold water!?"

50. Some of the boomers, such as the *Thomas Jefferson,* weren't even fitted with enough auxiliary pumps to begin with. As Stephens recalled, "You might have a compartment a gajillion feet long with a suction here, and a suction [there], and nothing in the middle. We had lots and lots of [bucket brigades] through the mouse house."

51. However, to the credit of the SUBSAFE program, no SUBSAFE-certified submarine has ever been lost. The *Scorpion,* which went down five years after the *Thresher,* had not yet been certified.

52. Norman Polmar, *The Death of the USS* Thresher: *The Story Behind History's Deadliest Submarine Disaster* (Guilford, CT: Lyons Press, 2004), 36–38, 124–26, 137–38.

53. Collins's actual replacement was HMC (SS) Andrew J. Gallant Jr., an experienced chief and no newcomer to the service. Of course, this does not make the loss any less tragic.

54. Stephen Johnson, *Silent Steel: The Mysterious Death of the Nuclear Attack Sub USS* Scorpion (Hoboken, NJ: John Wiley & Sons, 2006), 98–99, 102–09, 114–23, 146–66, 180–95, 219–34. Even the torpedo theory comes with two versions—an accidental explosion in the torpedo room caused by an overheating torpedo battery, and a hot-running torpedo that was ejected, only to turn back and strike the *Scorpion.*

55. The USS *Stickleback* (SS-415) sank in May 1958, during a training exercise after she collided with a destroyer escort on the surface. Fortunately, there were no casualties. The *Kursk* was a Russian Oscar II-class submarine that sank in the Barents Sea on August 12, 2000. In a very publicized incident, some crewmembers

survived the initial explosion, but later perished after what many US submarine veterans saw as a political mishandling of an emergency situation by the Russian government, in their initial refusal to accept outside help.

56. The crewmembers referred to as "nukes" received special training and certification, focused on the operation of a submarine's nuclear reactor.

57. Jackson noted that he "Made a lot of money in port, standing other people's watches."

58. Vrooman.

59. Sumner.

60. Macaluso.

61. Collins.

Chapter 3

1. Stafford.

2. In addition to the white hats, other items that often went missing included shoes and tools.

3. Manzer's anecdote prompted a playfully disgusted response of "What curtains!?" from the older diesel boat veterans, for whom such a seemingly insignificant measure of privacy was an unthinkable luxury.

4. To provide an example, Sumner recalled an instance when "Somebody goosed [the captain] as he was going up to the conning tower. [And] that was accepted; just the way it was."

5. LDO: limited duty officer. A restricted officer billet mostly held by mustangs with specialized technical expertise.

6. Nolan also appreciated how his captain would often come hang out in the sonar room with the sonar technicians who were on watch.

7. Horse and Cow: The infamous haunt of submariners, who packed the bar in droves, before and after deployments. Located initially in San Francisco, then in Vallejo, the bar was stuffed to the seams with submarine memorabilia.

8. Sumner.

9. This tradition was carried out, regardless of location. As Lascink noted, "Napa River [near] Mare Island—we used to blow sanitaries in there, but the guys still went off into that river."

10. Nelson was our other volunteer assigned to a new construction crew; he participated in the launching of the USS *Lewis and Clark* (SSBN-644).

11. Some captains, such as one aboard the *Mariano G. Vallejo*, would continue an old tradition known as "splicing the mainbrace," when the crew would be served alcoholic punch in a celebratory occasion after some significant accomplishment had been achieved.

12. Nolan noted how, "Not only did it make you want to . . . a lot of people did puke; so you're crawling through all that too."

13. Walters also described how the *Caiman*'s dispensary fed the pollywogs their "medicine" via "Some sort of a big hypodermic needle. You [just] open your mouth."

14. Nolan.

15. Lascink.

16. Stafford.

17. Webb noted that even though life jackets were usually available, in the early 1960s, it was not yet common practice to use them while working topside.

18. Gentian Violet is a medical dye, and is also used to treat fungal infections. It creates long-lasting stains on skin and cloth.

19. Walters.

20. "List of Z-grams," Elmo R. Zumwalt Jr., US Navy, last modified August 11, 2017, https://www.history.navy.mil/research/library/online-reading-room/title-list-alphabetically/z/list-z-grams.html. For Lascink, Zumwalt's greatest accomplishment was to allow "Beer in the barracks, legally! So then we had a refrigerator with the beer all stuffed inside, [at] Pearl."

21. Lascink.

22. Lascink also brought up a most unusual uniform customization: "I knew a guy that had a plate, a knife, and a fork on his flap, and it said 'Marines' Dinner Plate.' When I saw that, I says, 'I will not be anywhere around this guy,' cause who knows, if a Marine [sees that], there's going to be a big fight!"

23. And as Walters observed, the flat hat "Had a little pocket, and that pocket was just right for a condom!"

24. "History of US Navy Uniforms, 1776–1981," Bureau of Naval Personnel, US Navy, last modified January 23, 2017, https://www.history.navy.mil/research/library/online-reading-room/title-list-alphabetically/h/history-of-us-navy-uniforms-1776-1981.html.

25. Ibid.

26. Chiefs and petty officers are the NCOs of the US Navy.

27. For these reasons, the crew of the USS *Archerfish* (AGSS-311) was given the nickname "Playboys of the Pacific."

Chapter 4

1. Sumner.

2. In the colloquial practice of many veterans, the terms "Russian" and "Soviet" are used interchangeably, have the same lexical connotation, and are not used to distinguish between the change in government that occurred in 1991. As such, no further distinction will be made in this book.

3. Lascink.

4. Ironically enough, the Mark 37 torpedo was designed for antisubmarine warfare (ASW).

5. Sherry Sontag and Christopher Drew, *Blind Man's Bluff: The Untold Story of American Submarine Espionage* (New York: PublicAffairs, 1998), 412.

6. Walters added, "I got to develop pictures, and I tried to talk somebody into . . . 'Can I have a copy?'" Alas, the Office of Naval Intelligence didn't quite see things the same way.

7. Sontag and Drew, *Blind Man's Bluff,* 197–220.

8. Vrooman himself only found out about the award thirty-some-odd years later, after reading a comprehensive list published in *Blind Man's Bluff.*

9. According to Vrooman, the award was most likely given for a seventy-eight-day deployment in the fall of 1966, when the *Plunger* operated in Soviet waters with spooks onboard, under the command of CO Robert Doelling. However, according to the *Plunger*'s official command history for 1966, the only deployment during the latter half of that year was from July 15 to September 25, a period of seventy-three days, for "independent operations." Via a Freedom of Information Act (FOIA) request, the Office of the Chief of Naval Operations instead verified the award for the period of December 16, 1966 to March 15, 1967. With respect to this time frame, the command history notes two separate nonroutine events: (a) The installation of a new periscope "of advanced design" on January 9, 1967, followed by post-availability sea trials; and (b) Participation in a submarine vs. submarine exercise between March 6 and March 22 with three diesel-electric boats, focusing on leadership, sonar, and fire control operations. But these aforementioned possibilities all occurred under Doelling, who by many accounts was an unpopular skipper, and during his tenure on the *Plunger,* crew morale was unnecessarily low. This makes it seem unlikely that the boat could have accomplished a feat that would warrant a NUC, especially under the command of a captain who was certainly faced with several shortcomings. Further adding to the discrepancy is the hypothesis of former *Plunger* XO Fred Kollmorgen, who believes that the NUC was awarded for a much earlier operation under the command of CO Robert Styer, when the *Plunger* was involved in advanced weapons and sonar tests off Guam, with the USS *Blueback* (SS-581) serving as the target . . . Lascink's *Mariano G. Vallejo* received a Meritorious Unit Commendation (MUC) for special operations conducted in conjunction with the USS *Flasher* (SSN-613) in July 1969 . . . Two of Stephens's boats, the USS *Florida* (SSBN-728) and the USS *Tennessee* (SSBN-734), also received MUCs.

10. The Secretary of the Navy, "Navy Unit Commendation," United States Department of the Navy, FOIA request.

11. But as Stafford aptly noted, "Sure is nice in the engine room though!"

12. Other sailors, such as Stafford, weren't as lucky. As he remarked, "I could've been in the Sahara Desert, and I would've never known!"

13. Previous submarines dedicated to special operations included the USS *Halibut* (SSGN-587), USS *Seawolf* (SSN-575), and USS *Richard B. Russell* (SSN-687). In 2005, the newly commissioned USS *Jimmy Carter* (SSN-23) replaced the *Parche.* Some of the modifications made to the *Parche* during her special operations refit were described by Macaluso in Chapter 3: Blurring of Rank.

14. The plot overlay was never found, and some sailors surmised that it was shot out with the garbage in the TDU.

15. "History of USS SEA FOX (SS-402) During Operation DOMINIC," Ships History Branch, Naval Warfare Division, Washington Navy Yard.

16. Carneau's USS *Entemedor* (SS-340) was also indirectly involved with a nuclear weapons test. She participated in the sinking of the heavy cruiser USS *Salt*

Lake City (CA-25) after the obsolete target was used in the Operation Crossroads tests at Bikini Atoll.

17. "Cuban Missile Crisis, 1962: Online Documentation," Department of Defense, US Navy, last modified April 2, 2015, https://www.history.navy.mil/research/library/online-reading-room/title-list-alphabetically/c/cuban-missile-crisis-1962.html.

18. Ibid.

19. Local newspapers reported this incident before the *Sea Poacher* even arrived back at Key West.

20. The Mark 80 Polaris fire control system had been developed in the haste to deploy the *George Washington* and was installed onboard the first two SSBN classes (*George Washington* and *Ethan Allen*) the US Navy built. The Mark 80 supported Polaris A-1, A-2, and A-3 missiles, and was later replaced by the Mark 84 Polaris system, which delegated final responsibility to the weapons officer. Future fire control systems for the Poseidon and Trident missile programs would utilize the same precedent set by the Polaris Mark 84.

21. Lascink. DCT: depth control tanks.

22. Dave Oliver, *Against the Tide: Rickover's Leadership Principles and the Rise of the Nuclear Navy* (Annapolis, MD: Naval Institute Press, 2014), 148–49.

23. Alfred Scott McLaren, *Unknown Waters: A First-Hand Account of the Historic Under-Ice Survey of the Siberian Continental Shelf by USS* Queenfish *(SSN-651)* (Tuscaloosa: University of Alabama Press, 2008), 7–8.

24. McLaren, *Unknown Waters*, 41–42. In this book, Captain McLaren also recounts the proceedings of several other memorable interviews he witnessed as a PCO.

25. Collins.

26. Herman.

27. While departing Kings Bay, the *Tennessee* faced a more proactive challenge, and encountered protestors in small boats attempting to block her passage to sea. The protestors were escorted away by security boats.

Chapter 5

1. Walters.

2. Stafford.

3. Stafford.

4. Lascink.

5. These vehicle inspections were not always thoroughly performed because, as Sumner noted, "As many times as I was restricted, I went out of the gate in the trunks of cars!"

6. In 1959, the USS *Trutta* (SS-421) rescued five political refugees escaping the turmoil in Cuba. They had been adrift in a small boat for two days prior to being picked up near Key West.

7. Bryan. The *Thornback*'s stay in Lebanon coincided with the American inter-

vention and brief occupation of Beirut, in support of the incumbent pro-Western government fighting against rising political opposition.

8. TTF: Trident Training Facility, Kings Bay, Georgia.

9. Macaluso.

10. This state of affairs remained in effect until September 2008, when the US Navy for the first time forward-deployed a nuclear-powered vessel to Yokosuka, the aircraft carrier USS *George Washington* (CVN-73).

11. Because Tahiti did not yet have an airport in the mid-1950s, Walters noted how the island was only accessible to tourists via seaplane or cruise ship.

12. Webb, Walters et al.

13. Another reason for the Canadians' popularity was because they were impeccable hosts. As Nelson recalled, "We were up in Victoria, tied up outboard [of] a supply ship for the Canadian Navy. And they came down and invited us all over to have a drink. And I don't think anybody that went up there left the ship!"

14. Commanding Officer, USS CAPITAINE (AGSS-336), "Combined Republic of Viet Nam—U.S. ASW Exercise, 7–14 April 1963; report of," Ships History Branch, Naval Warfare Division, Washington Navy Yard.

15. With the Italian Navy devoid of aircraft carriers during this post–World War II era, the aircraft carrier that joined the Italian fleet during this particular multinational exercise was most likely a contribution by the British Royal Navy.

Chapter 6

1. Webb.

2. Webb.

3. Manzer.

4. Lascink. Although boomers operated a standard deployment of approximately three months, he noted how during the new construction period, "That first year, we were gone all the time."

5. Collins.

6. Lascink.

7. Bryan.

8. GI Bill benefits were paid to the veterans as a monthly stipend, designed to cover school tuition as well as living expenses; and, as Jackson noted, "Back [then] of course, education was a little bit cheaper, but you lived on $135 a month."

9. DD-214: An official US military document, certifying a service member's discharge or retirement from active duty.

Epilogue

1. Blue-water: A term of naval strategy, in reference to open ocean or "high seas" operations or capabilities; contrasted with brown-water operations and capabilities, which occur in or are limited to riverine, coastal, and/or littoral regions.

2. Macaluso.

3. Having no concern of overstaying their welcome, the Russians came fully prepared to settle in. As Stephens noted, "They [even] had their own buses, their own camper vans."

4. Carneau.

Bibliography

Primary Interviews

Conducted at the Oregon Museum of Science and Industry (Portland, OR). Archived in the Oral History Collection, Department of the Navy Operational Archives, Washington Navy Yard (Washington, DC). Permissions required.

Bryan Jr., William M. Group Interviews by Jonathan Leung. June 16, June 23, June 30, July 7, July 14, July 21, July 28, August 4, 2008.

Carneau, Fred A. Group Interviews by Jonathan Leung. June 16, June 23, June 30, July 7, July 14, July 21, July 28, August 4, 2008.

Collins, Elbert H. Group Interviews by Jonathan Leung. June 16, June 30, July 7, July 21, July 28, August 4, 2008.

Herman, Herbert A. Group Interviews by Jonathan Leung. June 16, June 30, July 7, July 14, July 28, August 4, 2008.

Jackson, Robert Austin. Personal and Group Interviews by Jonathan Leung. June 23, June 30, July 7, July 21, July 28, August 4, 2008, August 3, 2009.

Lascink, Garth. Group Interviews by Jonathan Leung. June 16, June 23, June 30, July 7, July 14, July 21, July 28, August 4, 2008.

Macaluso, Charles Fredrick. Group Interviews by Jonathan Leung. June 16, June 23, July 7, July 14, July 21, 2008.

Manzer, Mark A. Group Interviews by Jonathan Leung. June 16, June 23, June 30, July 7, July 21, July 28, August 4, 2008.

Nelson, Evert Charles. Group Interviews by Jonathan Leung. June 16, June 23, June 30, July 7, July 14, July 21, July 28, August 4, 2008.

Nolan, Alan L. Personal and Group Interviews by Jonathan Leung. June 23, June 30, July 14, July 21, July 28, August 4, 2008, June 16, 2009.

Stafford, Christopher. Personal and Group Interviews by Jonathan Leung. June 23, June 30, July 7, July 14, July 21, July 28, August 4, 2008, June 14, 2009.

Stephens, Michael A. Group Interviews by Jonathan Leung. June 16, June 23, July 7, July 14, August 4, 2008.

Sumner, Robert W. Group Interviews by Jonathan Leung. June 16, June 23, June 30, July 7, July 14, July 21, July 28, August 4, 2008.

Vrooman, David Meade. Group Interviews by Jonathan Leung. June 16, June 23, June 30, July 7, July 14, July 21, July 28, August 4, 2008.

Walker, Richard G. Group Interviews by Jonathan Leung. June 16, June 23, June 30, July 7, July 14, July 21, August 4, 2008.

Walters, Robert. Group Interviews by Jonathan Leung. June 16, June 23, June 30, July 7, July 14, July 21, July 28, August 4, 2008.

Webb, Gary W. Group Interviews by Jonathan Leung. June 16, June 30, July 14, July 28, 2008.

Miscellaneous Interviews

Joyner, Kenneth. Telephone Interview by Jonathan Leung. June 17, 2009.

Kollmorgen, Frederick. Telephone Interview by Jonathan Leung. May 5, 2010.

Command Histories

Accessed on location at the Ships History Branch, Naval Warfare Division, Washington Navy Yard (Washington, DC).

USS *Barbel* (SS-580): 1967–1968.

USS *Baya* (AGSS-318): 1961–1962.

USS *Blueback* (SS-581): 1962–1963.

USS *Caiman* (SS-323): 1955–1957.

USS *Capitaine* (AGSS-336): 1962–1964.

USS *Catfish* (SS-339): 1960–1961.

USS *Dace* (SSN-607): 1965–1966.

USS *Entemedor* (SS-340): 1947.

USS *Ethan Allen* (SSBN/SSN-608): 1977–1981.

USS *Florida* (SSBN-728): 1984–1986.

USS *George Washington* (SSBN-598): 1979–1980.

USS *Kentucky* (SSBN-737): 1994–1996.

USS *Lewis and Clark* (SSBN-644): 1964–1966.

USS *Mariano G. Vallejo* (SSBN-658): 1965–1969.

USS *Parche* (SSN-683): 1988–1991.

USS *Patrick Henry* (SSBN/SSN-599): 1967–1969, 1980–1982.

USS *Plunger* (SSN-595): 1966–1968.

USS *Pomfret* (SS-391): 1954–1956.

USS *Robert E. Lee* (SSBN/SSN-601): 1982–1984.

USS *Sam Houston* (SSBN/SSN-609): 1979–1982.

USS *Sea Fox* (SS-402): 1959–1962.

USS *Sea Poacher* (SS-406): 1960–1963.

USS *Snook* (SSN-592): 1972–1976.
USS *Tennessee* (SSBN-734): 1990–1994.
USS *Thomas Jefferson* (SSBN-618): 1963, 1976–1980.
USS *Thornback* (SS-418): 1956–1958.
USS *Trutta* (SS-421): 1958–1959.

Other Documents

Accessed on location at the Ships History Branch, Naval Warfare Division, Washington Navy Yard, (Washington, DC), or obtained through the United States Department of the Navy via the Freedom of Information Act (FOIA).

"Combined Republic of Viet Nam—U.S. ASW Exercise, 7–14 April 1963; report of." From Commanding Officer, USS CAPITAINE (AGSS-336), to Chief, Navy Section Military Assistance Advisory Group, Republic of Viet Nam. April 18, 1963.

"History of USS SEA FOX (SS-402) During Operation DOMINIC." [Author and Recipient unknown]. 1962.

"Master List of Unit Awards and Campaign Medals." From Chief of Naval Operations, to All Ships and Stations; OPNAV NOTICE 1650. March 9, 2001.

"Navy Unit Commendation." From The Secretary of the Navy, to USS PLUNGER (SSN-595). 1967.

"Summary of Events from the Court of Inquiry concerning the loss of the USS THRESHER (SSN 593) on April 10, 1963." 1963 and 1964.

"U.S. Navy Court of Inquiry Record of Proceedings and the Supplementary Record of Proceedings concerning the loss of the USS SCORPION (SSN 589) on May 22, 1968." 1968 and 1969.

Books (Naval History)

Anderson, William R., and Don Keith. *The Ice Diaries: The Untold Story of the USS* Nautilus *and the Cold War's Most Daring Mission*. Nashville, TN: Thomas Nelson, 2008.

Craven, John Piña. *The Silent War: The Cold War Battle Beneath the Sea*. New York: Simon & Schuster, 2001.

Duncan, Francis. *Rickover and the Nuclear Navy: The Discipline of Technology*. Annapolis, MD: Naval Institute Press, 1990.

———. *Rickover: The Struggle for Excellence*. Annapolis, MD: Naval Institute Press, 2001.

Friedman, Norman. *U.S. Submarines Since 1945: An Illustrated Design History*. Annapolis, MD: Naval Institute Press, 1994.

Hinkle, David Randall, Arne C. Johnson, and Harry H. Caldwell, eds. *United States Submarines*. New York: Barnes & Noble Books, 2004.

Johnson, Stephen. *Silent Steel: The Mysterious Death of the Nuclear Attack Sub USS* Scorpion. Hoboken, NJ: John Wiley & Sons, 2006.

Knoblock, Glenn A. *Black Submariners in the United States Navy, 1940–1975*. Jefferson, NC: McFarland, 2005.

Maas, Peter. *The Terrible Hours: The Man Behind the Greatest Submarine Rescue in History*. New York: HarperCollins, 1999.

McHale, Gannon. *Stealth Boat: Fighting the Cold War in a Fast-Attack Submarine*. Annapolis, MD: Naval Institute Press, 2008.

McLaren, Alfred Scott. *Silent and Unseen: On Patrol in Three Cold War Attack Submarines*. Annapolis, MD: Naval Institute Press, 2015.

———. *Unknown Waters: A First-Hand Account of the Historic Under-Ice Survey of the Siberian Continental Shelf by USS* Queenfish *(SSN-651)*. Tuscaloosa: University of Alabama Press, 2008.

Oliver, Dave. *Against the Tide: Rickover's Leadership Principles and the Rise of the Nuclear Navy*. Annapolis, MD: Naval Institute Press, 2014.

Polmar, Norman. *The Death of the USS* Thresher*: The Story Behind History's Deadliest Submarine Disaster*. Guilford, CT: Lyons Press, 2004.

Polmar, Norman, and K. J. Moore. *Cold War Submarines: The Design and Construction of U.S. and Soviet Submarines*. Dulles, VA: Potomac Books, 2004.

Silverstone, Paul H. *US Warships Since 1945*. Shepperton, UK: Ian Allan, 1986.

Sontag, Sherry, and Christopher Drew. *Blind Man's Bluff: The Untold Story of American Submarine Espionage*. New York: PublicAffairs, 1998.

Stillwell, Paul, ed. *Submarine Stories: Recollections from the Diesel Boats*. Annapolis, MD: Naval Institute Press, 2007.

Summitt, Dan. *Tales of a Cold War Submariner*. College Station: Texas A&M University Press, 2004.

Vyborny, Lee, and Don Davis. *Dark Waters: An Insider's Account of the* NR-1, *the Cold War's Undercover Nuclear Sub*. New York: New American Library, 2003.

Waller, Douglas C. *Big Red: The Three-Month Voyage of a Trident Nuclear Submarine*. New York: HarperCollins, 2001.

Whitlock, Flint, and Ron Smith. *The Depths of Courage: American Submariners at War with Japan, 1941–1945*. New York: Berkley Books, 2007.

Williamson, Gordon. *Wolf Pack: The Story of the U-Boat in World War II*. Oxford, UK: Osprey, 2005.

Books (Oral History)

Ritchie, Donald A. *Doing Oral History: A Practical Guide*. Oxford, UK: Oxford University Press, 2003.

Simpson, Craig S., and Gregory S. Wilson. *Above the Shots: An Oral History of the Kent State Shootings*. Kent, OH: Kent State University Press, 2016.

Terkel, Studs. *"The Good War": An Oral History of World War II*. New York: New Press, 1984.

Newspapers

Drew, Christopher. "Adrift 500 Feet Under the Sea, a Minute Was an Eternity." *New York Times,* May 18, 2005. http://www.nytimes.com/2005/05/18/us/adrift-500-feet-under-the-sea-a-minute-was-an-eternity.html.

Kakesako, Gregg K. "Sub Accident Eerily Similar to 1981 Incident." *Honolulu Star-Bulletin,* February 27, 2001. http://archives.starbulletin.com/2001/02/27/news/index.html.

Websites

"Blueback Base—Portland, OR." http://www.bluebackbase.org.

"Cuban Missile Crisis, 1962: Online Documentation." US Navy. Last modified April 2, 2015. https://www.history.navy.mil/research/library/online-reading-room/title-list-alphabetically/c/cuban-missile-crisis/online-documentation.html.

"Historic Naval Ships Association." http://www.hnsa.org.

"History of US Navy Uniforms, 1776–1981." US Navy. Last modified January 23, 2017. https://www.history.navy.mil/research/library/online-reading-room/title-list-alphabetically/u/uniforms-usnavy/history-of-us-navy-uniforms-1776–1981.html.

"List of Z-grams." US Navy. Last modified August 11, 2017. https://www.history.navy.mil/research/library/online-reading-room/title-list-alphabetically/z/list-z-grams.html.

"Naval History and Heritage Command." https://www.history.navy.mil.

"Naval Vessel Register." http://www.nvr.navy.mil.

"Submarine—OMSI." https://omsi.edu/submarine.

"US Submarine Veterans Home Page." https://www.ussvi.org/home.asp.

Museums

This list only includes submarine museums visited in preparation for this book. A comprehensive list is available at the Historic Naval Ships Association website (hnsa.org).

Soviet *B-39*
Maritime Museum of San Diego
1492 North Harbor Drive
San Diego, CA 92101

USS *Becuna* (SS-319)
Independence Seaport Museum
211 S Columbus Boulevard
Philadelphia, PA 19106

USS *Blueback* (SS-581)
Oregon Museum of Science and Industry
1945 SE Water Avenue
Portland, OR 97214

USS *Bowfin* (SS-287)
USS Bowfin Submarine Museum & Park
11 Arizona Memorial Drive
Honolulu, HI 96818

USS *Dolphin* (AGSS-555)
Maritime Museum of San Diego
1492 North Harbor Drive
San Diego, CA 92101

USS *Growler* (SSG-577)
INTREPID Sea, Air & Space Museum
Pier 86, W 46th Street
New York, NY 10036

USS *Lionfish* (SS-298)
Battleship Cove
5 Water Street
Fall River, MA 02721

USS *Nautilus* (SSN-571)
Submarine Force Library & Museum
1 Crystal Lake Road
Groton, CT 06340

USS *Pampanito* (SS-383)
San Francisco Maritime National Park Association
Pier 45, The Embarcadero
San Francisco, CA 94133

German *U-505*
Museum of Science and Industry, Chicago
5700 S Lake Shore Drive
Chicago, IL 60637

Index